AN ADVANCED
ENGLISH PRACTICE COURSE

AN ADVANCED ENGLISH PRACTICE COURSE

James Day MA,PhD

*Principal, Davies's School of
English, Cambridge*

LONGMAN

LONGMAN GROUP LIMITED
London

*Associated companies, branches and representatives
throughout the world*

*First published 1968
New impressions *1969; *1970 (twice);
*1972; *1974; *1975*

ISBN 0 582 52106 8

*Printed in Hong Kong by
The Hong Kong Printing Press Ltd*

To my colleagues, and especially O.C.D.

Contents

Part 2 SENTENCES IN PARAGRAPHS

Part 3 SELF-EXPRESSION IN A WIDER CONTEXT

Acknowledgments

We are grateful to the following for permission to reproduce copyright material:
George Allen & Unwin Ltd for an extract from *New Hopes for a Changing World* by Bertrand Russell; Edward Arnold (Publishers) Ltd and Harcourt, Brace & World Inc for an extract from *A Passage to India* by E. M. Forster; Edward Arnold (Publishers) Ltd for an extract from *The Human Situation* by MacNeile Dixon; author and author's agents and Michael Joseph Ltd for extracts from *Fair Stood the Wind for France*, *The Purple Plain* and *The Jacaranda Tree* by H. E. Bates; author, author's agents and Jonathan Cape Ltd for extracts from *Cut and Come Again* by H. E. Bates; Miss Sonia Brownell and Secker & Warburg Ltd and Harcourt, Brace & World Inc for extracts from *The Road to Wigan Pier* by George Orwell; Cambridge University Press for an extract from *Language and the Pursuit of Truth* by John Wilson; Jonathan Cape Ltd for an extract from *Magnus Merriman* by Eric Linklater; The Clarendon Press for extracts from *Doubt and Certainty in Science* by J. Z. Young, and for extracts from *Selected Modern Essays* by Sir Walter Raleigh; Collins Publishers for an extract from *The Murder at Crome House* by G. D. H. and M. Cole; Chatto & Windus Ltd and Columbia University Press for an extract from *Culture and Society 1780–1950* by Raymond Williams; Constable & Co. Ltd for extracts from *Modern Irish Short Stories* by Mary Lavin; Constable & Co. Ltd and McGraw-Hill Book Company for extracts from *The Reason Why* by Cecil Woodham Smith; Andre Deutsch Ltd for extracts by Christopher Hollis, Theodora Bosanquet and Graham Greene from *Time and Tide Anthology*; Faber & Faber Ltd and Coward-McCann Inc for extracts from *Lord of the Flies* by William Golding, Copyright © 1954 by William Golding; Victor Gollancz Ltd and Harcourt, Brace & World Inc for extracts from *That Uncertain Feeling* by Kingsley Amis; author, author's agents and Collins-Knowlton-Wing Inc for extracts from *The Crowning Privilege* by Robert Graves, Copyright © 1956 by Robert Graves; author, author's agents and Michael Joseph for extracts from *Odd Man Out* by F. L. Green; author, author's agents, William Heinemann Ltd and The Viking Press Inc for extracts from *Brighton Rock* by Graham Greene; Hamish Hamilton Ltd and The Society of Authors for an extract from *A Perfect Woman* by L. P. Hartley; Hutchinson & Co. (Publishers) Ltd for an extract from *Poetry of This Age* by J. M. Cohen; Mrs Laura Huxley, Chatto & Windus and Harper & Row, Publishers Inc for extracts from *Antic Hay*, *Beyond the Mexique Bay*, *Eyeless in Gaza* and 'Selected Snobberies' from *Music at Night* by Aldous Huxley; Michael Joseph Ltd and Harper & Row, Publishers Inc for extracts from *To Be a Pilgrim* by Joyce Cary; Martin Secker & Warburg Ltd and The Viking Press Inc for extracts from *Anglo-Saxon Attitudes* by Angus Wilson; proprietors of New Statesman for 'The Killer Cars' by Richard Carr from *New Statesman* of 30.10.64; Oxford University Press for extracts from *The Individual and the Universe* by Sir Bernard Lovell and *The Language of Music* by Deryck

Cooke; agents of the late Hesketh Pearson for extracts from *The Life of Oscar Wilde* by Hesketh Pearson; Penguin Books Ltd for extracts from *Uses and Abuses of Psychology* by H. J. Eysenck, *The Contemporary Cinema* by Penelope Houston, *Contemporary British Art* by Sir Herbert Read, *The Vocabulary of Politics* by T. D. Weldon, *The Age of Illusion* by Ronald Blythe, *Has Man a Future* by Bertrand Russell, and *European Painting and Sculpture* by Eric Newton, Penguin Books 1941; The Public Trustee and The Society of Authors for an extract from *The Apple Cart* by G. B. Shaw; Putnam & Company for an extract from *Out of Africa* by Karen Blixen; author, author's agent, Jonathan Cape Ltd for extracts from *Four Frightened People* by E. Arnot Robertson; author and author's agent for extracts from *Selected Short Stories* by William Sansom, Copyright © William Sansom 1960; author and B.B.C. Publications for an extract from *A University in the Making* by Dr Albert E. Sloman; The Society of Authors as the literary representative of the Estate of the late John Middleton Murry for extracts from *Selected Modern English Essays* by John Middleton Murry; author and author's agents for an extract from *The Straight and Narrow Path* by Honor Tracy; author and author's agents for an extract from *Brideshead Revisited* by Evelyn Waugh; the Executors of H. G. Wells for an extract from *Points of View* by H. G. Wells; Mr Henry Williamson and Faber & Faber for an extract from *Salar the Salmon* by Henry Williamson.

We have been unable to trace the copyright holders of the extract from *Modern Short Stories* by Constance Holme, sel. P. M. Jones (World Classics 447) and shall appreciate any information which will enable us to do so.

General introduction
The aims and scope of this course

This course has three aims. The students using it will probably have done anything up to six years' fairly intensive study of English at school and possibly at university. There are, however, certain mistakes which even advanced students make again and again. These mistakes vary from nationality to nationality, and largely depend on the mother tongue of the students. The first aim of the course is remedial. It tries to demonstrate how native English writers use certain tricky structures that overseas students sometimes mismanage, and then gives them practice in the correct use of those structures.

The second aim is to improve the students' powers of self-expression by expanding their vocabulary and repertoire of structures. The third is to stimulate them, through reading and discussion of sometimes provocative material, to think about and criticise both the form and the content of the passages that have been chosen to illustrate the structures practised.

The basis of any language communication depends largely on the verb, and the majority of sentences result from the interplay of static elements – nouns and adjectives – with dynamic ones – verbs and adverbs. Most students find that the English tense system needs careful study. So, although the course has been designed so that any one section of it may be used in isolation to illustrate and practise a particular structure, it develops out of a detailed examination first of tense, then of mood, then of the satellites of the verb (adverbials), via verb forms that operate as nouns (gerunds and infinitives), through noun clauses and nouns to adjectivals and adjectives. It thus leads from the simple to the compound; from the immediate to the contingent; from the definite to the indefinite; and from the concrete to the abstract. Each pattern of structures has a group of exercises attached to it. These develop from the almost absurdly simple, which aim at simply drilling the student in the correct use of the structure considered, via exercises with a closed system, where the most suitable answer is probably the most correct one, through exercises involving the student's imaginative use of the structure in a 'controlled' situation, to those where the student is allowed much more freedom of self-expression, still practising the structure required, in a precise but not too restricted context-situation.

In each section, the purely structural exercises are preceded by a number of comprehension questions about the vocabulary and argument of the passage, and followed by suggestions for discussion and/or essays about the material touched on in the passage and related topics. This constitutes Part 1 of the book.

Part 2 concerns more extended forms of self-expression. Examples are given of different types of style, of ways of constructing a paragraph, of methods used by authors to suit vocabulary to subject, not simply as a technical device, but in order to make the writer's intention absolutely clear. Some of these examples also show how the choice of vocabulary may influence the shape of the paragraph itself.

Part 3 makes suggestions concerning the organisation of students' self-expression on a larger scale still, notably in class-discussion and in essays. So while Part 1 consists largely of expository and practice material, Part 2 attempts to develop the students' imagination, and Part 3 merely gives him what it is hoped is useful advice.

It is not necessary to use the book as a consecutive course, though it has been planned as such. It is perfectly possible to arrange work on it using related themes from certain passages on similar topics, or simply to use sections at random for purely remedial purposes. Nor is it necessary to use all the exercises from one section. The teacher may omit such exercises as he considers too easy for his students. All the same, it is often both useful and encouraging to students to give them something that they are almost certain to get 100 per cent correct first go off, particularly in remedial work. Moreover, what has been designed as a step-by-step process should be more effective when used that way, and it is hoped that the individual steps involved are not so great as to confuse or irritate either teachers or their pupils.

Part I
STRUCTURES IN THE SENTENCE

Subdivision I
The verb and
its appendages

A
The tenses

Nearly all communications in any language fall into three categories. They may convey information, in which case they are called *statements*. They may seek information, in which case they are called *questions*; or they may require action, in which case they are called *commands*. A statement may convey information about an activity or a state of being. The state or activity may be considered as independent of any time context; it may be bound to a particular instant of time; it may be continuous; it may be repeated or habitual, not bound to a given moment or period of time, but liable to recur.

Moreover, a statement need not necessarily involve the present or actual situation. It may describe a past state or action; it may be a conjecture about the future or a wish-projection about the present; it may express regret about a past opportunity missed or mishandled. So when using language, the questions of tense, time and mood are vitally important.

Most important of all for the overseas student is the fact that the two words *tense* and *time* mean different things in English, although certain languages (e.g. French, German, Italian) use one word to name both concepts. A tense is simply a conventional verb form. It may involve a mutation of the basic form of the verb (the infinitive). It may involve, instead or in addition, the use of an auxiliary verb. It may have no time-connotation at all. It may be rigidly tied to a particular aspect of time or action. Some tenses even appear to have contradictory usages.

Traditionally the tenses in English are divided into past, present and future; their aspects into simple, continuous and perfect. Some describe states, some activities. Some indicate that the activity or state described is complete in itself, others that it is incomplete, habitual or repetitive. Some forms not normally considered as tenses indicate such things as predictions, suggestions or wish-projections. The auxiliary verbs used in some of these cases overlap with those used to form certain tenses.

The first section of this course attempts to illustrate how certain modern writers have used the various tense forms that exist in English. As far as possible the author has tried to choose texts where the tenses are used in relation to one another, so that their various uses may be more easily differentiated. The whole of Section A of the course is devoted to this work.

Section B gives examples of conditional or conjectural statements. The writer tries to say what he wishes to happen, what he thinks or hopes will happen, or what he feels might have happened, should happen, or should have happened. This inevitably involves a study of the uses of the so-called anomalous finite verbs. Section C examines how adverbial expressions of all kinds affect the structure of the sentence.

If the verb in any sentence is regarded as the central force upon which all the others depend, the nouns or pronouns acted on by the verb may be regarded as the static force which the verb is trying to shift, so to speak. The Subdivisions II, III and IV of Part 1 deal with aspects of nouns and adjectives in a manner similar to that used in Subdivision I with verbs and adverbials. The Introductory Notes to each section should help indicate its purpose.

The use of the simple present tense
to express universal statements

The simple present usually refers to a repeated action or else forms part of a statement whose validity is independent of any time context. It is often, therefore, not a *present* form at all. It is true that certain verbs (see below, §4, page 18) are rarely used in the true present (i.e. present progressive) form. But most verbs used in the simple present form occur in a context which clearly indicates a permanent state or repeated action. The latter case is usually indicated through an adverb or adverbial clause of frequency (such as one beginning with *whenever*). The following passage from a book on evolution shows how verbs, both active and passive, are used in the simple present form to express facts that the author considers to be true at all times anywhere.

PASSAGE I
No animal or plant *lives* in a vacuum. A living organism is constantly exchanging substances with its environment. A tree *absorbs* water and salts through its roots, and *loses* water and *absorbs* carbon dioxide through the leaves. A mammal *absorbs* water and food substances in the intestine and oxygen in the lungs. Without these exchanges, life is impossible, al- 5
though some seeds, spores, and encysted animals[1] *can maintain* their organization in a vacuum, and *resume* their living activity when normal conditions *are restored*. Life therefore is an active equilibrium between the living organism and its surroundings, an equilibrium which *can be maintained* only if the environment *suits* the particular animal or plant, which 10
is then said to be 'adapted' to that environment. If the animal *is placed* in an environment which *differs* too greatly from that which it *is adapted*, the equilibrium *breaks down*; a fish out of water will die.

JOHN MAYNARD SMITH: *The Theory of Evolution*

Comment
At first sight it appears that there are two exceptions to the principle stated in the introduction. In the second sentence there is the phrase 'A living organism *is constantly exchanging* substances . . .' This unusual idiom is found with certain adverbs implying a frequency so great that

[1] *encysted animal*; an animal which can enclose itself in a kind of bladder.

the constant repetition of the process almost becomes a continuous event in itself. The commonest are *always* (when it means _incessantly_, not when it means *on every occasion*), *for ever*, _continually_ and _constantly_. In the last clause of the paragraph the verb *will die* occurs; this is probably intended as a prediction of what is to happen as an inevitable and customary consequence of the main action whenever it occurs (cf. She is an industrious girl, but she *will make* silly mistakes when she doesn't concentrate).

QUESTION PAPER:

Comprehension

1 What examples does the author give of 'living organisms constantly exchanging substances with their environment'?

2 Define the following terms used in the passage:
   mammal   seeds
   roots   spores
   intestine

3 What does the author mean when he talks of *an active equilibrium*?

4 Use the following words from the passage in sentences of your own to show that you understand their *figurative* use as well as the literal one found in the passage:
   absorbed   seed
   plant   a fish out of water

5 The following words in the passage are used as nouns. Use them as *verbs* in sentences of your own.
   plant   water
   root   fish

Structures

6 Complete the following sentences in a suitable manner, putting whatever verb you use into the simple present tense:
   (*a*) Whenever he comes to a party, he ......
   (*b*) Every day, scientists ......
   (*c*) If you don't feed it regularly, a plant ......
   (*d*) I have told you at least ten times that you ......
   (*e*) They always ......
   (*f*) Nobody ever ...... nowadays.
   (*g*) She is the type of girl who regularly ......
   (*h*) She only ...... occasionally.
   (*i*) When ......?
   (*j*) Why does that student always ......?
   (*k*) How does that machine ......?

7 Write an account of the methods used by your teacher to develop your vocabulary. Your account should make use of the following adverbs: *usually, often, rarely, sometimes, frequently, never, regularly.* Remember where the adverbs should go in the sentence! (*about* 150 *words*)

8 Write a letter to an English friend describing some local festival or custom of your country which he will not have seen. (*about* 150 *words*)

Suggested discussion topics

The influence of environment on character.
Customs and habits in popular culture.
Man and his influence on the balance of nature.
The population problem and its solution.

§2 *The use of the simple future to express predictions or intentions*

One of the commonest – and most understandable – mistakes made by overseas students is that of using the simple present form in a main clause to refer to some action due to take place in the future. English speakers tend to do this only when some arrangement almost involving a set time table is concerned (e.g. your train *leaves* at 10.15; I *go* on holiday next week, so you must discuss the matter before then. The Prime Minister *sees* the T.U.C. leaders next Wednesday).

In this passage – which may be used in conjunction with §15 (page 65) – the author is comparing the present situation at some of the older English universities with the system he proposes to establish at the new University of Essex, of which he is Vice-Chancellor.

PASSAGE 2

All our courses *will be* for honours. Most English universities have a pass course which is less rigorous than the honours course, and is followed mainly by students who, at the end of their first year, are thought not to be of honours calibre. It is primarily a course for casualties. Often it consists of bits and pieces taken in several departments and lacks cohesion   5 as well as depth. In Essex, all students *will read for* honours, although someone who, in the final examination, is not good enough to be awarded third class nor bad enough to be failed outright may be awarded a pass. There *will* obviously *be* an occasional student who *will find* the course too demanding and *will not complete it.* But the advantage for the   10 weaker students of continuing with the honours course is that, as well as following an integrated scheme, they are working together with all their original colleagues. They can be helped by contact with them and they do not bear the stigma of inferior status.

A word about examinations. Only systematic research can show how   15 far the British system really measures intellect and originality, and not simply the ability to pass examinations. At this stage we propose no radical change. But we *shall vary* the circumstances under which a student is assessed: *have* some short examinations and some long, *allow* students in certain subjects to make use of text books and reference books,   20 and *take into account* research projects. The student of physics, for example, *will be required* in his final year to study and report on at least

9

one specialized topic, either experimental or theoretical, and the class of
his final degree *will be determined* in part by this individual research
project. It *will* thus *reflect* the student's ability to practise science.   25

ALBERT E. SLOMAN: A University in the Making

Comment

It can be argued that there are no future *tense forms* in English, but only
certain ways of expressing predictions. These ways depend on the like-
lihood of the prediction coming true. Here, Dr Sloman is talking about
his *intentions* and *plans* for his new university. The predictions are firm;
the future forms may be regarded as tense forms rather than mood
indicators.

Note, however, that in some of the dependent clauses, the future is not
used. In the sentence beginning 'In Essex, all students . . .' (*line* 6), the
concessive clause introduced by *although* has the verb 'is', not 'will be',
even though it refers to something which has not yet happened. The
point here is that the clause does not refer to a *prediction*. It refers to the
students' actual state of mind on the day they take the examination, not to
any prophecy about their future.

Similarly, in the sentence beginning 'But we shall vary . . .' (*line* 18),
the sequence of tenses is quite logical, though at first sight surprising.
Once it is established, assessing a student is a repeated and regular
process. The act of establishing it lies in the future – but its dependent
verb *is assessed* represents a permanent fact independent of any prediction. Note also the two passives: *will be required* and *will be determined*.

QUESTION PAPER:

Comprehension

1 Give a word or phrase of similar meaning to:
  (*a*) of honours calibre (*line* 4)
  (*b*) bits and pieces (*line* 5)
  (*c*) lacks cohesion (*line* 5)
  (*d*) too demanding (*line* 10)
  (*e*) they do not bear the stigma of inferior status (*lines* 13–14)
  (*f*) radical (*line* 18)
  (*g*) assessed (*line* 19)
  (*h*) take into account (*line* 21)

2 Use the following words in sentences of your own to show that you understand their meaning. Do NOT define them.
  (*a*) rigorous, severe, austere, strong
  (*b*) primarily, firstly, at first

(c) to neglect, to ignore, to be ignorant of
(d) physics, physic, physique
(e) topical, actual, present
(f) outright, downright, forthright
(g) cohesion, coherence

3   What do you think of Dr Sloman's scheme for examinations at the University of Essex?

Structures

4   Complete the following sentences, using the verb given in brackets in a suitable tense:
  (a) At the end of his course next week, he (*leave*) England for good.
  (b) After school this evening, she (*go*) to the theatre.
  (c) In 1970 there (*be*) a thousand miles of motorway in Britain.
  (d) I wonder if Britain (*go over*) to the metric system this century?
  (e) Any new applicant (*require*: PASSIVE) to pass a physical fitness test as from next week.
  (f) The final plan (*decide*: PASSIVE) at next month's meeting.
  (g) You (*allow*: PASSIVE) to go home in ten minutes' time.

5   Complete the following sentences, using a verb in the *simple future* form:
  (a) When I have finished reading this book ......
  (b) If we go to tea with Mrs Williams, you ......
  (c) By 1984 there ......
  (d) When I retire, I ......
  (e) As soon as I get home, we ......
  (f) Next year this class ......
  (g) By the time the Government has been in power three years, we ......
  (h) If you don't go away soon, I ......

6   Complete the responses in the following imaginary telephone conversation:
  A: Good morning. Is that the Chairman of the Committee?
  B:
  A: Can you tell me what was decided about the future of my plan?
  B:
  A: But if that is correct, doesn't that only give me six days to get it ready?
  B:
  A: I must discuss this with you personally. When will you be free?
  B:
  A: May I come and see you at lunch-time, then?
  B:
  A: Well, that means we shall have to get the matter over by two-thirty, doesn't it? Thank you very much for asking me. When shall we meet, and where?
  B:
  A: Thank you so much. I shall see you there at half past twelve, then. Good-bye.

7 Imagine that you are a political commentator predicting the policies of a newly elected government. Write a paragraph of about 120/150 words setting out what it is expected to do in the field of *either* foreign affairs *or* education.

8 Describe life in an ordinary provincial town in your country as you imagine it will be in about fifty years' time. (*about* 150/180 *words*)

Suggested discussion topics

The faults and merits of modern universities.
Intellectual snobbery: its causes and its cure.
Are examinations fair or useful?
Research is a nobler activity than teaching.

Because the so-called present perfect consists of a past participle and the auxiliary verb *have*, all too many students tend to confuse it with forms similarly constructed in their own language. It cannot be too strongly emphasised that this form is *not* a past tense. Zandvoort (*A Handbook of English Grammar*, §140) says that it usually denotes an action that falls within the time-sphere of the present. He gives three uses, *continuative* (§130) denoting an action or state beginning at some time in the past and continuing up to the present, *resultative* (§140) denoting a past action CONNECTED THROUGH ITS RESULT WITH THE PRESENT MOMENT, and the *perfect of experience* (§141), which 'expresses what has happened, once or more than once, within the speaker's or writer's experience'. As the speaker or writer cannot be other than alive at the moment of speaking or writing, the idea here, too, is one which is CONNECTED WITH THE PRESENT MOMENT. Hence it is quite un-English to use this tense in conjunction with any adverbial which indicates that there is no connection with the present. And – the converse error – students often use the simple past tense when they are talking about a state or action which comes under one of the three headings mentioned above.

The following passage (3*a*) shows the present perfect used in close connection with the simple present.

PASSAGE 3*a*

But it IS in the field of national differences that stereotypes APPEAR with particular virulence, possibly because in the case of most other groups reality and appearance IMPOSE a certain check on us, whereas in so far as other nations are concerned, we CAN rationalise our preferences in the complete absence of factual knowledge. Nor IS it the un-   5
educated who HOLD views of this kind; many a learned professor *has written* tomes on the national characteristics of various groups, based almost entirely on passing fancies and stereotyped prejudices ... It *has been* well *said* that one CANNOT indict a whole nation. Neither CAN one DESCRIBE it, and what is true of a whole nation IS also true of the con-   10
stituent parts of each nation. .... There *have been* a number of attempts at

the experimental definition of national differences and there ARE quite a
number of theories in this field, but it CANNOT truthfully BE SAID
that any reasonable progress *has been made* so far. It seems probable
that anthropological evidence regarding differences between different 15
tribes IS reasonably satisfactory, and there *have been* a number of attempts
recently to apply these methods to the larger and more complex groups
which we call civilised nations.

H. J. EYSENCK: *Uses and Abuses of Psychology*

The second passage (3*b*) shows the present perfect used almost exclusively, in two paragraphs where the emphasis is on the aspect of
'up-till-now', i.e. mainly what Zandvoort calls the *resultative* use of this
tense.

PASSAGE 3*b*

The development of the idea of culture *has* throughout *been* a criticism
of what *has been called* the bourgeois idea of society. The contributions
to its meaning *have started* from widely different positions, and *have
reached* widely various attachments and loyalties. But they *have been alike*
in this, that they *have been unable* to think of society as a merely neutral 5
area, or as an abstract regulating mechanism. The stress *has fallen* on the
positive function of society, on the fact that the values of individual men
ARE ROOTED in society, and on the need to think and feel in these
common terms. This WAS, indeed, a profound and necessary response
to the disintegrating pressures that WERE FACED. 10

Yet, according to their different positions, the idea of community,
on which all in general AGREE, *has been* differently *felt* and *defined*. In our
own day, we HAVE two major interpretations, alike opposed to bourgeois liberalism, but equally, in practice, opposed to each other. These
ARE the idea of service, and the idea of solidarity. These *have* in the main 15
been developed by the middle class and the working class respectively.
From Coleridge to Tawney the idea of function, and thence of service
to the community, *has been* most valuably *stressed*, in opposition to the
individualist claim. The stress *has been confirmed* by the generations of
training which SUBSTANTIATE the ethical practice of our professions 20
and of our public and civil service. As against the practice of *laissez-faire*,
and of self-service, this *has been* a major achievement which *has done*
much for the peace and welfare of our society. Yet the working-class
ethic, of solidarity, *has* also *been* a major achievement, and it is the
difference of this from the idea of service which must now be stressed. 25

RAYMOND WILLIAMS: *Culture and Society 1780–1950*

Comment

The instances of the simple present tense in the above passages all conform to the patterns set in the previous texts. The two passages in this

section show the relationship between the simple present and the present perfect. In doing so, they demonstrate that the present perfect is essentially a *present* and not a *past* tense.

The first thing to notice about both passages is the absence of any adverbials which tie the author's meaning to a point or period in the past. In Passage 3*a*, there is one continuative (*line* 14: 'that any reasonable progress *has been made* so far'), and three perfects of experience (*lines* 6–7: 'many a learned professor *has written* tomes'; *line* 11: 'there *have been* a number of attempts'; and *lines* 8–9: 'it *has been* well *said*'). None of these is qualified by any adverbial of definite time, but two of them are qualified by the adverbials of relative time *so far* and *recently* respectively. The meaning of both of these adverbials implies a continuity between the past and the present. In Passage 3*b*, the first adverbial of time related to a present perfect is the phrase 'from Coleridge to Tawney'; this implies a continuity between the lifetime of Coleridge (d. 1834) and Tawney, who was still alive when the passage was written. None of the other examples of the present perfect in Passage 3*b* is qualified by an adverbial of time at all.

If either of the authors had used a simple past form of the verb throughout his passage, the meaning would change completely, as indeed it does when Williams (*line* 9) writes: 'this *was* a profound and necessary response'. The *response itself* lies completely in the past; its *results* are still with us. Similarly the idea of culture; the bourgeois idea of society; the contributions to its meaning; the stress resulting from them; the two major interpretations of it – all these things still exist, as the passage implies. The verbs associated with them therefore go into the present perfect form.

QUESTION PAPER:

Comprehension

PASSAGE 3*a*
1 Give a word or phrase of similar meaning to:
   stereotypes (*line* 1)   passing fancies (*line* 8)
   virulence (*line* 2)   constituent parts (*lines* 10–11)
   rationalise (*line* 4)   anthropological evidence (*line* 15)
   tomes (*line* 7)

2 Do you think it is true that 'one cannot describe a whole nation'? In what sense do you think Professor Eysenck intends the phrase to be understood?

3 Explain what you think the author means by the following:
the bourgeois idea of society (*line* 2)   solidarity (*line* 15)
an abstract regulating mechanism (*line* 6) laissez-faire (*line* 21)
stress (*line* 6)   self-service (*line* 22)
disintegrating pressures (*line* 10)

4 What is your own conception of society? Do you consider it as 'a merely neutral area', or has it a positive function in human life?

Structures

5 Complete the following sentences, putting the verb in an appropriate tense:
   (*a*) Ever since the dawn of history ......
   (*b*) Up till now, nobody ......
   (*c*) Since the launching of the first sputnik in 1957 ......
   (*d*) Throughout the Christian era ......
   (*e*) From the Middle Ages until the present day ......
   (*f*) For the last twenty years the United Nations ......
   (*g*) Since its foundation this University ......
   (*h*) From the moment the House of Commons began discussing financial questions ......
   (*i*) Throughout their history some countries ......
   (*j*) Having got the vote in this country, women ......

6 Imagine you are applying for a job. Answer the following questions with complete sentences.
   (*a*) Have you ever been abroad in your life?
   (*b*) How long have you held your present post?
   (*c*) Have you ever been arrested by the police?
   (*d*) How many books have you written?
   (*e*) How many times have you been sacked from a job?
   (*f*) Have you ever been asked such impertinent questions before?

7 Write a paragraph of about 150 words on 'National Heroes', making use of the present perfect tense as naturally and frequently as you can. Try to use it in each of the three senses described by Zandvoort and mentioned in the introduction to this section.

Suggested discussion topics

Is there such a thing as national character? If so, what is it?
Class-consciousness and its effects.
The influence of social pressures on moral values.
The virtues and defects of patriotism.

The present progressive, the simple present and the present perfect

The next passage (4*a*) contains a number of examples of the three main present tenses in a scientific exposition. You will notice that the author uses the true present (the so-called Present Progressive or Continuous) very sparingly. He uses it to draw attention to what is actually happening *as he speaks* (the text is taken from a broadcast lecture). Students who have already read §3 should carefully note the uses of the present perfect in the passage below:

PASSAGE 4*a*

I *do not think* that since the time of Newton *it has ever been seriously contended* that the solar system *is* an accidental aggregation of bodies in space. By terrestrial standards the distances separating the sun, earth, and planets *are* very large. We *are* about ninety-three million miles from the sun, and the distant planet Pluto *is* over three and a half thousand 5 million miles away. On the other hand, the nearest star *is* over twenty billion miles distant. To bring these dimensions down to more manageable quantities, one *can say* that light from the sun *takes* 8 minutes on its way to the earth, over 5 hours to the planet Pluto, but 4 years to the nearest star. By the standards of the cosmos, the solar system *is* there- 10 fore an extremely compact unit. Moreover, the planets and the earth *move* around the sun in orbits which *are* almost circular, and all these orbits *lie* nearly in the same plane. The sun *is rotating* in the same sense as the planets, and the entire system *is moving* as a unit through interstellar space with a speed of about forty-five thousand miles per 15 hour.

SIR BERNARD LOVELL: *The Individual and the Universe*

The next passage (4*b*) is taken from a broadcast talk on art. The speaker imagines that the listener has a reproduction of the painting described before him *at the moment of speaking*. The painting, moreover, catches *a moment of time* and, so to speak, 'freezes' it, so that it is forever 'present' once the painting is completed. So when he describes it, the speaker uses the continuous form:

There is a picture by Metsu,[1] also formerly called 'The Music Lesson' but now 'A man and a woman seated by a virginal'. Here the girl *is paying* no more attention to the virginal than the young man *is* to his fiddle. She *is turning* towards him with a noticeable leer and *handing* him a song: he *is* sufficiently *entertained* by it to be about to spill over the glass of wine 5 he *is holding*. There *is* also an Ochtervelt[2] of a lady standing at a harpsichord and gazing into the eyes of a young man. And then there *are* those two strange pictures by Vermeer,[3] which *are* perhaps his latest works. In one a girl *is standing* at a harpsichord and *gazing* with a sly smile at the spectator: behind her *is* a painting of a Cupid holding up a blank card (or 10 a *billet-doux?*).

ELLIS WATERHOUSE in *The Listener*, 13 January 1966

Comment

The first of the passages shows the natural relationship between the present continuous and the other two forms. In general, as Zandvoort (§89.2) says, the verb takes on a 'dynamic' character when this form is used. In Passage 4*a*, Lovell uses the form only when he wishes to emphasise what the sun and the solar system are doing at the moment of speaking; when he wishes to emphasise what repeatedly and regularly happens, he uses the simple form. Just as 'I am English' may be clumsily paraphrased as 'My state of being is one of Englishness', so 'I am reading' may be paraphrased as 'my (present) state of being is one of reading'. One would thus expect that certain verbs indicating either a permanent state of being or an action so short that it cannot reasonably be considered as having any duration would rarely be used in the progressive form. Zandvoort (§93) gives the following list, to which one would add *to last* and *to continue*:

> to believe, to belong, to deserve, to hate, to know, to love, to mean, to own, to please, to possess, to prefer, to recognize, to remember, to resemble, to satisfy, to seem, to sound (intr.), to suffice, to suit, to surprise, to understand.

Scheurweghs (*Present-Day English Syntax*, §544, p. 319) gives as an explanation: 'Progressive tenses cannot normally be used with verbs that do not denote duration in a limited time', and adds to Zandvoort's list:

> to desire, to detest, to feel, to forget, to recollect, to refuse, to smell, to think.

[1] Dutch painter (1629–67) who painted many interiors and genre pieces.
[2] Dutch painter (*c.* 1635–*c.* 1710).
[3] Dutch painter (1632–75) whose works are internationally famous.

But he also continues; 'In present-day English, especially in spoken English, the progressive forms of these verbs are found more and more frequently, either because the verb is taken in a slightly different meaning or because it is desired to give special emphasis to their particular application to this very moment.'

Thus it would be natural in a conversation to hear the following:

'There are six of us coming.'
'*Aren't you forgetting* Jack? That makes seven, surely.'

Or this:

'Are you coming with us?'
'Be quiet. *I'm thinking.*'

These last two examples illustrate another use of this form with certain verbs – that of *indicating a future intention*. Zandvoort (§95) gives the following list of verbs frequently used in this way:

to arrive, to come, to go, to leave, to sleep, to stay; to dine, to lunch; to issue, to publish; to wear; to do; to play.

The next passage (4c) gives some examples of some of these verbs used thus.

PASSAGE 4c
'What *are you doing* tonight?' I asked him.
'*I'm going* to the Pavilion. It's packed jammed full, but there's a fellow over the road who's wonderful, and he's got me a ticket that had been returned. You can often get one seat, you know, when you can't get two.'   5
'Why don't you come and have supper with me? *I'm taking* some people to the Haymarket, and *we're going on* to Ciro's afterwards.'
                              W. SOMERSET MAUGHAM: *Virtue*

Comment
Where the statement or question refers to a present intention the speaker naturally uses a progressive form (e.g. 'What *are you doing* tonight?'; '*I'm going* to the Pavilion'; '*I'm taking* some people'; '*we're going on* to Ciro's').

In a negative question, however, this form implies a certain surprise, even portentousness – perhaps a protest. An example of this is 'Why *aren't you coming?*' If Maugham had used that instead of '*Why don't you come?*' the questioner would have implied that something had already arisen to prevent the other person from coming. '*Why don't you come?*'

however is simply an open suggestion which may be either accepted ('Yes, I will') or rejected ('No, thank you').

QUESTION PAPER:

Comprehension

1 Find words in Passage 4*a* whose meaning corresponds to the following definitions:
   to maintain in dispute,
   formation into a mass,
   closely packed or fitted together,
   path in which a heavenly body moves round another,
   flat or level surface,
   to turn like a wheel,
   in the intervals between the stars.

2 Give a phrase of similar meaning to (Passage 4*a*):
   By terrestrial standards (*line* 3)
   On the other hand (*line* 6)
   in the same sense as (*line* 14)
   as a unit (*line* 15)

3 Explain the difference between the following astronomical terms:
   (*a*) star *and* planet
   (*b*) solar system *and* cosmos
   (*c*) orbit *and* plane

4 What is the difference in meaning between:
   (*a*) sly, crafty, cunning, astute, shrewd.
   (*b*) to gaze, to stare, to leer, to glare, to simper, to grin.

Structures

5 Answer these questions with complete sentences. Put the verb into the most suitable tense.
   (*a*) Where's George? ......
   (*b*) What's he doing? ......
   (*c*) Does he do this often? ......
   (*d*) How long has he done it? ......
   (*e*) What's he doing this evening? ......
   (*f*) When does he normally arrive back home? ......
   (*g*) What does he usually do in the evenings? ......
   (*h*) Why doesn't he come and play bridge with us this evening? ......

6 Imagine that you are a radio commentator describing the arrival of an important foreign guest in your country. Using the present progressive tense *when necessary*, set the scene for your listeners at home and give an account of what happens.   (*about* 120/150 *words*)

7   Imagine that you are sitting in a railway train, writing a letter to a friend at home. The train is crowded, and standing at a large station. Compose a paragraph taken from your letter about what is happening.

(about 120/150 *words)*

Suggested discussion topics

Space travel and space research – are they worth it?
Man in the universe.
Modern art.
Patronage of the arts and sciences.

§5 *The present perfect in relation to the simple past*

Although the present perfect has already been considered in its aspect as a present tense, you must not forget that it does form a link between the present and some moment in the past. When wishing to describe a process, state or action which lies completely in the past, an English speaker normally uses the simple past tense.

Zandvoort (§135) illustrates its use when drawing attention to the time in the past at which an action or event took place. This obviously implies that it is necessary with any adverbial of definite past time, such as *yesterday, three minutes ago, last January* and so on. He also mentions its *iterative* aspect (§136); English speakers use it to refer to a former habit or custom now abandoned. Students should remember that the adverbial expression of past time demanding a simple past need not necessarily be a simple adverb or adverbial phrase; it may be a temporal clause beginning with such a conjunction as *when, whenever,* etc. Adverbials of place, too, may require a simple past when they refer to a place no longer 'inhabited' by the speaker or writer.

PASSAGE 5

When I *wrote* 'Murder in the Cathedral' I *had* the advantage, for a beginner, of an occasion which *called for* a subject generally admitted to be suitable for verse. Verse plays, it HAS BEEN generally HELD, should either take their subject matter from some mythology, or else should be about some remote historical period, far enough away from the present for the   5 characters not to need to be recognizable as human beings, and therefore for them to be licensed to talk in verse. Picturesque period costume renders verse much more acceptable. Furthermore, my play *was to be produced* for a rather special kind of audience – an audience of those serious people who go to festivals and expect to have to put up with 10 poetry – though perhaps on this occasion some of them *were* not quite prepared for what they *got*. And finally, it *was* a religious play, and people who go deliberately to a religious play at a religious festival expect patently to be bored and to satisfy themselves with the feeling that they HAVE DONE something meritorious. So the path *was made* easy.   15

T. S. ELIOT: *Poetry and Drama*

Comment

The first thing to notice in this passage, once again, is how the present perfect is brought into relation with the simple present. In *line 3*, the phrase 'it has been generally held' is related to the modal *should*, which is certainly a present here. Similarly, in *lines* 14-15, 'feeling that *they have done something meritorious*' (not they *did*) is a case where the *effect* of the act performed lasts until the moment of speaking or writing (in this case, of feeling). The act itself is not tied to the past; the statement is a generalization believed to be true independently of any time context (hence the present simples: 'people who *go . . . expect*').

The case is quite different, however, when Mr Eliot considers actions which are now complete and cannot be renewed, or for which the conditions cannot be re-created. The other verbs are related to one single past event – the first performance of *Murder in the Cathedral*. So Mr Eliot *had the advantage* (*line* 1) when he wrote the play; the occasion *called* for a particular subject; the play *was to be produced*; that first-night audience *were* (*on this occasion*) not quite prepared for what they *got*. And it *was* a religious play (at a particular religious festival). Thus the path *was* made easy.

QUESTION PAPER:

Comprehension

1 Give examples of Mr Eliot's use of perfectly normal words or expressions with a slightly ironic flavour throughout this passage.

2 The adjectives *religious, meritorious* (and *serious*) are members of that very large group of English adjectives ending in *-ious*. Find out, if you do not know it already, what the following ones mean:

meretricious, insidious, fastidious, bilious, contagious, obnoxious, fractious, rumbustious, obsequious, specious.

Now use them in sentences of your own as effectively as you can.

3 What, in your opinion, are the advantages and disadvantages of verse drama?

Structures

4 Fill the gaps in the following passage, putting the verbs in a suitable tense:

Up till now, it (*be*) possible to absorb most of the new immigrants in this country without too many of them feeling like fish out of water. Occasionally English people (*behave*) badly, some immigrants (*feel*) out of things, and many of those who (*believe*) that they (*bear*) the stigma of inferior status (*return*) home. It (*be*) not always easy to feel completely integrated in any strange society, and this (*be*) always particularly the case in England,

23

where so many quaint customs (*be*) still maintained, and so many social conventions (*rest*) on unexplained, and often inexplicable minutiae of conduct. This (*be*) the case in previous ages, too, as satirists (*show*) from the earliest times until the present. The most adaptable immigrants of the past, however, always (*take*) into account that they (*must*) understand the customs of their hosts, even if they (*adopt*) them (*not*).

5 Complete the following sentences in a suitable manner:
   (*a*) Last week, when going up to London, I ......
   (*b*) When she was a student, she often ......
   (*c*) In 1492, when Columbus ......, Britain ......
   (*d*) The last time I went ski-ing, I ......
   (*e*) At the first production of this play, in 1953, ...
   (*f*) As a student in America, that Thai girl ......

6 Write a paragraph describing your first day in a strange foreign city.
                                                         (*about* 150/180 *words*)

7 Write a paragraph from an imaginary guide-book describing a famous historic building in your country, concentrating on how and when it was built rather than what it now looks like.   (*about* 120/150 *words*)

Suggested discussion topics

The present and future of the theatre.

Art festivals are a cunningly disguised tourist-trap and are artistically worthless.

The Church and the theatre.

§6 The use of the past and present progressive forms in relation to other tenses

Just as the present progressive form inevitably refers to an action not yet completed, i.e. in progress, at the moment of speaking or writing, so does the past progressive refer to one not yet completed at a given and stated instant of time in the past. It is therefore most unusual to find this form used unless it either indicates the background to another action going on at the same time or illustrates a longer action in progress which a short, sharp action interrupts in some way. The shorter action may be implied rather than stated, and in any case ties the longer, progressive action down to a stated time. The following passage, a grim description of a scene that fortunately·could not be paralleled in modern Britain, takes its setting in time from the first sentence. The actions set in the past progressive form must be considered as taking place within the context of that one action; 'we walked up to the top of the slag-heap' is, so to speak, the adverbial of definite time that ties the other actions to a given moment in the past.

PASSAGE 6

We WALKED up to the top of the slag-heap. The men *were shovelling* the dirt out of the trucks, while down below their wives and children *were kneeling*, swiftly *scrabbling* with their hands in the damp dirt and *picking out* lumps of coal the size of an egg or smaller. You WOULD SEE a woman pounce on a tiny fragment of stuff, wipe it on her apron, scrutinise it to 5 make sure it was coal, and pop it jealously into her sack. Of course, when you *are boarding* a truck you DON'T KNOW beforehand what is in it; it may be actual 'dirt' from the roads or it MAY BE shale from the roofing. If it *is* a shale truck, there WILL BE no coal in it, but there OCCURS among the shale another inflammable rock called cannel, which LOOKS 10 very like ordinary shale, but IS slightly darker and IS KNOWN by splitting in parallel lines like slate. It makes tolerable fuel, not good enough to be commercially valuable, but good enough to be eagerly sought after by the unemployed. The miners on the shale trucks *were picking out* the cannel and *splitting it up* with their hammers. Down at the bottom of the 15 'broo'[1] the people who had failed to get on to either train *were gleaning*

[1] 'broo'; North-country and Scottish dialect word. The meaning here is 'hill', 'ridge'.

the tiny chips of coal that came rolling down from above – fragments no bigger than a hazel-nut, these, but the people were glad enough to get them.

GEORGE ORWELL: The Road to Wigan Pier

Comment

Since the progressive forms are all conjugated with the verb *to be*, a complete series of them exists if a verb possesses them at all, and their use depends in any given context on the normal conventions governing the use of the tenses. In this passage the seven (eight, if you count the idiomatic *came rolling*) past progressive forms all relate to the completed action 'We walked up to the top'. It is their point of reference in time. Implicit in every clause where Orwell uses a past progressive here is the idea 'at that particular moment'. Taken together, however, the moments form a closed, completed action. It lasts a short span of time – the time required to reach the top of the slag-heap. And so the modal verb *would* has an iterative sense (see §11). As that verb is iterative, so it implies another adverbial: 'every now and then'; 'at certain moments when one looked'. The other tenses are used in ways already discussed.

QUESTION PAPER:

Comprehension

1 Orwell uses the words *lumps*, *fragments* and *chips* to describe the various-sized pieces of stuff in the passage. Make a list of other words which signify a particular kind of *piece* of solid matter.

2 Use the following verbs in sentences of your own – figuratively if possible – showing that you know what they mean:

to scrabble	to pop (into)
to pounce (on)	to pick out
to wipe	to glean
to scrutinise	

3 The following words are used literally in the text. In the examples below, they form part of idioms. What do these idioms mean?
   (*a*) You can like it or *lump* it. (Slang)
   (*b*) He's tied to his mother's *apron*-strings. (Informal)
   (*c*) I never had any *truck* with fellows of that sort. (Informal)
   (*d*) The opposition *hammered* at the point until they succeeded. (Informal)
   (*e*) He's a *chip* off the old block. (Colloquial)

4 The following technical terms all relate to the mining industry. Find out what they mean, if you do not already know.

slag-heap	roofing
shale	fuel

Structures

5   Put the verbs in brackets in an appropriate form:

While I (*sit*) in the garden, it (*begin*) to rain. Some men (*work*) in the adjacent field, and soon it (*rain*) so hard that they (*run*) for shelter. Then the storm (*begin*). It (*be*) a most impressive sight. All the time it (*last*), hailstones as big as pennies (*fall*) and (*rattle*) against the window-panes of our house. The wind (*howl*) about the chimneys, and the doors (*shake*) from time to time. In neighbouring houses, slates (*rip* – PASSIVE) from the roofs, and while it (*continue*), many people (*wonder*) whether some of the houses (*will*) get blown down. Just as we (*worry*) about possible damage, the storm (*die down*) as quickly as it (*begin*).

6   Write sentences illustrating or referring to the following situations, using a past progressive where appropriate, and beginning with the openings suggested in brackets.

(*a*) You have just arrived at a party, looking rather distraught. Your host asks you what is wrong. You explain that a dangerous driver nearly involved your car in an accident. (When I was on the way here ......)

(*b*) You are in the theatre. Someone sitting in front turns round and tells you off for whispering so loudly. Your companion asks you what is wrong. You explain what happened (I was just ......)

(*c*) You are in the middle of writing a letter to a friend. A ball bounces through the window, spilling ink all over the table. Your hostess comes in and asks you to explain what has happened. (I was ......)

(*d*) You meet a friend. The last time you saw him, he was dressed in a very strange costume, in a disreputable part of the town. You want to know the reason. (What were you .....?)

(*e*) You are in a train. A fellow-passenger pulls the communication-cord, and leaps out of the window as the train slows down. The guard comes and asks you what happened. (The train was ......)

7   Write a paragraph of about 120/150 words describing what happened during a long wait at some office before an interview about a job.

Suggested discussion topics

The State and the poor.
From each according to his ability; to each according to his need.
The difficulties of working in a foreign country.
Industrialisation and the problems it brings.

§7 The past perfect in relation to the simple past

The past progressive tends to be used in relation to the simple past when one wishes to describe any action not yet completed as a kind of background to a point of time in the past. This point of time might well be that of an action referred to in the simple past tense. The past perfect tense is used to illustrate an action which is complete before another action starts, both actions being completely in the past. It is thus often used in narratives relating to past time, and above all in reported speech and, as will be shown in §12, in what are called rejected conditionals. In Passage 7 the point of time to which all the past perfect forms refer is not actually mentioned in the paragraph quoted. It is the entry of a friend into the room described here. The fact that this entry takes place at the end of the day is not really relevant; it is the entry itself that constitutes the point of time.

PASSAGE 7

I *had drawn* my curtains early that evening and *not moved out*. The kitchens *had sent up* a meal, and I *had eaten* it as I read by the fire. The fire *had been kept* high and bright all day; though it was nearly ten o'clock now, I stoked it again, shovelling coal up the back of the chimney, throwing it on so it would burn for hours. It was scorchingly hot in front of the fire,   5 and warm, cosy, shielded, in the zone of the two armchairs and the sofa which formed an island of comfort round the fireplace. Outside that zone, as one went towards the walls of the lofty medieval room, the draughts were bitter. In a blaze of firelight, which shone into the sombre corners, the panelling on the walls glowed softly almost rosily, but no   10 warmth reached as far. So that, on a night like this, one came to treat most of the room as the open air, and hurried back to the cosy island in front of the fireplace, the pool of light from the reading-lamp on the mantelpiece, the radiance which was more pleasant because of the cold air which one *had* just *escaped*.   15

C. P. SNOW: *The Masters*

Comment

A straightforward piece of visual description of a scene lying completely in the past, so the writer uses the simple past throughout the narrative for the actions described, whether he is describing a single action (*line* 4: *I stoked it again*) or a habitual reaction (*line* 11: *one came to treat . . . and hurried back . . .*). The past perfect is used for those actions already in the past before his narrative takes place. You will notice that the past perfect may be used either to refer to a finished action (*lines* 1-2: *the kitchens had sent up a meal, and I had eaten it*) or to a continuous process lasting up to the time-reference (*lines* 2-3: *the fire had been kept high and bright all day*), so it can, as it were, be regarded as a kind of 'indirect perfect' or as an 'indirect simple past'. It can also be used with reference to a single action or state, as in the cases mentioned above, or with reference to a habit or custom (as in the last sentence, where *had just escaped* is tied to the iterative simple pasts *came*, *hurried* and *was*).

QUESTION PAPER:

Comprehension

1 Differentiate between:
   cosy, comfortable; medieval, middle-aged; high, tall, lofty; sombre, dark, obscure, gloomy; pool, pond.
   Use them in sentences of your own.

2 Do you think you get a good picture of the actual features of the room described, or more of the atmosphere? Why?

3 Can you infer from the passage roughly what the time of year was, what sort of a building the room was in, and what sort of job the writer did? What details of the description help to tell you?

Structures

4 Complete the following sentences with a suitable clause:
   (*a*) I began writing letters after . . . . . .
   (*b*) When she arrived home, she found that the fire, formerly so bright . . . . .
   (*c*) It was now six weeks since John . . . . . .
   (*d*) He told her about his previous career; he . . . . . .
   (*e*) He said he wouldn't buy the car until . . . . . .

5 Write an imaginary report on an interview you have conducted with an applicant for a job, telling a friend how the applicant described the various stages of his career to you.   (*about* 150 *words*)

6 Write a dialogue between two friends, informing one another about a swindler who has played different tricks on each of them.
                                                      (*about* 180/200 *words*)

Suggested discussion topics

If men value comfort more than justice, they will soon find
that in losing justice they will lose comfort, too.
Some animals hibernate; all men ought to, particularly politicians.
Styles and fashions in furniture and interior decoration.

§8 The past perfect in relation to time and other contingencies

In §7, we considered the use of the past perfect as an absolute tense, occurring in its own right in main clauses. This tense, like some others, is found far more frequently, however, as a subsidiary in subordinate clauses, such as temporal or conditional clauses, or in reported speech.

PASSAGE 8

Our real trouble WAS that we WERE short of capital, for it *had* all *been spent* in the old days before I TOOK OVER the running of the farm. We COULD NOT carry through any radical improvements, but HAD TO live from hand to mouth – and this in the last years, BECAME our normal mode of living on the farm.   5

If I *had had* the capital, I THOUGHT, I WOULD HAVE GIVEN UP coffee, have cut down the coffee trees, and have planted forest trees on my land. Trees GROW UP so quickly in Africa, in ten years' time you WALK comfortably under tall blue gum trees and wattle trees which you HAVE yourself in the rain CARRIED in boxes from the nurseries, twelve 10 trees in a box. I WOULD HAVE HAD then, I REFLECTED, a good market for both timber and firewood in Nairobi. It IS a noble occupation to plant trees, you THINK of it many years after with content. There *had been* big stretches of native forest on the farm in the old days, but it *had been sold* to the Indians for cutting down, before I TOOK OVER the 15 farm; it WAS a sad thing. I myself in the hard years HAD HAD TO cut down the wood on my land round the factory for the steam-engine, and this forest, with the tall stems and the live green shadows in it, *had haunted* me. I HAVE NOT FELT more sorry for anything I HAVE DONE in my life, than for cutting it down. From time to time, when I COULD AFFORD 20 it, I PLANTED UP bits of land with eucalyptus trees, but it DID NOT COME TO much. It WOULD BE, in this way, fifty years before I *had got* the many hundred acres planted up, and *had changed* the farm into a singing wood, scientifically run, with a sawmill by the river. The squatters of the farm however, whose ideas of time WERE different from those of the 25 white people, KEPT ON looking forward hopefully to the time when everybody WOULD HAVE abundance of firewood – such as the people *had had* in the old days – from the forest that I WAS now soon GOING TO plant.

KAREN BLIXEN: *Out of Africa*

Comment

This whole passage is not, officially, a piece of reported speech, but the author treats the tense system throughout much of it as if it were. The informal, almost conversational narrative slips quite easily from a direct address to the reader into a more formal attitude, where the author is recounting her own reflections about the past – a past previous to the point that she had reached in her narrative. Occasionally she slips in a general observation which is independent of her main narrative, and for that she resorts to the immediacy of the simple present and present perfect forms (e.g. *line* 8: *Trees grow up so quickly in Africa; line* 19: *I have not felt more sorry* . . . etc.).

The first and third sentences of the second paragraph constitute together a *rejected condition*. Conditional sentences often cause difficulty, particularly those involving the use of the words *would* and *should*. This will be dealt with more fully in Section B (§§ 10–13). It should be noted here, though, that the tense in the subordinate clause with *if* is a past perfect:

If I *had had* the capital, . . . I *would have given up* coffee.

Similarly, in the third sentence of that paragraph:

I *would have had* . . . a good market for both timber and firewood in Nairobi.

Implicit in this statement is the unstated 'If I *had had* the capital'.

QUESTION PAPER:

Comprehension

1 The words *nurseries* and *squatters* are used in a rather special sense here. What do they mean, and what other meanings have they?

2 Why was the writer genuinely sorry to have coffee trees instead of forest trees? And why, do you think, did she regret cutting down the wood on her land round the factory?

3 What do the following expressions mean?
   living from hand to mouth   this forest . . . had haunted me
   timber and firewood   it did not come to much

Structures

4 The following sentences have been taken from the passage and put into direct speech, as if they were the actual thoughts going through the writer's mind. Change the words *I think* back to *I thought*, alter the tenses to fit the

sequence of tenses in reported speech, and then see whether your answer has the same tenses as the original passage:

If I had the capital, I think, I should give up coffee, cut down the coffee trees, and plant forest trees on my land. I should then have a good market for both timber and firewood in Nairobi. There were big stretches of native forest on the farm in the old days, but it was sold to the Indians for cutting down, before I took over the farm; it is a sad thing. I myself in the hard years had to cut down the wood on my land round the factory for the steam-engine, and this forest haunted me. It will be, in this way, fifty years before I have got the many hundred acres planted up, and have changed the farm into a singing wood. From time to time, when I can afford it, I plant up bits of land with eucalytus trees, but it does not come to much.

5 Complete the following sentences, using an appropriate verb expression:
   (a) He would have got the job, if ......
   (b) You wouldn't have missed the train, if ......
   (c) She wouldn't agree to his suggestion until ......
   (d) There would have been plenty of time to finish the job, if ......
   (e) What would you have done, if ......

6 Compose sentences of your own, using the openings suggested, to illustrate or refer to the following situations:
   (a) A friend has forgotten his wallet, and there is not enough money to pay the taxi. (If you . . .)
   (b) A politician has made a speech, but has had difficulty dealing with the questions afterwards. (As soon as . . .)
   (c) After long negotiations your manager has agreed to your suggestions for a new sales process. (Until I . . .)
   (d) A friend has passed a vital examination, yet his name didn't appear on the list and you are discussing it with him. (When I saw the list, I thought . . .)
   (e) Because a train service has been withdrawn, you have difficulties in getting to London. (If this service . . . .)

7 Write a paragraph of about 150/180 words on the subject: *If I had lived two hundred years ago.*

Suggested discussion topics

   Planning too much in advance is irresponsible.
   Striking a balance between social needs and individual wishes.
   Men are not evil so much as greedy, short-sighted and lazy.
   Why not allow women to run the world? Men have made a bad enough mess of it for too long.

§9 *The perfect progressive forms*

The three main perfect progressive forms – past, present and future – are not common, but it is necessary to know how to use them. Their time connotations are easy enough to understand; but as they consist of a perfect from the verb *to be* + the *present* participle of the main verb, they tend, like all progressive forms, to throw the interest not on to the action of the verb itself, but on to the state of being of the subject at the time the action was performed. This is so whether the auxiliary verb is in the past, present or (very rarely indeed) future perfect form.

Compare the two sentences 'What have you learnt?' and 'What have you been learning?'; the former seems to stress rather THE ACTION of learning; the latter THE STATE REACHED BY THE SUBJECT of the action. If one heard a crash during the washing-up in the kitchen, one would surely ask '*What have you broken?*' not '*What have you been breaking?*' If one met a friend one had not seen for years, one's first question would almost certainly be '*What have you been doing?*'

Since these tenses are not common, isolated examples of them are quoted in their immediate context instead of extended passages.

PASSAGE 9*a*

When Ashenden met her she *had been leading* this riotous life, *dancing* and *gambling* all night, *racing* most afternoons a week, for twelve or thirteen years and she was no longer very young; but there was hardly a line on that lovely brow, scarcely a crow's foot round those liquid eyes, to betray the fact. The most astonishing thing about her was that notwith- 5
standing this feverish and unending round of senseless debauchery she HAD PRESERVED an air of virginity.

W. SOMERSET MAUGHAM: His Excellency

Comment

The past perfect simple (*had preserved, line* 7) contrasts sharply with the progressive *had been leading* (*line* 1) and the three present participles connected with it. It would have been absurd to say '*She had been preserving* an air . . .' That would imply either a conscious or a frequentative process rather than a continuous one.

PASSAGE 9*b*

It occurs to me that during these talks *I have been depicting* the countryside as a sort of paradise in which every prospect pleases and where no man is vile. That, of course, is not true. Countryfolk have the same share of worries as townsfolk, and there is just as much envy, hate and uncharitableness in our rural districts as there is in our towns – but no 5 more. That is the point which *I have been trying* to make – the townsfolk and countryfolk on this island are not inhabitants of *different* countries but very near neighbours in a small one.

A . G . STREET: Fit for What?

Comment

The continuous perfect tenses are frequently used when a *series* of actions, repeated (usually at regular or short intervals) are considered as constituting together a kind of unified process. Such is the case with the examples here. Mr Street spoke, not once, but several times, in a series of broadcasts about the relationship between town and country life. The verb *have been depicting* in *line* 1 implies three things. Firstly, the action started in the past, and is still going on at the moment of speaking (present perfect) or at any rate has only just finished. Secondly, the action consisted of a repeated process. Thirdly, the repetitions constituted a kind of 'chain' of actions, each of which could be considered either separately or as part of that chain.

It is sometimes argued that this tense is only used when the action under consideration is to be continued in the future. This is not always so. Certainly a caption in *The Times* under a photograph of Signor Danilo Dolci to the effect that he *had been fighting* the Mafia in Sicily would imply that he intended to continue doing so there, whereas *he has fought* the Mafia in Sicily would probably imply that if he intended continuing, it would be somewhere else, or even that he was now going to stop; but it cannot fairly be argued that any of the examples chosen here falls into this category.

QUESTION PAPER:

Comprehension

1 In Passage 9*a*, Mr Maugham uses the following descriptive expressions. Explain what he means by them:

    a crow's foot   senseless debauchery
    liquid eyes   an air of virginity

2 What do you think the phrase means in Passage 9*b* 'where every prospect pleases and where no man is vile'?

3 Put the verbs in an appropriate tense:

I (*wait*) here daily since last November for the nine o'clock bus. It always (*come*) at least five minutes late, so that every day since I (*start*) my new job, I (*have*) to run from the bus-stop to my office. Unfortunately, I (*get*) rather fat lately, the result of too little exercise, so I (*arrive*) recently at the office rather out of breath every morning. As a result, I (*think*) about various ways to slim. I (*study*) the newspaper advertisements every day, and I think I (*find*) what I want. It (*be*) a kind of stationary rowing-boat, which (*sell*) rather well in this country lately. A friend of mine who (*buy*) one last week already (*lose*) ten pounds, as he (*use*) it for an hour every day since he (*buy*) it.

4 Write a paragraph from a letter to a friend describing the changes in your home town since he last visited it six years ago. (120/150 *words*)

5 Write an account of a talk by an explorer who has just returned from a remote part of the world. (150/180 *words*)

Suggested discussion topics

The advantages and disadvantages of life in the country.
The State and the gambling public.
Racing.

B
Moods and contingencies

Relatively few statements are completely bound to a definite point or period of time. Some are independent of any time context, merely held to be generally true. Others 'project' a situation on to reality, or are based on the assumption that the past did not develop as it actually did. Others still predict what may happen, or what it is hoped will happen. It may even be argued that the future form is not a tense, but a projection of a present feeling about or attitude towards what will probably happen. Other 'projections' may express one's *desire* to do something, one's *regret* that one cannot do or has not done a particular thing, one's assertions that one is *in a position* to do it, that one has the *skill* or *capacity* to do it, that it is one's *duty* to do it, that one is *forbidden to*, and so on. The aim of the following ten sections is to show how these various ideas may be expressed in English.

Many of the mistakes overseas students make result from misuse of tense forms in contexts of this kind. This is understandable, as English uses the various auxiliary verbs conventionally found in such statements with some freedom. But many mistakes can be avoided if the student remembers that grammatically speaking, it is the *main* clause that matters. It is the tense of the verb in that clause, not in the subordinate one, which shows whether the statement is a fact or a projection. The subordinate clause may well be the more significant of the two syntactically, and it is usually the more 'real' of the two from the tense point of view. The subordinating conjunctions that seem to present most difficulty are those of time: *when, whenever, until, as soon as,* etc.; and those of conditional contingency: *if, unless, in case, supposing,* etc.

Obviously any time clause is a kind of adverb. It may be an adverbial of definite time, defining the exact moment or period when something happened; it may be an adverbial of relative time, or one of frequency. And it may have overtones which are not simply temporal but relate, for example, to ideas of cause and effect. There are cases, too, when *if* and *whenever* are so close in meaning as to be practically interchangeable.

In such cases the sequence of tenses within the sentence must be consistent.

Because clauses of this kind often involve imagining that things are different from what they actually are, we often find the so-called modal verbs in the main clause. The verbs which occur most frequently in such cases are *will, shall, can, could, would* and *should*. Some languages use a subjunctive form to show the relationship between what is actual and what is conjectural; English does not. These verbs often correspond to what would be a subjunctive in other languages, but it is misleading to call them subjunctives. They have a wide range of meanings, some of which are not 'subjunctive' at all.

A word about inversions

It is perfectly natural English in certain forms of conditional sentence to omit the conditional conjunction *if* and invert the verb–subject order, as if the sentence were a question, in the subordinate clause. No examples of this procedure are found in the texts chosen here to illustrate contingencies. If the student wishes to study this type of conditional form as well, he is asked to look ahead to §23, which deals with inversions of the normal word order. This convention is commonest in rejected conditions and certain types of open condition.

§10 *Open conditions with a present tense in the subordinate clause*

The first type of conditional sentence dealt with here is that which has a main verb form relating to a future event. Since a contingency presents two statements, one hypothetical or predictive, and the other the direct consequence of it, it is normal in English to regard the hypothetical or predictive statement as 'real', and the consequence as 'future' in this type of sentence. The 'real' statement is represented by a clause with a *present* tense; the consequence indicates or implies the future by use of a modal verb or an imperative. Passage 10*a* illustrates this type of conditional sentence.

PASSAGE 10*a*

If I take it for granted that the sea exists, none of you *will contradict* me. *If I say* that the sea is sometimes furiously violent and always uncertain, and that those who are most familiar with it trust it least, you *will not* immediately *shriek out* that I do not believe in the sea; that I am an enemy of the sea; that I want to abolish the sea; that I am going to 5 make bathing illegal; that I am out to ruin our carrying trade and lay waste all our seaside resorts and scrap the British Navy. *If I tell you* that you cannot breathe in the sea, you *will not take* that as a personal insult and ask me indignantly if I consider you inferior to a fish. Well, you must please be equally sensible *when I tell you* some hard facts 10 about Democracy.

GEORGE BERNARD SHAW: Preface to *The Apple Cart*

Comment

The commonest form of conditional sentence in English with a verb in the present is the *open present* condition, such as the above passage illustrates. In it the subordinate verb goes into the present tense (usually either simple or perfect; sometimes, though more rarely, progressive) and the verb in the main clause into the simple future. Neither the form nor the meaning needs any further explanation. But perhaps students' attention should be drawn to the last sentence of the above example. The convention that the verb in the subordinate clause is a *present*, even though the main verb is a *future* holds good in temporal clauses as well as conditionals. Conjunctions such as *When, Until, Before, After, Whenever,* and conjunctional phrases such as *As soon as, The moment that,* etc., all require the observance of this convention.

PASSAGE 10*b*
He that is unfaithful in little is unfaithful also in much; *if* a common court case *cannot be* correctly *reported,* how *are we to believe* the reports of world events? *If* an interviewer *misinterprets* the novelist whom we have all seen, what *does he do* with the foreign statesman whom *we have never seen?* *If* the papers *can be convicted* of False Emphasis, Garbling, 5
Inaccuracy, Reversal of the Fact, Random Invention, Miracle-Mongering, and Flat Suppression in cases where such distortions are of advantage to nobody, what *are we to suppose* about those cases in which vested interests are closely concerned? And, above all, what are we to make of the assumptions on which all this is based – that the reader is too stupid 10
to detect falsehood and too frivolous even to resent it?
DOROTHY L. SAYERS: *How Free is the Press?*

Comment
This passage illustrates another kind of conditional sentence, this time where both verbs, main and subordinate, are in a present tense. Notice, by the way, that Miss Sayers treats the present perfect as a present tense, not a past, and that her suppositions refer, not to a single future event, but to a habitual course of action not restricted to any given time or reaction.

QUESTION PAPER:

Comprehension

1   The word *shriek* (used by Shaw in *line* 4 of Passage 10*a*) is commonly used of the human voice. Make up sentences of your own, using the following words of related but different meaning:
   to screech, to squeal, to scream, to squeak.

2   Give a word or phrase of similar meaning to:
      lay waste   scrap (Passage 10*a*)
   and:
      garbling   vested interests
      random invention   frivolous
      miracle-mongering   to resent (Passage 10*b*)
      distortions

3   In Passage 10*a*, Shaw states that he is going to tell the reader some 'hard facts' about Democracy. Write a further paragraph to the passage stating some of these hard facts.

4 To what extent do you think Miss Sayers's criticisms of the modern popular press are justified? Mention some of the 'vested interests' that she might have had in mind (Passage 10*b*, *lines* 8-9).

5 There are two allusions to Biblical quotations in Passage 10*b*. Can you find them? How many other common idiomatic phrases can you think of in English which come from the Bible?

Structures

6 Put the verb in a suitable form:
   (*a*) If you (*come*) tomorrow, I (*have*) the book ready.
   (*b*) If he (*keep*) his promise, you (*be able to*) pay for the car next month.
   (*c*) If you (*light*) that fuse now, the rocket (*go*) off.
   (*d*) Unless you (*enter*) for the exam now, it (*be*) too late.
   (*e*) Supposing you (*tell*) your father later, what (*do*) he then?
   (*f*) If you (*ask*) him for help nowadays, he (*be*) always ready to give it.
   (*g*) If you (*jump*) this queue, of course people (*get*) angry.
   (*h*) People (*send*) to prison if they (*convict*) of stealing. (BOTH VERBS IN THE PASSIVE)

7 Complete the following sentences with a suitable expression:
   (*a*) You will lose your money if you ......
   (*b*) We shan't catch the train unless ......
   (*c*) Suppose you stop shouting; ......
   (*d*) Don't lock the door, in case ......
   (*e*) I shall send the letter by registered post, in case ......
   (*f*) He only gets angry if ......
   (*g*) Nobody will mind if you ......
   (*h*) You'll catch a cold if you ......
   (*i*) Don't bother to wait up for me unless ......
   (*j*) We always underline such words, in case ......

8 Compose sentences of your own, using a condition-sentence framework, to illustrate or refer to the following situations:
   (*a*) A friend has decided to walk along the parapet of a high building.
   (*b*) Someone wants you to lend him a large sum of money.
   (*c*) You have been asked out to dinner, but the date is unsuitable; however, you would like to go.
   (*d*) Your car has broken down on the open road. You want your companion to stay in it while you fetch help.
   (*e*) You are commenting on a lazy fellow student's chance of passing an exam. He is quite clever.
   (*f*) Some friends of yours have been staying at your house at your expense for rather longer than you like.
   (*g*) You are going out for the evening; there have been some robberies in the neighbourhood recently.
   (*h*) A rich friend offers you a chance to go on a summer cruise with him.

9 Write a letter of complaint to a hotel suggesting improvements they might make in their service to guests. Use *if*, *unless*, *in case*, and *supposing* at least once each when making your suggestions. (*about* 120/150 *words*)

Suggested discussion topics

Mass-communications and mass-democracy.
The Age of the Common Man is the Age of Mediocrity.
Public and private morality in the twentieth century.

§11 *Conditions with the simple past tense in the subordinate clause*

A very common mistake in students' English is the over-use of the so-called conditionals. One of the reasons for this is probably that the verbs *would* and *should*, commonly used to signal the conditional in English, also have other idiomatic uses (see below, §§17, 18). The passages in this section have been chosen to demonstrate the uses of these conditional forms (and, of course, when they are NOT used) in conditional sentences. Students should remember that the conditional *form* as such occurs in the MAIN CLAUSE ONLY; and that if the verb *would* or *should* happens to occur in the subordinate clause, it is there as a modal verb or as a substitute for the conjunction *if*. The verb in the subordinate clause, whatever it may be, will be found to be in the simple past tense in all these examples.

PASSAGE 11*a*

If our estimate of Handel *were based* as it was in contemporary London upon his forty-two Italian operas, instead of upon 'Messiah' and 'Israel in Egypt', *we should see* nothing but common sense in the contemporary judgement as to the rivalry between Handel and Bononcini: 'Strange that such difference should be 'Twixt Tweedledum and Tweedledee.' 5
Most of us know little of Handel except 'Messiah' and 'Israel in Egypt'. Both of these works were failures in their own day. To his contemporaries Handel *was* the great man *if* (and *only if*) *you happened* to live in London, where the rivalry with Bononcini took place. *If* you *lived* in Germany, you *would* probably *know* far more of Graun and Hasse. *If* 10
you *lived* in Paris your great master *would have been* Rameau. Nowhere in the world *would* you *find* Johann Sebastian Bach *regarded* as more than an astonishing player on the organ, a writer of extremely complicated music in obsolete styles, the third choice for the post of Cantor in St Thomas's in Leipzig, and the idol only of a small group of pupils who 15
found it wise to keep to themselves their personal conviction of his greatness.

SIR DONALD TOVEY: *The Main Stream of Music*

Comment

There are two quite different types of conditional sentence in this excerpt, and yet both of them employ the standard conditional verb *would/should*. The first one, in *line* 1, is an *unreal* or *rejected* condition, depicting a situation such as does *not* exist at present and would require changing before the condition itself could be realised. Sir Donald Tovey states that our estimate of Handel is NOT based on his forty-two Italian operas.

Many students often confuse this type of condition with the type used in *line* 7: 'To his contemporaries Handel *was* the great man *if (and only if)* *you happened* to live in London.' This type of condition we call a *past open* condition. Some people did live in London; they thought Handel the great man (note the use of the definite article, which would probably be stressed in pronunciation: [ð:]). Others did not, and they did not consider him so. The uses of *would* in the next examples are interesting. They are not, as might appear at first sight, unreal present conditions, like the example in *line* 1. The verb *would* is not a conditional auxiliary, but a simple past. One of the idiomatic uses of *will* is a kind of conjecture ('You will know that already, of course'). So if this sentence is translated into a present context, the form will be:

> If you live in Germany, you will probably know more of Graun and Hasse.

Paraphrase the main clause here, and it becomes something like this:

> it is probable that you know more of G. & H.

The same is true of the sentence beginning: 'Nowhere in the world *would you find* . . .' There remains the other example (*line* 11). This is a rejected condition, of the past type, such as normally has a past perfect in the subordinate clause. The point about all these examples is that a past open condition and a past rejected condition are in many respects similar, but they must not be confused with the similar-*looking* but syntatically *different* present unreal or rejected type. The next passage gives further examples of the latter kind of condition.

PASSAGE 11*b*

If the authors and publishers of 'Dick Deadshot' and such remarkable works *were* suddenly *to make a raid* on the educated class, *were to take down* the name of every man, however distinguished, who was caught at a University Extension lecture, *were to confiscate* all our novels and warn us to correct all our lives, *we should be* seriously annoyed. Yet they 5
have far more right to do so than we, for they, with all their idiocy, are normal, and we are abnormal. It is the modern literature of the educated, not of the uneducated, which is avowedly and aggressively criminal. Books recommending profligacy and pessimism, at which the high-souled errand-boy *would shudder*, lie upon all our drawing-room tables. 10

If the dirtiest old owner of the dirtiest old book-stall in Whitechapel *dared* to display works really recommending polygamy or suicide, his stock *would be seized* by the police.

G. K. CHESTERTON: A Defence of Penny Dreadfuls

Comment

The conditionals in this excerpt are all unreal present types. The vestigial subjunctive in English (*were to*; *If he were*, etc.) is merely a strengthened form of this. Note again that in the subordinate clause the verb is in the simple past form; the *would* occurs in the main clause. Cases of *would* in the subordinate clause are rare and always involve an idiomatic use of *would* as a modal, not a contingent, auxiliary verb. In such cases the meaning may be either iterative (e.g. 'If he *would behave* more kindly to animals . . .') or optative, expressing some kind of wish (e.g. 'If you *would open* the window . . .'). It may occasionally express some form of insistence (e.g. 'I told him that if he *would make* such silly mistakes, he would fail'). But students are warned that such cases are very rare, whether involving *would* (which is here a past tense) or its present form in such instances (which is of course *will*).

QUESTION PAPER

Comprehension

1 Give the verbs from the following nouns in Passage 11*a*:
    estimate, rivalry, difference (2), failure, idol, conviction.
    Now make up sentences illustrating their meaning.

2 Give a word or phrase of similar meaning to:

raid	profligacy
to confiscate	shudder
annoyed	polygamy
avowedly	

3 How far do you agree with Chesterton's statement in Passage 11*b* that 'it is the literature of the educated, not of the uneducated, which is avowedly and aggressively criminal'? Which modern authors do you think Chesterton would have condemned?

4 In what way, and for what reasons, do you think that the state of affairs described by Sir Donald Tovey in Passage 11*a* has changed since the piece was written in 1938?

Structures

5 Put the verb in a suitable form:
    (*a*) If you (*listen*), which you don't, you (*learn*) more.

(b) In the olden days, if you (*happen*) to be a man, you (*occupy*) a much more dominant position than if you (*be*) a woman.

(c) Supposing you (*try*) cleaning the carburettor, (*go*) the car better then?

(d) If the manager (*approve*) the idea, which is very unlikely, it (*improve*) labour relations considerably.

(e) He's not very reliable; but if he (*agree*) to your plan, he (*assist*) you whole-heartedly.

(f) The train isn't likely to be late, but in case it (*be*), we (*can*) always warn your friends that we (*may*) be late.

(g) (*Suffer*) you less from coughs if you (*smoke*) not so much?

(h) Fifty years ago in Britain, if you (*be*) a woman, you (*not allow* – PASSIVE) to vote.

(i) If wishes (*be*) horses, beggars (*ride*).

(j) If she (*marry*) him, which I don't think (*happen*), her parents (*be*) horrified.

6 Complete the following sentences with a suitable expression:

(a) It would be better if you ......

(b) It wouldn't be worth going unless ...

(c) She didn't buy the new dress, in case ......

(d) Supposing you ...... would that ......?

(e) When my sister was a student in England, if you ......

(f) When my mother was a girl, you didn't ...... unless ......

(g) The company would make a bigger profit if it ......

(h) People wouldn't be dissatisfied with the government unless ......

(i) She didn't say a word, in case ......

(j) He's unlikely to agree, but if ......, you would ......

7 Write sentences of your own, using a condition-sentence framework, to illustrate or refer to the following situations:

(a) The government have introduced what seems to you an unjust tax change. You suggest what they should do.

(b) You are describing a disappointing holiday. The weather was bad.

(c) An old relative is criticising modern youth's morals and blaming the popular press.

(d) A friend is offering you advice about preparing for examinations, suggesting how you could change your methods.

(e) You are learning a new game, sport, or musical instrument. Your teacher offers you advice about how to correct a fault.

(f) There is a distinct chance that an unpleasant acquaintance is going to ask you out for the evening. You ask a friend's advice.

8 Imagine that you are a teacher or parent telling off an unruly student. Write a dialogue between yourself and the student, making use of the words *if, unless,* and *supposing,* and suggesting various possible changes in the present attitude of the two. (*about* 180/200 *words*)

Suggested discussion topics

Fashions in the arts.
Art and morals.
All power corrupts; absolute power corrupts absolutely.
Censorship of the press, the cinema, and radio and television.

§12 Rejected conditions

Many students confronted with a rejected condition flounder around vaguely hoping that the insertion of *woulds* and *shoulds* more or less at random will solve their problems for them. As the excerpts in this section show, the solution is normally quite simple: the *would* or *should* comes in the MAIN clause only. This is the case even if the conjunction *if* is left out and the subordinate verb inverted to show that this has happened. The first passage in this section – written in a chatty, colloquial style – is almost entirely conceived as a rejected condition. The student will notice that in some cases the subordinate clause can be replaced by an infinitive phrase:

> PASSAGE 12*a*
> I didn't want to be a builder. At the time *I'd have been* anything. *I'd have gone* around the roads collecting fertilizer for the Allotment Union *if my father had managed* to get me a permanent bucket. But I wanted to get away from behind that door. I was sick of being posted there as a scarecrow for the bum bailiffs. I *croaked* that statement about death being   5
> in the house so often and with such passion it *wouldn't have surprised* me *to see* death sitting down with us at meals, chatting cosily and complaining about the quality of the grub, which it *would have had* every right to do, for the grub we had was rough.
>
> GWYN THOMAS: *And a Spoonful of Grief to Taste*

Comment
The only feature worth commenting on here is the use of the infinitive *to see* as the conditional subordinate in the fifth sentence. The principal clause in the conditional is of itself a subordinate clause anyway, being a consecutive clause dependent on the main *I croaked that statement*. The tense of a consecutive clause in English depends entirely on the time-relationship it has with the event it describes; there is no complication about special forms for it. The student should note that the verb in the subordinate clause in *line 3* is in the past perfect, as is always the case with rejected conditions.

If Joan[1] *had been* malicious, selfish, cowardly or stupid, she *would have been* one of the most odious persons known to history instead of one of the most attractive. *If* she *had been* old enough to know the effect she was producing on the men whom she humiliated by being right when they were wrong, and *had learned* to flatter and manage them, she *might have* 5 *lived* as long as Queen Elizabeth. But she was too young and rustical and inexperienced to have any such arts.

GEORGE BERNARD SHAW: Preface to Saint Joan

Comment

Again notice that the *would have* form occurs in the MAIN clause only, and that the alternative *might have* is sometimes preferred when the conjectured outcome of the condition is considered not inevitable, but possible (see below, §15). Notice also that the final sentence of the excerpt shows that the condition is a rejected one.

PASSAGE 12*c*

Over the five years from the beginning of 1952 to the end of 1956 there was an average current surplus each year of £160m. This makes up a big sum when added together; *if* it *had all been tucked away* it *would have been* enough to double the size of the British gold and dollar reserve by the end of those five years. This is exactly what Germany has been doing[2] 5 with its current account surplus. And the reason why Britain's position has appeared weak and precarious by comparison with Germany's is not simply that our current surplus is smaller than theirs. *If* the situation *had been reversed* and the Germans *had had* a surplus only the size of the British, they *would* still *have looked* strong. 10

ANDREW SHONFIELD: British Economic Policy since the War

Comment

The only necessary comment here concerns the fact that the first of the conditionals (*line 3*) is a passive and that in the main clause of the second (*line 10*) there is an adverb of relative time. Note that it goes between the auxiliary *would* and the infinitive *have*.

QUESTION PAPER:

Comprehension

1 Find a word in the passage mentioned corresponding to the definition given
   a piece of ground let out for spare-time cultivation (12*a*)
   badly dressed figure intended to frighten birds (12*a*)

---

[1] St Joan of Arc.
[2] Written in 1958, and thus referring to events up till that date.

sheriff's officer who attempts to confiscate debtors' property to realise their debts (12*a*)
to utter a low hoarse sound (12*a*)
comfortably and warmly (12*a*)
food (colloquial) (12*a*)
moved by hatred or ill-will (12*b*)
hateful (12*b*)
to lower a person's dignity or self-respect (12*b*)
to praise or compliment insincerely (12*b*)
unrefined, unsophisticated (12*b*)
sum of money in excess of one's expenditure (12*c*)
unsafe, insecure (12*c*)

2 Make up sentences of your own, using the following words of related but different meaning:
   (*a*) to croak, to growl, to snarl, to grunt, to snort
   (*b*) selfish, egocentric, self-righteous, egotistical, self-seeking
   (*c*) malicious, acrimonious, invidious, truculent, malevolent
   (*d*) rustic, rural, country, countrified
   (*e*) surplus, profit, excess, surfeit
   (*f*) current, actual, topical, present, modern

Structures

3 Put the verb in a suitable form:
   (*a*) Why didn't you come? If you (*come*), we (*enjoy*) ourselves much more.
   (*b*) We (*catch* – NEGATIVE) the train if we (*take* – NEGATIVE) that taxi; thank heaven one was waiting.
   (*c*) If Ludwig II (*pay* – NEGATIVE) Wagner's debts, the opera house at Bayreuth (*build* – NEGATIVE PASSIVE).
   (*d*) If the Crusades (*take place* – NEGATIVE), we (*have* – NEGATIVE) all the scientific progress of later ages.
   (*e*) If Julius Caesar (*murder* – NEGATIVE PASSIVE), Shakespeare probably (*write* – NEGATIVE) a play about him.
   (*f*) If Beethoven (*be*) a modern pop-singer, he (*die*) a rich man.
   (*g*) If Wren (*design*) our school, it (*look*) much more attractive.
   (*h*) If those people (*talk* – NEGATIVE) so loudly, we (*hear*) what the lecturer actually said.
   (*i*) If you (*be born*) in England eight hundred years ago, you probably (*be*) a serf on some great estate.
   (*j*) If Shakespeare (*live*) in the twentieth century, he quite possibly (*write*) plays for television.

4 Complete the following sentences with a suitable expression:
   (*a*) Nobody would have noticed if . . . . . .
   (*b*) If you . . . . . ., the whole operation would have . . . . . .
   (*c*) Supposing they had . . . . . ., what . . . . . .?
   (*d*) Everyone would have been delighted if . . . . . .

(*e*) In prehistoric times you would have ...... if ......
(*f*) If there had been a World Cup for football a hundred years ago ......
(*g*) The police would not have caught the thief if ......
(*h*) If Columbus ...... that the world was round, ...
(*i*) That student wouldn't have passed the exam if ......
(*j*) If you had shut the door properly, it ......

5   Write sentences of your own, using a conditional-sentence framework of the rejected type, to refer to the following situations:
(*a*) A friend has forgotten to fill the petrol tank of his car; consequently it has stopped in a rush-hour traffic jam.
(*b*) A friend has fallen in love with a mean, selfish and deceitful girl whom he met on a pleasure cruise.
(*c*) You have been listening to a piano recital, and regret giving up the piano after ten lessons.
(*d*) The aeroplane in which you intended to return home has crashed, with heavy loss of life.
(*e*) Your friend is so busy complaining about the English weather that he walks into a lamp-post.
(*f*) You read in the newspaper about a school friend who has become a famous television star.
(*g*) Your teacher has made what you consider a wrong decision.
(*h*) A party of friends has been caught out in the rain without raincoats.
(*i*) You have been so busy talking to a friend on the telephone that the coffee has boiled over.
(*j*) Your room-mate has been to a rather too gay party and is suffering from a hangover.

6   Write a short composition (*about* 200/250 *words*) on the subject:
    If I had been born five hundred years ago.

Suggested discussion topics

    The great might-have-beens of history.
    National heroes and myths.
    Money doesn't make you happy.
    World financial troubles and their remedies.

The next passage is intended to form a bridge between the previous sections on tense and contingency and the next group on the modal auxiliary verbs and their uses.

PASSAGE 13*a*

Apart from the question of food, there is the question of energy. It seems clear that, *if* it *were* financially worth while, fairly economical methods *could be discovered* by which more use *could be made* than at present of energy from the sun. And in theory there is no calculable limit to what *can be got* out of atomic energy. When people *have discovered* how to 5 turn hydrogen into helium, sea-water *will become* their raw material, and it *will be* a long time *before* this source of supply *is exhausted*. Speaking of less specific possibilities, we *have to reflect* that man *has existed* for about a million years, and scientific technique for at most two hundred years. Seeing what it *has already accomplished*, it *would be* very rash to place any 10 limits upon what it *may accomplish* in the future. Scientific knowledge is an intoxicating draught, and it *may be* one which the human race *is unable to* sustain. It *may be* that, like the men who built the Tower of Babel in the hope of reaching up to heaven, so the men who *pursue* the secrets of the atom *will be punished* for their impiety by providing by accident the 15 means of exterminating the human species, and perhaps all life on this planet. From some points of view such a consummation *might not be* wholly regrettable, but these points of view *can* hardly be ours. Perhaps somewhere else, in some distant nebula, some unimportant star has an unimportant planet on which there are rational beings. Perhaps in an- 20 other million years their instruments will tell them of our fate, and lead them to agree on an agenda for a conference of foreign ministers. If so, man *will not have lived* in vain.

BERTRAND RUSSELL: The Limits of Human Power

Comment

Grammatically there is little in this passage that has not been considered before under the heading of tenses save for one important feature. The fourth sentence (*line* 5), begins: 'When people *have discovered* how to turn hydrogen into helium, sea-water *will become* their raw material', and similarly, there is a clause in *lines* 14/15: 'the men who *pursue* the secrets of the atom *will* be punished'. These sentences illustrate an aspect of English tense sequences which is sometimes forgotten, namely that in modern English it is unusual to find a future tense in an adverbial or adjective clause when the main verb of the sentence is in the future. The contingent adverbial clause beginning *when people have discovered* is one such case, the relative clause *who pursue* etc. another. Notice, however, that in an adjectival clause this convention only operates if the adjectival clause is of the identifying kind (see below, §28). If the adverbial clause is considered as a point of time (and one could easily substitute *at that moment* for it), then it becomes clear that it can be considered relatively to the main verb as a PRESENT, even though it refers to a FUTURE time.

Remember, however, that these principles apply only when the subordinate clause is so closely bound to the main verb as to be adverbial to it. When the words *if* or *when* are part of a *noun* clause ('I shall not tell you *when she will arrive*', for example) rather than an adverbial expression as here, they do not apply.

It is not, therefore, mere hair-splitting to say that there is a difference between:

I shall not tell you *when she will arrive*,

which may be paraphrased as 'I shall not tell you the time of her arrival', and

I shall not tell you when she arrives,

which, though ambiguous, more probably means: 'When she actually gets here, I shall not inform you of the fact.' In order to make things quite unambiguous, it is better to put an adverbial clause beginning with *when* at the beginning of the sentence. If it is a reported question, and therefore a noun clause, it should of course follow the verb on which it depends.

PASSAGE 13*b*

After dressing for dinner, which he *would have* at the Savoy or elsewhere, he *might drop in* to see an act of his play, confer an epigram on some acquaintance, and go to a party and a late supper. In March 1893 he took rooms at the Savoy Hotel, explaining that he *could not* go home as he had forgotten the number of his house, and was not quite certain of   5
the street, though he believed the district was Chelsea. Whenever the rooms were changed to suit his taste, he *would tell* a friend about his magnificent new suite, and the colossal weekly bill he *had to pay*, exactly like a youngster who is thrilled by some new possession and impressed by its cost.   10

HESKETH PEARSON: *The Life of Oscar Wilde*

Comment

There are two examples here of the verb *would* used as a tense-indicator rather than a modal verb (*lines* 1 *and* 7). The student will notice that it is frequentative on both occasions, and implies 'he was in the habit of . . .' This is also true of the verb *will*, which can be shown by simply turning the other verbs in the sentences into simple presents. Students should watch this – *will* does NOT indicate a future when it is used in this way; it indicates a persistent or repeated habit – often a wilful one. Notice also the verb *had to* (*line* 8), not *must*.

PASSAGE 13c

The poet, the painter, the architect, the sculptor, the dress-designer, the house-decorator, the furniture-maker, the printer: these had reacted against the stereotyped art and craft of the period, and their general tendency was called aesthetic, the work of each being in some way related to the rest, though the relationship was never clearly defined, and   5 few of the artists *would have claimed* kinship with others working along the same lines. Such diverse characters as Ruskin, Morris, Pater, Swinburne, Whistler, Woolner, Rossetti, Burne-Jones, Henry Irving, and even those satirists of the 'Movement', Gilbert and Sullivan, were part of the tendency; but it *may be doubted* if any of them *would have cared* to 10 be called aesthetes, and the last two *would have rejected* the appellation with scorn. Each of these artists was playing his own game; and though some *might have recognized* that the others were on their side, none *would have called* it a team.

HESKETH PEARSON: *The Life of Oscar Wilde*

Comment

The only points worth noting here are that conditional sentences do not necessarily need an *if* clause at all – all the conditional tense forms in this passage are reactions to a suppressed supposition of the nature of 'if they had been asked'. Note, however, that one should distinguish between *if* (conditional conjunction, rarely followed by a *would* or *should*) and *if* (conjunction introducing a noun clause – in this case an indirect question) which of course requires the tense sequence normal in such cases (see below §27).

Students should not forget that *should* is a conditional auxiliary in the FIRST PERSON ONLY, and that it has other uses besides those of helping to form a conditional, as the next sections will show. This may at once be seen if one conjectures what Gilbert or Sullivan's words might have been in direct speech compared with the above passage. Surely, they would have been:

'I *should not claim* kinship with others . . .' (*line* 6)

'I *should not care* to be called an aesthete' (*line* 10)

Again, although the condition 'If you asked me' is implicit in the sentences, it is noticeable once again that the relationship between a time contingency, a modal usage (*might have recognized* – *line* 13) and a conditional usage is quite close, and needs to be watched carefully.

The reason for this is that all these usages project the effect of an imaginary or predicted situation on to an actual one in their various ways; which is why they have been placed in the same section of this course.

QUESTION PAPER:

Comprehension

1 Explain what is meant by the following words or phrases: sea-water will
    become their raw material (Passage 13*a*, *line* 6)
    Scientific knowledge is an intoxicating draught (13*a*, *lines* 11–12)
    such a consummation might not be wholly regrettable (13*a*, *lines* 17–18)
    man will not have lived in vain (13*a*, *line* 23)
    he might ... confer an epigram on some acquaintance (13*b*, *lines* 2–3)
    few of the artists would have claimed kinship with others working along
        the same lines (13*c*, *lines* 6–7)
    Each of these artists was playing his own game (13*c*, *line* 12)

2 Illustrate the difference in meaning between the following groups of words
    by using them in sentences:
    (*a*) economical, economic, economics
    (*b*) technique, technology, technical
    (*c*) conference, reading, lecture, lesson
    (*d*) diverse, diversity, diversion, divert
    (*e*) aesthete, intellectual, dilettante, amateur, connoisseur

3 Give a word or phrase of similar meaning to:
    source (Passage 13*a*, *line* 7)
    specific (13*a*, *line* 8)
    rash (13*a*, *line* 10)
    agenda (13*a*, *line* 22)
    bill (13*b*, *line* 8)
    thrilled (13*b*, *line* 9)
    appellation (13*c*, *line* 11)

4 Give a suitable definition to the nouns taken from the texts (left-hand
    column) and the adjectives derived from them.
    nebula   nebulous
    craft   crafty
    side   sidelong

5 Examine and comment on Russell's viewpoint in Passage 13*a*. From what points of view do you imagine he might consider the extermination of mankind 'a not wholly regrettable consummation'?

6 Why do you think Russell refers to scientific knowledge as 'an intoxicating draught'?

7 What do you learn about Oscar Wilde's character from Passage 13*b*? Would you have liked such a person?

8 Passage 13*c* a number of artists are mentioned. Find out what you can about the life and work of any *four* of them.

Structures

9 Put the verb in a suitable form:
   (*a*) When she (*finish*) making-up, she (*come*) with you.
   (*b*) Science (*transform*) human life in the last 300 years.
   (*c*) I (*not, can*) join you until I (*write*) this letter.
   (*d*) When he (*pass*) his exam next year, he (*take*) a job as a teacher.
   (*e*) It (*be*) unlikely that William Morris (*like*) Picasso.

10 Write sentences of your own, using constructions involving the verbs *will* or *would* to refer to the following situations:
   (*a*) You are discussing the behaviour of an eccentric uncle, now dead.
   (*b*) You are expressing a nostalgic regret at your country's present foreign policy.
   (*c*) A friend has just mentioned an embarrassing happening from your schooldays together.
   (*d*) You are warning a class-mate about his carelessness in leaving things lying about.
   (*e*) You are looking forward to your holiday.

11 Write a paragraph (*about* 120 *words*) on your ambitions after you finish studying.

Suggested discussion topics

The dangers and opportunities offered by atomic power.
World Government.
Taste in art.
Artists are always odd and usually unpleasant.

The modal [anomalous finite] verbs

INTRODUCTORY NOTES

Of all the structural devices in English that are difficult for the advanced student, these verbs are perhaps the most irritating. One of the troubles is that they are similar to, but not identical with, many cognate verbs in other languages.

The two most important uses of these verbs are to indicate prediction and permission. That is to say, in one sense they imply, in various degrees, that a given situation may develop in a particular way, and in another sense they imply that if the subject takes a certain initiative, the situation may be *made* to develop in a particular way. The presence or absence of an *initiative* from the subject is the key to understanding how the verbs are used.

If the idea of *permission* is uppermost, the commonest modal verbs fall into a sequence as follows:

could
can
may
should
ought to
need to
(had better)
must
(have got to)
shall

Set out like this, the sequence clearly runs from a mild suggestion to an outright enforcement of a recommended action. (Note that all these verbs as used in the above sequence are present in form and future in implication.)

The idea of *prediction* is expressed by a sequence running thus:

might
may
should
will
(am, are, is going to)
(can't help)
shall

From the above sequences, it appears that these verbs operate in a kind of tense-limbo. They refer to what is potential rather than actual, yet they cannot be said to be future tense forms. They seem to refer to the future as a kind of extension or manipulation of the present situation. The only one of which this is not entirely true is the verb *can*, which conveys not only the idea of *being in a position to do something* (e.g. 'There's a lovely fresh breeze; good – we can go sailing') but of having the capacity, skill or knowledge to do it ('Can you swim?'). In the second case *can* is of course just as much a simple present as a verb like 'do'. It is interesting to note in passing that English speakers do not use verbs of the senses (*see, hear*, etc.) in the present progressive form very much. They tend to use them with *can* in such cases ('Can you see that aeroplane up there?' 'Can you hear that scratching sound next door?')

Try paraphrasing examples of the verbs in the two sequences as given above, and the result will be something like the following:

SEQUENCE 1 [PERMISSION]:
I could = it is open to me to . . . should I wish
I can = it is open to me if I take the initiative to . . .
I may = I am allowed to . . .
I should = I am advised to; it is my duty to . . .
I ought to = I am recommended to . . .
I need to = it would be good for me if I . . .; it is necessary for me to . . .
I had better = there might be difficulty or trouble if I don't . . .
I must = I am required or obliged to . . .
I have got to = it is more or less unavoidable for me to . . .
I shall = (*a*) a simple future (1st person only)
        (*b*) The speaker will compel you (or the 3rd person) to, e.g. 'You *shall not* pass.'

The second sequence may be roughly paraphrased as follows:

SEQUENCE 2 [PREDICTION]:
I might = it is possible, but not likely, that I shall . . .
I may = it is possible that I . . .
I should = it is probable that I . . .

I shall = (simple future; 2nd and 3rd persons *will*)
I am going to = it has been arranged that I . . .; it is almost inevitable
   that I . . .
I can't help = it is impossible for me to avoid . . .
I will = (2nd and 3rd person *shall*) I am determined that . . . (Again,
   as in Sequence 1, the speaker will compel the subject to.)

Obviously, Sequence 2 would be the only possible choice with an impersonal verb such as *to rain*, and even then 'it shall rain' is a sentence one can only imagine emanating from a grand vizier, demiurge or deity.

Further difficulties arise when these verbs are prefaced with a negative particle of some kind. If you wish to construct a sequence involving prohibition instead of permission, on the lines of Sequence 1, it would run:

> need not
> haven't got to
> should not
> had better not
> must not
> cannot
> may not
> shall not

The negative forms of Sequence 2 are much more straightforward:

> might not
> may not
> should not
> will not (won't)
> is not going to
> cannot
> shall not

Here the negative obviously means exactly the opposite of the affirmative. In the negative forms given of Sequence 1, however, the paraphrase equivalents are more or less as follows:

I need not = it is not necessary for me to
I haven't got to = I am not forced to
I should not = I am not advised to; warned against (+ Gerund!)
I must not = I am forbidden to
I may not = I am forbidden to
I cannot = I am not in a position to
I shall not = I refuse to

The past forms of these verbs often require great care. In many cases, there is no actual past *form*, only past equivalents. It is very often necessary to use a paraphrase of some kind in past contexts. One very tricky case is the verb *can*. Where it means possessing the skill or knowledge to do something, the simple past form is *could*; where it means being in a position to do something, English speakers prefer *was (were) able to*. If the context makes it clear that the subject had the chance to do something but did not take advantage of the opportunity, the form used is *could have* + the past participle. For further examples of this, see §16, page 68.

With the exceptions of *may* and *must* in their meanings as given in Sequence 1, the so-called perfect infinitive (*to* + *have* + the Past participle) may be used with all these verbs. *May have* is exclusively used as an extension of *may* in Sequence 2. *Must have* implies 'the only possible inference is that . . .' and thus comes somewhere between *should have* and *will have*:

He *should have arrived* by now. (speculative)
He *must have arrived* by now. (assertive)
He *will have arrived* by now. (confidently predictive)

The student is warned that in some cases the printed page leaves a certain ambiguity about the exact meaning of e.g. *should have*. For example, 'he should have forgotten that' might be either Sequence 1 or Sequence 2. In the first case it would mean: 'It is his duty to have forgotten it', so to speak; in the second 'he has probably forgotten it'. In spoken contexts the ambiguity is absent, as the intonation gives the clue to which usage is intended.

Generally speaking, it is not advisable for the overseas student to depart from the uses given in the sequences above or the texts that follow. If he hears English speakers doing so, he should carefully note what they say and the context in which it occurs.

§14 Modality – 1: Permission, open possibility and ability (Sequence 1)

The idiomatic anomalous verbs in any language always cause confusion. This is because their meanings overlap with one another, and yet do not always overlap with the entire set of meanings idiomatically associated with what looks like the corresponding verb in other languages. The next six sections illustrate various uses of the so-called anomalous finite or modal verbs in English: *can, could: may, might: shall, should: will, would: must* and *ought to*. The reader will notice that in the first passage the verbs are used in the sense of simple presents, referring to something which is universally true.

PASSAGE 14*a*
We *may labour* with words, but to what purpose amid these incomprehensibles? We *can see* that time and space are unlike anything else with which we have any acquaintance. There is nothing with which to compare them. Whatever they *may be*, they appear to include all material things with which our immaterial minds are somehow associated; yet 5 this we *may say* with confidence, that things themselves in any sense of the word they *cannot be*. No tool of any kind bites on them. No rude hands *can be laid* upon these immortals. No chemical analysis *can tell* you their composition, no biology unfold their ancestry or relate the story of their evolution. There *cannot be* material bodies without the space they 10 occupy, but we *can imagine* space which contains no bodies. Time, too, without events – sometimes called 'duration' – we *can* indeed *imagine*, yet of empty, eventless time we *could not be* conscious. Of neither space nor time do our senses give us the slightest information. They *cannot be seen*, heard or depicted, space is not seen, nor time; there is nothing to see; 15 and travel fast or slow, you approach no nearer the terminus of either; and if time flows it is a flowing without anything that flows.
W. MACNEILE DIXON: *The Human Situation*

Comment
The differentiation between *can* and *may* here is quite marked. In the first line, *may* implies *it is open* (i.e. permitted) *to us*; in the fourth sentence, however, *can* cannot be substituted for *may*, and if *may* were substituted

for *can* throughout the passage afterwards, the meaning would be materially altered. Try it, and see! This is particularly so when a negative subject such as *No rude hands* etc. is involved. *You may not lay hands on someone* implies 'you are *not allowed to* do so', or alternatively 'it is open to you not to do so'. It doesn't mean 'you are not in a position to', or 'you haven't got the skill or ability to'. The following passage takes our exposition a stage further. Here the verb *may* does not appear at all. The emphasis is on our *ability* or *capacity* to do things, not merely the fact that *it is open to us* to do so. The ability is the result, as the passage implies, of *know-how* and not of situation. Where *can* and *may* are interchangeable, the former often implies initiative, the latter simply permission.

PASSAGE 14*b*
The phrase 'You *can't change* human nature' is repeated more often than it is understood. There is a sense in which geneticists WOULD REGARD it as at least approximately true, although not in the sense in which it is usually meant. If by 'human nature' is meant the 'nature' of individual human beings, that is to say, their genetically determined capacity, not 5
to develop into some one particular kind of person, but to develop in any one of a variety of ways according to the circumstances of their upbringing, then the statement is true. We do not know how to alter the genetic constitution of the human race so as to change the capacities of the individuals born, although we *can say* that the indiscriminate scattering of 10
radioactive substances into the atmosphere WILL INCREASE slightly but significantly the number of the genetically handicapped, and that the discouragement of marriages between close relatives WILL DECREASE that number. In fact, *we can be* fairly confident that the 'nature' (i.e. the genetically determined capacities) of human beings has not 15
greatly changed since the neolithic revolution, since 7,000 years is too short a period for major evolutionary changes. There are probably genetically determined differences of a statistical kind in temperament and talents as well as in physical type between human races, and the present increase in intermarriage between human races must have re- 20
sulted in changes in the genetic constitution of the population, although we *cannot* at present *say* whether the result has been an increase or a decrease in health, fertility or intelligence.

J.MAYNARD SMITH: *The Theory of Evolution*

Comment
The basic sense of *can* (and of *could* when it is used as a simple past of *can*) is that of possession of the skill or knowledge required to exploit a situation. So when *cannot* is used in this way, the implication is that the skill or knowledge is absent. Here it is utterly different from *may not*;

in such a context, *may not* would mean not the absence of knowledge or skill, but the absence of *permission* (e.g. You *may not smoke* in the classroom).

Where the skill or knowledge is barely enough to do what is required, an English speaker very often uses the verb *to manage to* (e.g. 'She *managed to swim* the river'). Note that the meaning of this particular verb in the negative depends on where the negative particle is placed ('*We didn't manage to hit* the other car' = 'We were unsuccessful when we tried to . . .'; '*We managed not to hit* the other car' = 'We were successful in avoiding . . .').

Where the skill or knowledge is not really adequate to do what is needed, and yet the thing is still successfully attempted, we often use the verb *to contrive to* (e.g. 'She *contrived to pass* the examination, despite her stupidity'). In this case it is much more probable that any negative will precede the dependent verb rather than the verb *to contrive* itself (e.g. 'I do not know how he *contrived not to get caught* by the Customs men').

Note *must have resulted* in *line* 20. It clearly means something like 'no other result was possible'; 'no other conclusion may be drawn from the evidence available'. This point is further developed in §17.

QUESTION PAPER:

Comprehension

1 Explain what is meant by the following phrases:
   our immaterial minds (Passage 14*a*, *line* 5)
   No rude hands can be laid upon these immortals (14*a*, *lines* 7–8)
   their genetically determined capacity (14*b*, *line* 5)
   indiscriminate scattering of radioactive substances into the atmosphere
     (14*b*, *lines* 10–11)
   the neolithic revolution (14*b*, *line* 16)
   differences of a statistical kind (14*b*, *line* 18)
   the genetic constitution of the population (14*b*, *line* 21)

2 What are the characteristics that Dixon (Passage 14*a*) asserts make it impossible to call time and space 'things'?

3 In what sense do you think Maynard Smith (Passage 14*b*) would agree that it is NOT true to say 'You can't change human nature'? What factors does he say will increase or lessen the chances of maintaining or improving what he defines as one type of 'human nature'?

4 What characteristics of these two passages seem to you to indicate that scientists rather than philosophers wrote them?

Structures

5 Insert *can* or *may*, affirmative or negative as seems most suitable:
   (*a*) That child is only six, and —— play the violin quite well.
   (*b*) We haven't decided where to go for our holiday this year; we —— stay at home, or we —— go abroad.
   (*c*) There is no school this afternoon, so we —— go swimming.
   (*d*) Look at that cloud; it —— rain at any moment.
   (*e*) —— you see that skylark?
   (*f*) The car won't start. What —— be wrong with it?
   (*g*) I don't know. Perhaps the tank —— be empty.
   (*h*) It —— be; I filled it up yesterday.
   (*i*) Yes, but there —— be a leak in the tank.
   (*j*) I suppose so; and, of course, the petrol —— be very good.

6 Complete the following sentences in two different ways, one using an expression with *can*, and one with *may*:
   (*a*) Hurry up and get ready; ......
   (*b*) Have you got an umbrella? It ......
   (*c*) Is this boat well equipped with lifebelts? I ......
   (*d*) Look; that notice says 'No Smoking'; ......
   (*e*) Oh, dear; Aunt Myrtle is coming to lunch; ......
   (*f*) If we get a taxi, we ......
   (*g*) Don't talk French to him; he ......
   (*h*) This party is terribly boring; ......

7 Write sentences of your own responding to the following situations, using *can* or *may*, as seems most suitable:
   (*a*) A friend rings up and asks if it is possible for him to stay in your house for a few days.
   (*b*) You are asked to take part in a swimming gala.
   (*c*) A friend, normally punctual, is very late for an appointment.
   (*d*) Someone asks you what your future plans are.
   (*e*) A newspaper asks you for an article on your home town.
   (*f*) Your flat-mate is suddenly taken seriously ill.
   (*g*) You don't feel very well yourself.
   (*h*) You are going out for the evening, and think the engagement will last until after midnight.

8 Write a paragraph of about 150 words, setting out your comments on the possible developments of world politics over the next fifty years.

Suggested discussion topics

Can you change human nature?
Problems in dealing with handicapped people.
Man is still at heart a savage, as he was 7,000 years ago.
Are science and religion incompatible?

A second important use of some modal verbs in English is that of indicating the *possibility* that a thing may happen. Whilst it is true that sometimes the verb *could* (and very occasionally the verb *can*) is used in such contexts, by far the commonest usages involve the verbs *will*, when the prediction is confident, and *may*, when it is not so confident. When it is so unsure as to indicate *improbability*, the verb to use is *might* (e.g. in the proverb: *Pigs might fly*).

This passage shows how a writer in the 1930s used the verb *may* in a passage which is very largely prediction:

> PASSAGE 15
> It is possible that the development of record-breaking and display athleticism *may be approaching* its maximum now, or that in America it *may* even *be passing* its maximum. All the rational feats of bodily strength and skill *may* presently *have been tried out* to the limit. People *will cease* to beat records and only aspire to touch them. If the world's prosperity 5 goes on increasing, the great majority of people *may tire* of the spectator's role in the stadium. They *may find* competing attractions. They *may go* to look on less frequently and less abundantly. There *may be* changes in the economic and industrial ordering of the world that *will diminish* the present supply of honourable amateurs for public games. Prosperous 10 people *may find* some better method of launching their sons and daughters upon life than in offering them up to athletic uses. Public shows of games *may become* mainly professional displays of an exemplary sort. But this *may not affect* the wide diffusion of open-air recreation. That *may be* a permanent gain. If leisure increases, it seems likely to become more and 15 more general, more and more a normal element in life.
> H. G. WELLS: 'The World of Sport', from *Points of View*

Comment
Notice how the writer makes a distinction between what may be happening at the present moment (progressive tenses in the first sentence) and what he thinks may happen *as a general rule* in the future (simple tenses in the rest of the passage). In the second sentence notice the expression

may have been tried out. Here, the author is writing about something that may already be an accomplished fact; hence the perfect infinitive. Notice, too, that when he writes about something he regards as almost inevitable, he switches from *may* to *will.* Notice also that he does not once use the verb *can* – or even *could.*

QUESTION PAPER:

Comprehension

1 What is the author's main argument in this passage? Do you agree with him?

2 What does he mean by the phrases:
    rational feats of bodily strength (*line* 3)
    the spectator's role in the stadium (*lines* 6–7)
    honourable amateurs (*line* 10)
    launching their sons and daughters upon life (*lines* 11–12)
    professional displays of an exemplary sort (*line* 13)
    wide diffusion of open-air recreation (*line* 14)

3 Replace the italicised phrases with a form of ONE word taken in each case from the passage:
    (*a*) She *has the ambition and desire* to become a singer.
    (*b*) Our firm is *offering its products in rivalry* with yours.
    (*c*) We want to erect a memorial to him *that will last for ever.*
    (*d*) There is *quite enough* food to avert famine.
    (*e*) He is *getting fed up with* his job.[1]

4 Use sentences of your own to illustrate the difference between:
    rational *and* reasonable   economic *and* economical
    industrial *and* industrious   amateur *and* amateurish
    to concur *and* to compete

Structures

5 Insert *can*, *may*, or *will*, as seems most suitable:
    (*a*) My brother —— come to England next year if he —— afford to.
    (*b*) I think he —— pass the examination; he —— certainly write good essays when he tries.
    (*c*) The trouble with air travel in winter is that your plane —— run into fog.
    (*d*) He —— have written to me; if so, his letter —— probably arrive tomorrow.
    (*e*) I imagine that their plane —— be taking off at this moment; if so, we —— expect them to arrive in two hours' time.
    (*f*) —— you row? If so, we —— go on the river.
    (*g*) Don't be so certain! All the boats —— be booked.

[1] In question 3(*e*) it will be necessary to replace the preposition *with* by another proposition.

(*h*) If the boats are booked, you —— have to think of something else to do.

(*i*) He —— run tremendously fast; do you think he —— become an Olympic champion one day?

(*j*) He —— do, if he —— find a good trainer.

6 Complete the following sentences, using a suitable expression with *can*, *may*, or *will*:

(*a*) I can't understand why he's so late; of course, he ......

(*b*) If you choose this colour, you ......

(*c*) Have you any idea who she is? I think she ......

(*d*) Ah, yes. I recognise you; you ......

(*e*) Please don't shout at me; people ......

(*f*) What's she doing now? I'm not sure; she ......

(*g*) If that car doesn't get out of the way, he ......

(*h*) This is a lovely country for sailing if you ......

7 Imagine that you are a sports-commentator. Write three sentences in reply to each of the following questions, one using a form of *can*, one of *may*, and one of *will*.

(*a*) What are your country's prospects in the next Olympic Games?

(*b*) Why were your forecasts about the winner of the Monte Carlo Rally so inaccurate?

(*c*) What are your reactions to the decision to cancel your country's most famous tennis-tournament?

(*d*) Why do you think the English are so fond of cricket?

(*e*) What are your reactions to an English journalist's statement that your country's best golfer is a 'worn-out has-been'?

8 Write a letter about 150 words long to a travel-agent, asking for detailed information about a holiday in America (North or South). Explain why you want to go there and what you want to do when you get there. Use the verbs *can*, *may* and *will* as often and as naturally as possible.

Suggested discussion topics

The purpose of record-breaking.

The amateur's place in modern sport.

The uses of increased leisure.

The dangers of being prestige-conscious.

§16 Modality – 3: Opportunity; possibility; impossibility (Sequence 1)

It is important to remember that even when certain modal verbs are rather similar in meaning in the affirmative, the negative forms may mean something quite different from one another. The following passage gives examples of *can* and *may* in affirmative and negative contexts. Notice that in some cases they may be used almost as synonyms; in others this is impossible. Notice also that POSSIBILITY (usually implied when we use *may*) and OPPORTUNITY (implied when we use *can* in the sense of 'being in a position to . . .') are not the same thing, and that both are different from PERMISSION.

PASSAGE 16*a*

To call the love of Shakespeare's romantic comedies itself romantic is meaningless, or it is the expression of a private and personal conviction concerning the nature of love. It *may mean* that in the opinion of the judge love is not in fact so happy, nor so secure, nor so deeply irradiated with the heart's delight as Shakespeare represented it; but it *can mean* nothing 5
more. And we *cannot tell* whether Shakespeare himself believed that love actually was as he chose to represent it. But we *can say* that he did believe either that it was so, or that it ought to be so; and that he found it natural to create men and women who are alive with a reality no other created characters possess, who love in the way he chose to make them love, 10
with a tenderness and gaiety, an open-eyed confidence in themselves and the future, a shyness and a humour, a marvellous equality in affection, which have made them for a whole world of mankind the embodiment of their experience if they were happy in love, or of their dreams if they were disappointed. 15

J. MIDDLETON MURRY: *Shakespeare and Love*

Comment

The student should particularly note the second sentence of this excerpt, which illustrates quite clearly the difference between *can* and *may*. As it stands, the phrase *it can mean nothing more* implies: it is impossible for it to mean anything more. If Murry had written *it may mean nothing more,* a possible paraphrase would have been: it is possible, but not unquestionable, that it doesn't mean anything more. At the beginning of the same sentence, *it may mean* is preferable to *it could mean* partly because it indicates a more definite possibility, and partly because there is no idea of the impersonal *it* taking any initiative. *It can mean* would be unacceptable to many English-speakers.

PASSAGE 16*b*
As daylight brightened, Lord Lucan and Sir Colin Campbell saw that the Russians were advancing towards them in enormous strength; two great columns of Russian infantry with artillery, numbering some 11,000 men and thirty-eight guns, were converging on the Causeway Heights, and Lucan sent an aide-de-camp to inform Lord Raglan that an attack on   5
the redoubts was imminent. Lord Raglan, however, *could do* nothing; no assistance *could be sent* in time, since two hours at least must elapse before a division *could be brought down* from the heights. Nor *could* Sir Colin Campbell or Lord Lucan *help*: Highlanders and cavalry must be kept for the defence of Balaclava itself. Once the Causeway Heights were 10
carried, only the Argyll and Sutherland Highlanders and the cavalry stood between the Russians and Balaclava. The Turks must be left *to do the best they could*, and for this unfortunate situation Lucan blamed Raglan.

CECIL WOODHAM-SMITH: *The Reason Why*

Comment
In this excerpt, it would clearly be absurd to replace the *could* forms by *might*. The meaning is that the subject was in a position to do something because the resources were available. Notice, though, that there is more than just the idea of simply *exploiting a situation*. To many English-speakers it is still rather unnatural to use *could* as a simple past in this sense. For example:

Yesterday was a public holiday, so we *could go* to the cinema instead of to school . . .

does not sound as natural as:

Yesterday was a public holiday, so we *were able to go* to the cinema instead of to school.

Passage 16*c* will help make this distinction clearer.

Another point to notice here is the use of negative subjects and objects with modal verbs rather than the simple use of the negative particle *not* with the verb itself. In Passage 16*b* there is, for example:

Lord Raglan *could* do *nothing* (*line 6*),
no assistance could be sent (*line 7*),

This tendency is quite common in English.

On both sides policies were overmuch coloured by escapist and wishful thinking based on things it was fashionable (and comfortable) to believe: that dictators *could be overthrown* by economic means, and *might* indeed *head* for ruin spontaneously; that military might *could not defy* the moral opinion of the world; that political predicaments *could be conjured away* 5 by finding the right ethical principle. Perhaps these ideas proved more pernicious than the simple longing for 'peace at any price'.

DAVID THOMSON: *England in the Twentieth Century*

Comment

The difference between ability and possibility is well shown in the first sentence in this passage: *could* and *might* are contrasted with one another. In each case *could* implies being in a position to do something, or of having the resources necessary to achieve it. *Might* is much less forceful in meaning. The same would apply if the verbs *could* and *might* were replaced by *can* and *may* respectively. With *may* and *might* there is no question of using one's own initiative to influence a situation. These verbs merely indicate that the situation is an open one.

The same is true if the verbs are used with a perfect infinitive. *Could have* nearly always implies, however vestigially, the idea of not taking advantage of, or not exploiting a situation when there was an opportunity to do so. *Might have* tends to imply rather that the situation would perhaps have developed differently whether anyone had taken advantage of it or not. But nowadays there is an increasing tendency to treat them as synonyms.

To be able to is so clumsy when followed by a perfect infinitive that it never occurs to any Englishman to use it so. The same is true of *to manage to* and *to contrive to*, though it is true that they are occasionally found with a perfect infinitive (e.g. 'Can *you manage to have finished* that job by eight o'clock?' 'How did he *contrive to have passed* such a difficult exam before going to University?') but even in the two examples given, a present infinitive would sound more natural.

Finally, a little advice about the nouns *possibility* and *opportunity*. Because an opportunity is something of which one can take advantage, it is perfectly natural English to talk of *having the opportunity* to do something. It is not natural English to use the verb *to have* in connection with the noun *possibility*, although overseas students frequently do so. The reasons for this apparently pedantic differentiation should by now be clear from the passages and comments in this section!

Comprehension

1 Explain what the author means by the following phrases:
   Shakespeare's romantic comedies (Passage 16a, *line* 1)
   deeply irradiated with the heart's delight (16a, *lines* 4–5)
   alive with a reality no other created characters possess (16a, *lines* 9–10)
   an open-eyed confidence in themselves (16a, *line* 11)
   equality in affection (16a, *line* 12)
   the embodiment of their experience (16a, *lines* 13–14)

2 Define the following terms as used in a technical (military) sense:
   in enormous strength (Passage 16b, *line* 2)
   a division (16b, *line* 8)
   carried (16b, *line* 11)

3 Mrs Woodham-Smith uses the terms *infantry, cavalry* and *artillery*. What are the following units responsible for?
   the Service Corps
   the Catering Corps
   the Ordnance
   Of which arms would one use the terms:
   squadron, battery, company?

4 Explain the difference in meaning between:
   romantic *and* sentimental
   actually *and* presently
   reality *and* topicality
   affection *and* affectation
   disappointed *and* deceived
   imminent *and* immanent
   assistance *and* presence
   defence *and* prohibition
   to blame *and* to disgrace

5 What do we learn about Shakespeare's attitude to love from Passage 16a?

6 What aspects of the vocabulary of Passage 16c indicate the author's disapproval of the attitudes he describes?

Structures

7 Insert *could* or *might*, as seems most suitable:
   (*a*) She was so tall that no one —— believe she was only eleven.
   (*b*) She calls it a *Gesamtkunstwerk*, whatever that —— mean.
   (*c*) When he was a student, he —— speak Italian fluently.
   (*d*) Did you think he —— forget to come?
   (*e*) He —— become Prime Minister one day. Yes; and pigs —— fly.
   (*f*) If you —— afford a Rolls-Royce, would you buy one?
   (*g*) If you lean so heavily against that fence, it —— collapse.

(*h*) When it stops raining, we —— go swimming.
(*i*) Only Shakespeare —— create such a character as Rosalind.
(*j*) He told us we —— be able to get seats for the concert.

8 Complete the following sentences, using an expression with *could* or *might*:
(*a*) Stand clear of that lift-shaft; ......
(*b*) You didn't help very much; after all, you ......
(*c*) I'm sorry the goods didn't arrive on time; ......
(*d*) If it's frosty tonight, ...
(*e*) She has always been intelligent; when she was small, she ......
(*f*) Don't talk so loud; ......
(*g*) He disinherited his daughter for becoming a schoolmistress; how......
(*h*) If you are going to town this afternoon, ...
(*i*) That's one rehearsal settled, then; when ......
(*j*) He considered that the play ......

9 Imagine that you are a theatre manager; a play has been submitted to you. You find that the following things are wrong with it. Make criticisms and suggest improvements, using *could* or *might*, as seems most suitable, in the form of a dialogue between yourself and the playwright.
(*a*) There are too many changes of scene.
(*b*) The minor characters do not contribute enough to the action.
(*c*) The military technical terms are inaccurate.
(*d*) The behaviour of the heroine is too volatile.
(*e*) The first act is too long.
(*f*) Certain sentiments expressed by the hero are rather too chauvinistic.
(*g*) The language is rather artificial.
(*h*) The action is too much held up by political diatribes.
(*i*) The imagery is unimaginative.
(*j*) The denouement is too melodramatic.

10 A boastful acquaintance has written you an unpleasant letter. Write a suitably firm but tactful reply putting him in his place.   (150 *words*)

Suggested discussion topics

War is too serious an affair to be left to the generals.
Finality is not the language of politics. (*Disraeli*)
Next to being married, a girl likes to be crossed in love a little now and then. (*Jane Austen*)
Should a dramatist aim at portraying character or purveying ideas?

§17 Modality – 4: Necessity, advice or warning (Sequence 1)

The normal manner of indicating compulsion in English, using a modal verb, is through the verb *must*. When a course of action is recommended rather than to be enforced, the verb used is *should*. The first passage in this section shows how the latter verb is used in such contexts.

PASSAGE 17*a*

There *should . . . be* an attempt on both sides, on the one hand, to increase mutual knowledge of each other's case, and, on the other hand, to disseminate information as to the disastrousness of a nuclear war *should* it *take place*.

The main work to be performed during the moratorium would be an 5 agreement to appoint a Conciliation Committee consisting of equal numbers of members from East and West and neutrals. I think such a Committee, if it were to perform its work efficiently, WOULD HAVE TO BE small. It might, for example, consist of four members from the West, four from the East, and four neutrals. It *should* – at least, at first – 10 *have* advisory powers only. Whenever it did not succeed in reaching unanimity, the opinions of both majority and minority, with the reasons for them, *should be made* public. Its decisions *should be governed* by certain principles. Of these, the first and most important *should be* that the proposals as a whole offered no net gain to either side, since, otherwise, 15 there WOULD BE no chance of their being agreed to. For example, Russia *should cease* to jam Western radios provided that they abstained from virulent hostile propaganda. The second principle to be adopted *should be* to seek ways of diminishing dangerous friction in areas where this is occurring – as, for example, between Israel and the Arab world, or 20 between North and South Korea.

BERTRAND RUSSELL: *Has Man a Future?*

Passage 17*b* illustrates the use of the verb *must* in a passage where the advice offered is framed in terms of recommending what is necessary rather than suggesting what is advisable.

PASSAGE 17*b*

I believe that film music is capable of becoming, and to a certain extent already is, a fine art, but it is applied art and a specialized art at that; it *must fit* the action and dialogue; often it becomes simply a background. Its form *must depend* on the form of the drama, so the composer *must be prepared* to write music which is capable of almost unlimited extension   5 or compression; it *must be able* to fade-out and fade-in again without loss of continuity. A composer *must be prepared* to face losing his head or his tail or even his inside without demur, and *must be prepared* to make a workman-like job of it; in fact, he *must shape* not only his ends, but his beginnings and his middles, in spite of the producer's rough hewings.   10

RALPH VAUGHAN WILLIAMS: *Composing for the Films*

Comment
Both these verbs clearly have a future aspect, as they recommend, or even, in the case of *must*, enjoin, definite action. Replacing one by the other in these texts would alter the emphasis rather than the actual meaning. But when followed by a perfect infinitive, their meaning diverges sharply. *Must* with the perfect infinitive implies 'the only reasonable assumption is that' (e.g. 'She *must have forgotten*'). *Should* + the perfect infinitive still retains the idea of need, duty or necessity (e.g. 'She *should have forgotten*'). If you replace all the present infinitives by perfect infinitives in either passage, they would have to be with *should* not *must* if the meaning is not to be altered beyond recognition.

Supposing Dr Vaughan Williams had used perfect infinitives in his second sentence. There is a world of difference between:

Its form *must have depended* on the form of the drama, so the composer *must have been prepared* to write music which is capable of almost unlimited extension or compression; it *must have been able* to fade-out and fade-in again without loss of continuity. . . .

and:

Its form *should have depended* on the form of the drama, so the composer *should have been prepared* to write music which is capable of almost unlimited extension or compression; it *should have been able* to fade-out and fade-in again without loss of continuity.

The first version implies, as suggested above, that the only reasonable assumption was that the facts as presented were so. In the second, however, the whole tone of the passage is that the form *didn't* depend on the form of the drama; that the composer *wasn't* prepared to write the kind of music required; that that music *wasn't* capable of being faded-out, etc. In other words, *should* + the perfect infinitive implies that for some reason the present situation is not what it is expected to be because *something has gone wrong*. Students are reminded, however, that in the first person, *should* may indicate a conditional form (see Passage 11a).

QUESTION PAPER:

Comprehension

1 Explain the following words or phrases:
>to disseminate information (Passage 17*a*, *lines* 2–3)
>moratorium (17*a*, *line* 5)
>advisory powers (17*a*, *line* 11)
>unanimity (17*a*, *line* 12)
>to jam (17*a*, *line* 17)
>to abstain from virulent hostile propaganda (17*a*, *lines* 17–18)

2 Dr Vaughan Williams uses the terms *fade-out* and *fade-in* in Passage 17*b*. Find out what they mean, and look up the meaning of the following terms if you do not know them:
>cutting, close-up, continuity, long-shot, zoom, pan, track, director, producer, credit-titles, to dub

3 What do you think Dr Vaughan Williams means by his final sentence? Do you think that writing music for films is a useful discipline for a creative musician?

4 Comment on Russell's suggestions about the work of his proposed Conciliation Committee.

Structures

5 Insert *must* or *should* as seems most suitable:
>(*a*) Do you really think you'll win the pools? You —— be mad!
>(*b*) A car as opulent as that —— cost at least £5,000 nowadays.
>(*c*) Be quiet, please! Why —— you talk so loudly when he's trying to explain?
>(*d*) That man —— think you're a fool, talking to your dog like that.
>(*e*) You —— trust her; it's your only chance.
>(*f*) If you —— waste so much time getting dressed, no wonder we shall be late for the party.
>(*g*) She's a very nice girl, but she insists that she —— practise singing in her bath.
>(*h*) I can't think why some painters feel that they —— always strive after originality.
>(*i*) Children —— be seen and not heard, said the Victorians.
>(*j*) You ——n't miss this film; it's a masterpiece.

6 Complete the following sentences, using an expression with *should* or *must*:
>(*a*) There is no necessity to shout, even if . . . . . .
>(*b*) I'm not ready yet; tell him . . . . . .
>(*c*) Fancy thinking I'd pay £20 for that bike; he . . . . . .
>(*d*) I don't like curtailing people's liberty, but . . . . . .
>(*e*) Did you call her a grumpy old battleaxe? Well, you . . . . . .
>(*f*) If you want to hear the dawn chorus, you . . . . . .

(g) Anyone who believes that you can abolish crime by purely educational means ......

(h) In order to be a successful creative artist, one ......

(i) She's the kind of girl who thinks ......

(j) No modern state ......

7 Imagine that you are the proprietor of a hotel. Devise suitable regulations to fit the following situations; use *must* or *should*:

(a) People have been washing their clothes in the swimming-pool.

(b) Guests have been holding noisy parties late at night.

(c) Some guests have been allowing their dogs to sleep in spare beds in their rooms.

(d) Cars have been left outside the hotel entrance all night with the ignition keys in.

(e) One of the guests has been very rude to a waiter.

(f) A handbag has been stolen from a lady's room.

(g) People have been forgetting to empty the bath out after taking a bath.

(h) Some of the male staff have arrived on duty unshaven.

(i) Children have drawn rude pictures on the wall of the lounge.

(j) Owing to the clumsiness of one of the guests, the hotel lift has jammed.

8 Imagine you are in charge of an office. Write a memorandum to the staff setting out your plans for improving its efficiency. Use *must* and *should* where it is suitable. (*about* 150 *words*)

Suggested discussion topics

How to put 'teeth' into international organisations.

The Cinema is not an art; it is a craft which makes use of art.

An Englishman thinks he is moral when he is only uncomfortable. (*Shaw*)

Let him who desires peace prepare for war.

This section overlaps in some measure with the previous one, but shows in addition how the verbs *can* and *could* fit into the sequence denoting necessity and advice rather than possibility. It also shows how the verb *might* is used in contexts suggesting possibility.

PASSAGE 18

It is now time that the motorist was given a decent road system, and, in return, punished heavily for misbehaviour. The annual conference of the Law Society has recently suggested, for example, that motorists *should be put* on probation if they commit certain types of driving offence and automatically disqualified if they do so again. At the same time, the   5
offences themselves *should be divided* into two broad categories, one involving immediate disqualification, the other a second chance, while special courts manned by expert motorists *should be set up* to deal with offences not in the criminal code. These offences *might include* inconsiderate driving, jay-walking and vehicle negligence. Another idea which   10
might help to reduce bad driving *would be* to make drivers convicted of this offence display a special bad conduct badge which *would hurt* the pride of any man behind the wheel. Police patrolling of roads *could be* greatly *improved* and the present system of speed checks, which in any case are of only marginal value, *should be replaced* by the French practice   15
of patrolling roads with a car fitted with two automatic cameras and a special tachymeter. The cameras *can be used* to record any incidents of bad road behaviour, including details of the vehicle concerned and the road situation, while the tachymeter records date, time and speed. Once the evidence of these devices is acceptable in court, they *can be used*   20
against such misbehaviour as dangerous overtaking, disregard of speed limits, blinding headlights and even excessive exhaust fumes. Police action *could* also *be made* more effective by a more frequent use of spot checks to include the driver's eyesight, his knowledge of the Highway Code and the state of his car, and penalties *should* certainly *be stepped up*   25
against those who run faulty vehicles . . . and garages who give 10-year-test certificates to cars whose brakes and steering are in bad repair.

'The Killer Cars' in *New Statesman*, November 1964

Comment

The difference between *could* and *might* is reasonably clear in this passage. Whereas *might* indicates mere possibility, *could* stands more for a suggestion to *improve* matters; *might* is MORALLY MORE NEUTRAL than *could* throughout the passage. If there is any distinction between *can* and *could*, as used here, it is that *can* is used in those sentences which take it for granted that a certain situation has become real, not projected (*lines* 17 *and* 20).

Should is here used much as Russell uses it in Passage 17*a*.

QUESTION PAPER:

Comprehension

1 What is the meaning of the following phrases?
     put on probation (*line* 4)
     jay-walking (*line* 10)
     of only marginal value (*line* 15)
     excessive exhaust fumes (*line* 22)
     spot checks (*lines* 23–24)
     the Highway Code (*lines* 24–25)
     penalties should certainly be stepped up (*line* 25)

2 What is the difference between:
     a conference and *a lecture*
     offending and *offensive*
     convicted of and *convinced of*
     to check and *to control*
     to overtake and *to take over*
     fumes and *smoke*
     faulty and *mistaken*

3 What do you think of the suggestions made in the passage for the improvement of road safety?

Structures

4 Read through Passage 18 and see in how many places you can substitute *might* and *need to* for *should*. Explain how, if at all, the sense of the passage is altered.
     Now do the same, substituting *may* and *might* for *can* and *could*. Note where the sense is altered, and how.

5 The following sentences have been framed around the concepts best expressed by the use of modal auxiliaries in English. Rewrite them so that they express the same basic idea but use a model verb instead of the words in italics, rearranging the syntax of the sentence where necessary.
     (*a*) She *found it within her capacity* to pass the exam.

(b) You *are under no obligation* to go to the party.

(c) *Has he got your permission* to leave early?

(d) *It is just about possible that* the train will be on time.

(e) *It is your duty to* read this book.

(f) Under the present tax system, we *are all obliged to* fill in complicated forms which *are outside our comprehension.*

(g) *The only possible conclusion is that* he has got lost.

(h) *I wonder what the explanation is of* what happened?

(i) If you hadn't wasted so much time, it *would have been possible to attend* the meeting.

(j) I don't know what has gone wrong; *it is*, I suppose, *quite possible that* his car has broken down.

(k) *Is it really necessary to* snore like that?

(l) We *had the opportunity to* play tennis yesterday, but we didn't.

(m) That's a pity; *it would have been a good thing if you had* taken advantage of the chance.

(n) She *has the unfortunate habit of picking* her teeth in public.

(o) If you don't come to school regularly, he said, *I insist on your doing* extra work at home.

6 Write an imaginary dialogue, using as many examples of different modal verbs as you can, between an irate landlord and a musical student who insists on practising his instrument and listening to records late at night.

(*about* 200 *words*)

Suggested discussion topics

Road safety and the prevention of road deaths.

The public and the police.

I tremble for my country when I reflect that God is just. (*Jefferson*)

§19 *Consecutive and final clauses*

These rather formidable-sounding titles are used to describe clauses which illustrate the consequence (consecutive) or the purpose (final) of an action. Students often find difficulty with them as, in some languages, they both require a form of subjunctive, whereas in English, they require quite different constructions, some of which may involve a modal verb – notably *might* or *could*. The passages in this section have been chosen to show how the ideas of consequence and purpose are variously expressed in English.

PASSAGE 19*a*
Nowhere, in this part of the forest, could we see more than twelve yards round us, and in most places much less. Our unaccustomed eyes reported all impressions at first as I suppose those of the colour-blind do, in a hundred tones of grey; though our grey was shot with green. Trunk, foliage and creeper in that unhealthy light took on a variety of shades, but one 5 predominant hue which swallowed all others for a while. Then I saw suddenly, when we had forced our way for some distance into this dim, monotonously coloured world, that the pale-grey mass above me was in reality an immense cluster of hanging yellow flowers busy with golden bees. A great tree, rotten at the core, had fallen *in such a way that it* 10 *would have blocked* the path here, where for a hundred yards or more the living roof pressed down *so that we walked stooping*, and at this point bent double, but the trunk was partially supported still by the mass of its attendant creepers intertwined with others: they had given and sagged but not broken. There was enough room at one side *for us to squeeze,* 15 carefully, for fear of parting the last strand of the sling, whose strength we could not gauge, under this barricade of the jungle's ingenious devising.

E. ARNOT ROBERTSON: *Four Frightened People*

Comment
The normal conjunction for introducing a consecutive clause in English is *so that*, and the mood and tense of the verb depend largely on the meaning of the main clause. In the example in *lines* 10–11 (*in such a way that it would have* . . .) the tense depends on the fact that the consecutive clause

is subordinate not only to the main verb *had fallen*, but also to the implied conditional: the tree didn't block the path because it was partially supported by creepers (see *line* 11). Within the same sentence a further consecutive occurs (*line* 12: *so that we walked stooping*) and this time it is indicative and past, like the verb on which it depends: *pressed down*.

Final clauses are usually introduced by an infinitive with or without some proposition. In line 15 *enough room . . . for us to squeeze*: the *for* goes of course with the *us*. It is when *so that* is used as a final conjunction that troubles arise. In the majority of cases the tendency is to use the modals *could* and *might;*

> There was enough room *so that we could* squeeze past.
> He left school at 16 *so that he could* start work in the bank

Occasionally *can* or *may* are used in such cases, if the main verb is in the present or future tense or an imperative:

> I shall leave early *so that you can get* some sleep.
> Tell him to be punctual *so that we may rehearse* as long as possible.

PASSAGE 19*b*
A fox had slipped across the grass from the edge of the plantation on the hillside. It *stopped* on the bank *to assay* the air, and then *crept down to the ford to drink*. First it must smell the hoofmarks of the horses, each one very carefully, as though its life depended on no strange horse having joined the herd since its nasal inspection of the night before. Satisfied 5 with the familiar scents, it drank a little, then *withdrew from the bank to sniff about*, as on second thoughts, possibly *to discover* a stranger which had not drunk, but stayed away from the river lest *it leave its scent there for the fox to detect*. Finding nothing new, *it raised its sharp snout to flair the breeze*, before *slinking* over Humpy Bridge *to follow* along the 10 other bank to the broken bay, where damp sand and silt held the press of many more hooves. The fox learned that pigs had been wallowing there during the day; and also that a dog of strange scent *had visited the ford to drink*. This was alarming, for it could not recognize the smell; so after wetting it, thereby removing the smell from the earth and the 15 doubt from its mind, the fox went away, satisfied, towards the hen-house and the rabbit-warrens by the avenue of chestnuts.

HENRY WILLIAMSON: Salar the Salmon

Comment
This passage contains more examples of the infinitive used to indicate purpose. In *lines* 8/9 there is one example of particular interest, involving a kind of indirect object + infinitive construction: *lest*[1] *it leave its scent*

---

[1]This vestigial subjunctive after *lest* is best avoided. It is affected. Nowadays, we prefer to use *in case* + an indicative. *In case* normally follows the same tense conventions as other contingency conjunctions.

there for the fox to detect. This is a common procedure in English when the object of the preceding clause and of the final clause infinitive are the same. The prepositional object (in this case *the fox*) of the *for* becomes the subject of the infinitive.

Williamson might have written:

lest it leave its scent there *so that the fox might detect it.*

This will be readily seen to be far clumsier than the other construction, and is preferable only when the subject of the final clause is impersonal or inanimate:

lest it leave its scent there *so that it might not be detected;*

or:

They left the car in the wood *so that it would not be noticed.*

In a negative final clause, the construction is *so as + not +* the infinitive:

She got up early *so as not to miss* the train,

when the implied subject of the infinitive is the same as the subject of the preceding finite verb. If the subject changes, then a *so that* clause is more usual (see the examples above in the previous paragraph).

A word is necessary here on the subject of *stopped to (line* 2). This is an infinitive of purpose. It does not depend on the verb *to stop.* Any verb form directly dependent on *to stop* must be a GERUND (see §25, page 115).

QUESTION PAPER:

Comprehension

1 Passage 19*a* is a description of a natural scene; 19*b* of events happening in a landscape peopled by animals. Which of the two descriptions seems to you to be the more evocative, and why?

2 Comment on the following phrases. How suitable do you think they are in their context? What improvements can you suggest if you find them unsuitable?

an immense cluster . . . busy with golden bees (Passage 19*a, lines* 9–10)
this barricade of the jungle's ingenious devising (19*a, lines* 17–18)
nasal inspection (Passage 19*b, line* 5)
removing the smell from the earth and the doubt from its mind (19*b, lines* 15–16)

3 Give a word or phrase of similar meaning to:
shot with green (Passage 19*a, line* 4)
one predominant hue (19*a, lines* 5–6)

rotten at the core (19a, *line* 10)
intertwined with others (19a, *line* 14)
sagged (19a, *line* 14)
sling (19a, *line* 16)
to gauge (19a, *line* 17)
to sniff about (19b, *lines* 6–7)
snout (19b, *line* 9)
slinking (19b, *line* 10)
wallowing (19b, *line* 12)
rabbit-warrens (19b, *line* 17)

4 Write sentences of your own, using the words *to sag, wallow* and *rabbit-warren* in figurative senses.

5 Imagine *either* that Passage 19a had been written by Williamson or that Passage 19b had been written by Arnot Robertson. Write a further paragraph, supplying the details you feel are missing from whichever paragraph you choose. Do not attempt to copy the style of the author.

Structures

6 Complete the following sentences with a consecutive clause using (*so*) *that*, or a final clause using a suitable infinitive construction:
   (*a*) He slunk cautiously out of the room ......
   (*b*) He found that the front door was locked ......
   (*c*) He climbed over the roof, but he was so heavy ......
   (*d*) Then he ran down the street as fast as he could ......
   (*e*) This exercise made him pant for breath, ...
   (*f*) After he had done this, he caught a bus ......
   (*g*) When the conductor asked for his fare, he found he hadn't got enough money ......
   (*h*) The conductor threatened to report him to the police, ...
   (*i*) The excuse he gave was carefully planned, ...
   (*j*) After all, he had only left the house ......

7 Answer the following questions, using a consecutive or final clause, as seems most suitable:
   (*a*) Why are you studying English?
   (*b*) Why couldn't your friend come with us this morning?
   (*c*) Why is that student copying out that article?
   (*d*) What does a country need weapons for?
   (*e*) Why is it necessary for firms to spend much money on advertising?

8 Link the following pairs of sentences together, using a final or a consecutive clause, as seems most suitable:
   (*a*) Many students work too hard. They become over-tired.
   (*b*) It is sometimes necessary to take examinations. Employers are often convinced that you know a lot.

(c) Many modern employers invest money in computers. This saves both time and money.

(d) Wild animals are often both afraid and suspicious. This makes it difficult to tame them.

(e) People ought to have a hobby of some kind. They can then relax and enjoy life more.

9 Write a letter to a prospective employer, explaining why you wish to apply for the following post:

WANTED: Secretary to Managing Director of small but rapidly expanding firm. Requirements: intelligence, ability to write well in three languages (English, French, Russian preferred), experience in shorthand-typing and sales promotion, willing to travel. (*about* 180/200 *words*)

Suggested discussion topics

Nature – man's enemy, or his friend?
Wild life and its effect on human life.
Animals in captivity.

C
Adverbials

In A and B there are examples of *clauses* used to amplify the meaning of a verb by giving it a setting in time, or expressing its relationship to a wish-projection or other mood and an attempt has been made to show how certain forms are used to indicate the repetitive or frequentative nature of an action. It may seem rather like putting the cart before the horse to consider such adverbials before considering simpler adverbial forms such as single words or phrases. But the problems involving the latter are of a different nature. Phrases and single words are less complex than clauses, and do not involve the relationship of two finite verbs to one another. They tend rather more to create problems concerning the position of the individual words and phrases within the clause itself. In other words, it is not so much *what* one is trying to say that raises the problem, but the *shape* of one's utterance.

It is a marked feature of all kinds of English to state first the general thesis of one's communication completely before modifying it by giving more precise details. By this is meant that whereas in some languages the conventional order of a sentence might well be:

> She (*subject*) wrote (*verb*) carefully (*adverb defining* HOW *the action of writing was carried out*) her letter (*object*)

thus defining the verb itself more closely before mentioning its object, in English the conventional order would be:

> She (*subject*) wrote (*verb*) her letter (*object of the verb*) carefully (*adverb defining* HOW *the action* was *performed*).

In fact the basic framework of the communication is established first and the 'frills' added afterwards.

Adverbials count as 'frills', and have to be squeezed into the sentence in a suitable position. There may be many reasons for this; one is certainly that English is peculiarly rich in verbs – presumably because it has the inestimable advantage of having no set ending for a verb infinitive, and it is thus theoretically possible to impress any part of speech without modification into service as a verb. (Certain experimental prose and verse depends for its originality on this very factor). This means that many verbs will have in themselves a precise meaning. So adverbs of manner tend to be tacked on as after-thoughts to the verb complement. Students are warned never to place an adverb, particularly an adverb of manner, between a verb and its object. Like many other rules of thumb, this is true only up to a point. The purpose of the next few sections is to try to indicate where that point is situated. It certainly begins when the verb complement is not the direct object of a transitive verb, but stands in some indirect relationship to a verb.

Any adverbial may apply either to the verb only or to the sentence as a whole. For example, if we say:

Clearly she has read the passage.

we mean: 'It is obvious that she has read the passage.' The adverb *clearly* refers, not simply to the *manner* in which the passage has been read, but to the *fact* that it has been read at all. But if we say:

She has read the passage clearly.

the adverb must refer to the style of her reading. Where the adverb is placed, therefore, depends on what function it fulfils in relation not only to the verb but to the sentence or clause as a whole. This process may be complicated by matters of rhythmic balance in the sentence. Students should never forget that a printed text is a visual aid, a reminder of what someone has said or thought. It is only when it comes to life as a spoken or imagined series of sound-patterns that it has its full effect. The sound-patterns will depend on the length of the various basic elements – subject, verb, verb complement – that go towards making up the conventional pattern of communication.

Adverbials are used with verbs, adjectives and other adverbs; they thus amplify the meaning of something already partly understood rather than complete the meaning of an unfinished communication. The student will thus understand why similes and other phrases and clauses involving descriptive comparisons have been included in this section.

Adverbs and prepositions very often overlap in meaning. They are thus quite often identical if they indicate place or direction. It is not so much these adverbials that cause difficulties to overseas students as those of manner, relative time and frequency. The following passage is rich in adverbials of all kinds. Students should note carefully where it is possible to place them, and, more important still, where it is *not* possible to do so.

PASSAGE 20*a*
It was a fine day for the races. People poured into Brighton by the first train; it was like bank holiday all over again, except that these people didn't spend their money; they harboured it. They stood packed deep on the tops of the trams rocking down to the Aquarium, they surged like some natural and irrational migration of insects up and down the front. 5
By eleven o'clock it was impossible to get a seat on the buses going out to the course. A Negro wearing a bright striped tie sat on a bench in the Pavilion garden and smoked a cigar. Some children played touch wood from seat to seat, and he called out to them hilariously, holding his cigar at arm's length with an air of pride and caution, his great teeth gleaming 10
like an advertisement. They stopped playing and stared at him, backing slowly. He called out to them again in their own tongue, the words hollow and unformed and childish like theirs, and they eyed him uneasily and backed further away. He put his cigar patiently back between the cushiony lips and went on smoking. A band came up the pavement 15
through Old Steyne, a blind band playing drums and trumpets, walking in the gutter, feeling the kerb with the edge of their shoes, in Indian file. You heard the music a long way off, persisting through the rumble of the crowd, the shots of exhaust pipes, and the grinding of the buses starting uphill for the racecourse. It rang out with spirit, marched like a regiment, 20
and you raised your eyes in expectation of the tiger skin and the twirling drumsticks and saw the pale blind eyes, like those of pit ponies, going by along the gutter.

GRAHAM GREENE: *Brighton Rock*

Comment
The first thing to notice is that, as is repeatedly emphasised, there is no

case here where the adverbial comes between any verb and its complement, unless that complement is itself an adverbial of some kind. Occasionally the personal part of the verb complement, if there is one, might itself be considered as an adverbial of direction, as in *line* 12: 'he called out *to them*'. There is an interesting case of careful choice of word order in *line* 16: 'He put his cigar (1) *patiently* (2) *back* (3) *between the cushiony lips*'. Strictly speaking, the adverb of direction *back* is part of the verb complement, of the phrasal verb *to put back*, and at first sight it seems that *patiently* should go after *back*. But *back* and *between the cushiony lips* are so closely connected that Greene prefers that order. Notice also how he prefers to put an adverbial of place or direction first; then one of manner, as in: 'People poured (*a*) *into Brighton* (*b*) *by the first train*' and in: 'holding his cigar (*a*) *at arm's length* (*b*) *with an air of pride and caution*'. This order is not, so to speak, compulsory, in the way that putting an *s* on the third person singular of a present simple of a regular verb is compulsory, but it is the commonest one where there are two or more adverbials referring to the same verb. Even where the verb complement is itself an adverbial of place, and is followed by another adverbial of place, the one most closely connected with the verb takes precedence, as in: 'sat *on a bench/ in the Pavilion garden*' (*lines* 7–8), and 'He called out *to them/ again/ in their own tongue*' (*line* 12). In this latter case the order is patently (1) verb complement itself an adverbial of direction; (2) abverb of relative time; (3) adverbial of manner.

PASSAGE 20*b*

The music began *again*. Teresa stood quite still *before the fire* and assembled her thoughts. Her left hand gripped the golden crucifix *on her bosom*, *while her right hand patted her hair*, which had been tossed by the wind. She was examining her reflection *in the big mirror above the mantelpiece*. She saw the iron-grey hair streaked with strands of black, and the eyes   5
that *formerly* had been full and dark but which were *now* hard and wide and coarse as her heavy lips, that *always* seemed to have lurking *behind them* the laugh of derision, the explosive threat, the coarse oath, or the soft tongue of blarney. She saw, too, the heavy jaw *under its fat*, which was that of self-indulgence and all the selfish complacency of a tyrant. And   10
on the big hands were the jewelled rings. *Now* they flashed *again* at her and excited her cruel instincts, for they were the visible things of success which her savage, pagan soul had *always* lusted after.

F. L. GREEN: *Odd Man Out*

Comment

The above passage has a large number of examples of adverbials of place and time (mostly relative time), together with two adverbial expressions of frequency. It is especially noteworthy that the favourite position for adverbials of relative time – *formerly, now, again* – is much more flexible than that of adverbials of frequency (*always*) or place. Only one of the adverbials of place comes before the verb – *on the big hands* (*line* 11) – the others always constitute a secondary part of the verb complement. Notice particularly that in the second and third sentences the adverbial is delayed until *after* the object of the transitive verb (*gripped, was examining*). With *always*, as with all adverbs of frequency, the normal position is between the subject and the verb if there is no auxiliary; and after the first auxiliary if there is one.

PASSAGE 20C

Sean stood *rigidly* in that place of narrow alleys and silent storeyards. His hands were thrust *deeply* into his overcoat pockets. Not far away there was a tall telegraph post whose wires hummed *loudly* in the high wind, sending out a note which the staunch post echoed, too. He heard it and did not like it. He kept lifting his shoulders as though to fold the 5 collar *closer* about his ears and neck where the freezing wind struck him and carried the post's note to him. Fear was moving like a live thing in him. He forced his senses *to remain alert* so that he might see anyone approaching him, and hear them, and hear, too, Dennis's whistle. But through the medium of those acute senses fear was travelling. It made 10 little deadly rushes towards his will, herding his thoughts and threatening them. For a little while it was quiescent. It seemed to have retreated or diminished. He drew a deep breath.

F. L. GREEN: Odd Man Out

Comment

Although only certain of the adverbials have been italicised in this passage, the paragraph contains a large number of them. In each of the first three sentences there is an example of an adverb of manner used in combination with a longer adverbial to qualify an intransitive or passive verb. In each case the author puts the adverb first and the longer adverbial afterwards. In the fifth sentence is an adverbial simile (*as though to fold*, etc.), of the kind which will be dealt with in §22. The next sentence has an adjectival simile (see also §22).

Certain verbs, all indicating a state of being or a change of state, are followed by adjectives, not adverbs (see §21). The commonest are:

to be, to seem, to appear, to look, to feel,

all of which indicate a state of being, and

to become, to get, to turn, to grow

(the so-called *inchoatives*) which are followed by an adjective complement when they signify a change of state (e.g. He grew *restive*; she got *angry*). When they signify a movement or activity, they are of course followed by an adverb in the usual way. Here (*line* 8) we have *to remain alert*.

QUESTION PAPER:

Comprehension

1 Comment on Graham Greene's use of the following verbs in Passage 20*a*:

harboured (*line* 3)   rang out (*line* 20)
rocking (*line* 4)   twirling (*line* 21)
surged (*line* 4)

Can you think of any other verbs he might have used which would have been as suitable?

2 Substitute a more expressive phrase, taken from one of the passages, for the phrase or clause in italics:

he called out to them *with noisy cheerfulness*
they were walking *in a single line, one behind the other*
she had iron-grey hair, *with lines of black occasionally breaking the mass of grey*
lying hidden behind them
the *firm and reliable* post
it *didn't show any sign of vitality*

3 Use the following words in sentences of your own, bringing out the difference in meaning between them:

stripe *and* streak   pagan *and* heathen
hollow *and* cavernous   rigidly *and* firmly
gripped *and* clasped   acute *and* sharp
patted *and* tapped   deadly *and* mortal
strands *and* wisps

Structures

4 Put the adverbials given in brackets in a suitable place in the sentence:
(*a*) She ate her breakfast. (this morning), (voraciously), (as if she had a train to catch)
(*b*) She stood looking. (there), (at the picture) (calmly)
(*c*) She threw the book at him. (angrily) (when she understood what he had said)
(*d*) That man mows the lawn. (always) (carefully) (on Sunday morning)
(*e*) They are leaving the airport. (now) (by the afternoon plane)
(*f*) He observes all the rules. (punctiliously) (always)
(*g*) She speaks English. (fluently) (without a trace of accent) (now)
(*h*) I can't understand her behaviour. (properly) (possibly) (however hard I try)

5 Complete the sentences with two suitable adverbials, and put them in a suitable place in the sentence:
   (a) He walks around ......
   (b) She practises her tennis shots ......
   (c) They like to go swimming ......
   (d) We shall visit the city museum ......
   (e) They won't understand a word he says ......
   (f) They have arrived back ......
   (g) They are complaining ......
   (h) You have written that essay ......

6 Write sentences to answer the following questions, using suitable adverbials, and putting them in suitable places in the sentence:
   (a) What would you do if you met a fierce tiger, escaped from a zoo?
   (b) How many times have you been asked to marry someone?
   (c) How often do you play golf?
   (d) When do you do your homework?
   (e) What would you do if your class-mates insulted your country?
   (f) How much Russian do you speak?
   (g) Where is the nearest cinema to your home?
   (h) When do you hope to return home?

7 Write a description of a cocktail party *or* a dance, taking care to make your description of the guests' movements and manner of speech as accurate as possible by using adverbials of manner. (*about* 120/150 *words*)

Suggested discussion topics

   Popular festivals.
   The treatment of the physically and mentally handicapped.
   A person's outward appearance is no indication of his inner character.
   The only thing we have to fear is fear itself. (*Roosevelt*)

§21 *Verbs not necessarily followed by an adverb*

Certain verbs in English, the commonest of which is of course the verb *to be*, may be followed by an adjective complement rather than an adverbial one. Chief among them are those which indicate a state of being rather than an activity of some kind, like to *seem, to appear, to look* (e.g. *you look ill*), or the so-called inchoatives, which denote a change of state: *to become, to grow*, and so on. (It is important to remember that some of the inchoatives, such as *to grow, to go, to turn*, also have active meanings, and may therefore have an adverb complement.) Passage 21 includes a number of examples of verbs of this kind used in this way.

PASSAGE 21

From childhood I *had been* nervously *aware* of the change which takes place in trees and earth a little while after dusk and of how familiar things recede and *grow antagonistic* then, like a lover when passion dies. In the jungle *it was* inescapably *strong* this sense of a new charge of life flowing through the inanimate forms. Before that night I should have said that I 5 already knew intimately that panic-edged writhing darkness of the forest. But lying out now by the banked fire, I learnt something that I have since partly forgotten: it *would not be possible to remain sane* and *hold it intact* in one's mind. In any case it *was incommunicable* in its entirety – partly a feeling, as nearly as I can recall or express it, of 10 close and unbreakable communion with every part of this savage, suffering earth, though this was but a fraction of the sudden extension suffered by my understanding. I fought against my realization of being bound up in it all, helplessly and for ever. One *grows light-headed* in extreme hunger, and my enormously enlarged consciousness of every 15 blade of grass and every grain of soil, here and elsewhere, may have been only that. Against this appalling sense of oneness with the night, and the forest, and with everlasting things whose images were these straining trees and this pointless wealth of air and water and ground, I could put only my wan faith in personal annihilation, clinging to the cold, comely pride 20 of the spirit in accepting no trumped-up mitigation of its hopelessness in the face of death. And soon the life in me seemed to flow away into the ground and *leave me empty and unexpectant*, more or less passive. The horror ebbed too, and I was unconscious for a blessedly long time, I think.

E. ARNOT ROBERTSON: *Four Frightened People*

Comment

The verbs which use this pattern of an adjective complement are few in number, and they fall into two important groups: those which have a simple adjective complement, and those which have a noun or pronoun, followed by an adjective not an adverb, as their complement. Examples of both types of construction are found in Passage 21. In *lines* 1 (*had been aware*), 3 (*grow antagonistic*), 8 (*remain sane*), and 14 (*grows light-headed*) there are examples of verbs followed simply by a plain adjective. The verbs most frequently used in this way are:

> to be, to become, to seem to remain, to stay, to keep (= *to maintain an identical state*, e.g. 'I hope the meat *keeps fresh*'); to feel, to appear; to go, to grow, to turn (*inchoative*); to stand, to lie, to sit.

The pattern where the adjective is used in close connection with the object of the verb, but *following* its noun, is found in *line* 9 (*hold it intact*), and *line* 23 (*leave me empty and unexpectant*). With these, the adjective indicates a condition or state resulting from the action described by the verb. Quite a number of verbs may be used in this way, but when they are used so, they always have this quasi-causative significance:

> This news *made him angry.*
> They *painted the floor red.*
> They *found the house empty.*

The commonest verbs used in this way are:

> to beat, to boil, to colour, to consider, to cut, to discover, to dye, to fill, to find, to get, to hold, to keep, to leave, to lick, to make, to paint, to render, to set, to think, to turn, to drive (in the sense of *to cause to become* – e.g. *She drove him mad* – and only with a limited number of adjectives), to wash, to wipe.

QUESTION PAPER:

Comprehension

1 Give a word or phrase of similar meaning to:

dusk (*line* 2)	straining (*line* 18)
antagonistic (*line* 3)	comely (*line* 20)
inanimate (*line* 5)	trumped-up (*line* 21)
writhing (*line* 6)	mitigation (*line* 21)
the banked fire (*line* 7)	ebbed (*line* 24)

2 The following verbs all describe certain types of movement. Find out what they mean, and use them in suitable sentences:

> to writhe, to slither, to twitch, to squirm, to wriggle, to flutter

3 Examine this passage as a description of the effect of night in the jungle on an observer. Write a short (*about* 100 *words*) appreciation of the author's style, method and ideas.

4 Why do you think the author uses the following images:
panic-edged, writhing darkness (*line* 6)
savage, suffering earth (*lines* 11–12)
my enormously enlarged consciousness (*line* 15)
no trumped-up mitigation of its hopelessness (*lines* 21–22)

Structures

5 Change the adjective in brackets to an adverb *if necessary*.
  (*a*) She drives the car (good).
  (*b*) That noise drives me (mad).
  (*c*) The decorators have painted the house (bad).
  (*d*) They have painted the front door (purple).
  (*e*) They discovered the house (quick).
  (*f*) They discovered the house (empty).
  (*g*) He will grow (clever) and (clever) as he gets (old).
  (*h*) Please keep the door (open).
  (*i*) I hope it will stay (cool).
  (*j*) One day he will learn to grow tomatoes (proper).
  (*k*) The guests left the house (tidy). (What's the difference?)
  (*l*) The guests left the house (angry).
  (*m*) Please keep that book (careful).
  (*n*) They filled the decanter (gentle) with sherry.
  (*o*) They filled the decanter (full) with sherry.

6 Complete the following sentences, using a suitable adjective or adverb as seems appropriate:
  (*a*) The film was terrible; it left the audience . . . . . .
  (*b*) I wish people would stop whistling pop-tunes like that; it drives . . . . . .
  (*c*) It's autumn now, and the leaves are turning . . . . . .
  (*d*) Do you think these flowers will keep . . . . . . ?
  (*e*) She keeps all the souvenirs of her former fiancé . . . . . .
  (*f*) That man appears . . . . . .
  (*g*) He always takes you by surprise, he appears . . . . . .
  (*h*) Let's go out and celebrate, and paint the town . . . . . . (Idiom)
  (*i*) Be careful when you colour your hair . . . . . .
  (*j*) We must consider the new plan . . . . . .
  (*k*) I consider the new plan . . . . . .
  (*l*) The cruel owner beat his donkey . . . . . .

7 Write sentences of your own, using the verb in brackets with an appropriate adverb or adjective complement as is most apposite, in response to the following situations:
  (*a*) A friend has been told about an unjustified accusation made against him. (to make)

(*b*) Your friend is very pale. (look)

(*c*) A friend you have not seem for some time has different-coloured hair from what you remember. (dye)

(*d*) Your favourite football team has played very badly in an important match. (to beat)

(*e*) Your little brother is behaving rather annoyingly. (to drive)

(*f*) The table in the restaurant is dirty. (to wipe)

(*g*) Some friends have not yet applied for a booking at a very popular hotel for a holiday next week. (to leave)

(*h*) A friend is wearing a very odd costume. (to think)

(*i*) You are expressing your admiration for a person who didn't get flustered in a dangerous emergency. (to remain)

(*j*) It looks like rain, and you want to go out bicycling. (to stay)

8   Write a paragraph (*about* 100/120 *words*) on the subject 'A nightmare journey', using the following verbs; make sure that they are used with a suitable adjective or adverb complement – or both, when indicated.

To feel; to consider (BOTH); to think (BOTH); to drive (BOTH); to discover; to turn; to seem; to keep (BOTH); to go (BOTH).

Suggested discussion topics

Memories of childhood, and their effect on character.

What makes people embarrassed?

Mercy-killing.

§22 *Adjectival and adverbial similes*

The conjunctions *as* and *like* (frequently misused by English people anyway!) often cause trouble to advanced students who are enterprising enough to try to use similes in their work. The purpose of this section is to illustrate when we use *as*, when *like*, when *as if*, and when *such as*.

PASSAGE 22*a*

The thunder did not break. Instead, the drops increased in number and suddenly became a flood. The trees, the hedges and the fields, the sky itself and all its gesticulating silent mobs wavered *like reflections in a stream*, and then dissolved into an air which was largely water. I found myself alone among warm cataracts, with no distinction of material for 5
the senses, except the variety of noise; the dashing of leaves, the roar of boughs, the hissing of a copse, the rustle of hedges, the tinkle of drains. Which proved so delusive that in the thickened twilight I lost my way and found myself walking in the stubble, mixed with new clover, of a field already cut; an accident not surprising on such an evening. But 10
now of such bewildering effect that, AS I STOOD, with every clover leaf pouring its waterfall into my boots, I felt *as if the very earth were liquefying under my feet, as if the familiar trees, fields and sky had actually melted into some primitive elementary form* and that the world of German philosophy, in which everything can be anything else, *as the philosopher* 15
pleases, had actually realized itself in a universal nothingness, whose very colour was uncertain. And I, the very last individual being of the old creation, though still solid in appearance and capable of supporting a hat; *as I ascertained by touch*; trousers, umbrella, etc., *as I perceived by sight*, was yet already wavering in essence, beginning to lose the shape 20
of my ideas, memory, etc., preparatory to the final and rapid solution of my whole identity.

JOYCE CARY: *To Be a Pilgrim*

Comment

None of the comparisons here is very striking, and the difference between *as* and *as if* is very clear. Where a finite verb is likened to another finite verb, *as if* is the usual conjunction:

I felt + *as if* + the . . . earth *were* liquefying
           + the . . . trees . . . *had actually melted.*

Where the comparison is between two nouns via a verb, and the implication is 'in the *manner* of', we use *like*:

the silent mobs wavered + *like* + *reflections in a stream.*

Here, the noun phrase *the silent mobs* is compared, via the verb *wavered,* to
reflections in a stream. *When they wavered*, they *resembled* those reflections.
They did not actually *function* as reflections; they merely resembled them.

The function of *as* is more varied, and more complex. It is not merely
a conjunction of comparison; it may also be a conjunction of time. In
Passage 22*a* the meaning is clear, but not easy to paraphrase without
absurd pomposity; that is usually the trouble with very short words!
The student will notice, however, that in each case it is followed by a
finite verb: *as the philosopher pleases: as I ascertained: as I perceived. Like*
always has a noun or pronoun – or occasionally an adjective – complement, never a verb. Please do not use *like* as a conjunction, even if
Americans do so.

PASSAGE 22*b*
We stood there and looked up at the church AS HE TOLD US in rising
voice of that long-ago night. With its eyed bell-tower questioning up-
right at one end, and the small nave beneath, it looked *something like a
lonely mountain goat*; it was the same shape, and alone in the mirage of
slopes one needed guidance to define exactly the size of any such distant   5
object. And now AS WE LISTENED and looked, the setting of the sun
told against the moonlit story – yet added to its magic. For with its
northern low slow setting, the horizontal sunglow made a fantasy of the
place: the sky turned soft lavender, the snow ranged luminescent from
rose to palest gold, what trees there were took a sacrificial copper to   10
their trunks, far-away clouds against the lavender sky showed bright
blue *like washed cloth*, and above all the moon shone out apple-green
like a bewitched jewel. Such colour looked impossible – but it was so.
And fixed so in the clear northern air, *as if all seen through glass*. Colour
in this strange North *such as is never seen* in the traditionally colourful 15
lands of the Mediterranean. The sun made magic of everything: and
within this magic – against which one could smell petrol fumes, smoke
cigarettes, blow one's nose and switch jazz from radio – there lived the
small curious Lapps, still in hide wigwams, still herding their fur-
horned reindeer *as through the immemorial cold past*.   20
                          WILLIAM SANSOM: *A Wedding*

Comment
The *as* clauses in the first and third sentences are temporal, and do not
come within the scope of this section. The similes introduced by *like* do
not differ from those in the Joyce Cary excerpt. The *as if* comparison

(*line* 13) depends upon the verb participle *seen*; the force of the simile is thus one of verb comparison rather than noun. In the next sentence the writer moves via a conjunction phrase from a general term *colour* to the particular instance of that term: SUCH AS *is never seen*. This is the normal conjunction-phrase to express 'of a kind that', 'of this sort . . .'. In the last line of the excerpt, the writer uses *as* meaning 'in the manner that'. The verb dependent on *as* has been suppressed; the clause expanded to its full form would be:

> still herding their . . . reindeer, *as they had done* through the immemorial cold past.

This is not merely a matter of likening one action to the other (in which case the conjunction would have been *as if*) but of stressing the identical nature of the actions compared.

PASSAGE 22*c*

If a theme of the type used in polyphonic music acts very much *like a brick or a block of stone* (*as something of no importance* in itself, *useful only as raw material* to be built into a structure), the thematic material of other types of music – opera, song, symphony – *is* important in itself, being emotionally expressive, *as is* the material of painting and literature. The 5
experience derived from a piece of polyphony, *like that derived from a piece of architecture*, consists mainly of a perception and admiration of its form; but in most cases, the experience derived from a piece of non-polyphonic music, *like that derived from a painting or a literary work*, is only partly referable to an appreciation of its form: much of it derives 10
from our emotional response to its actual material. A typical contrapuntal point or fugue-subject has no real significance until it takes its place in the construction *as a whole*; but a theme in a sonata, *like a hand in a painting* or a line in a poem, is already of absorbing emotional interest in itself, even if its full significance is only appreciated when its integration 15
into the overall form is understood. Indeed, in music, *as to a greater degree* in literature, a work can be outstanding in spite of being cast into a most unsatisfying form: we listen to *works like Boris Godunov* and Delius's Violin Concerto, *as we read books like Tristram Shandy* and *Moby Dick*, not for their formal beauty, but for the fascination of their material. 20

DERYCK COOKE: *The Language of Music*

Comment

The many comparisons here involving the use of *like* demonstrate quite clearly when it is used. In every case, two nouns are compared, not through a verb, but directly. Where a verb or an adverb is involved in the comparison (e.g. *lines* 16-17: in music, *as to a greater degree in literature*) it becomes necessary to use *as*. This is also the case in *lines* 18-20 (we *listen to works* like Boris Godunov ... *as we read books* like Tristram Shandy). Here, the comparison is a direct one between two verb activities. In the very same sentence, the comparison, made directly between the nouns *Boris Godunov* and *Delius's Violin Concerto* – where the two musical works are specific examples of the imprecise general term 'works' – requires the junction *like*, not *as*.

When the conjunction needed means *in the manner of, of a similar kind to,* then *like* is used; when it means *in the function of,* we use *as*; and when the comparison is between two verbs, meaning *in the same way that,* we use *as*.

QUESTION PAPER:

Comprehension

1 The author uses the words *rustle, hissing* and *tinkle* in Passage 22a. Make up sentences of your own, using the following words of related but different meaning:
    clink, jingle, ping, patter, sizzle, swish

2 What words might the author of Passage 22a have used instead of:
    bewildering (*line* 11), ascertained (*line* 19), perceived (*line* 19)?

3 Passage 22b, the author mentions the *nave* and the *bell-tower* of a church. Define those terms, and also the following:
    the chancel, the pulpit, the font, the aisles

4 What do you think the author of Passage 22b is trying to convey by the following phrases:
    the snow ranged luminescent (*line* 9)
    a sacrificial copper (*line* 10)
    traditionally colourful lands of the Mediterranean (*lines* 15–16)
    The sun made magic of everything (*line* 16)
    hide wigwams (*line* 19)

5 Examine and comment on Mr Cooke's argument in Passage 22c. What does he mean by *polyphonic music*? Name some composers whose works fall into this category.

Structures

6 Fill the blanks with *as, like, such as* or *as if*, as seems most suitable:
    (*a*) She sings —— an angel.
    (*b*) He looks —— Sir Winston Churchill.
    (*c*) That student behaves —— a child.
    (*d*) In his spare time, he works —— a pop-singer.
    (*e*) Men —— him deserve all they get.
    (*f*) She stood there —— she had been struck dumb with fear.
    (*g*) They reacted —— the world were coming to an end.

(*h*) Try to understand the passage —— a whole before examining the details —— new vocabulary, etc.

(*i*) Mozart was treated —— a serf by Archbishop Colloredo.

(*j*) Why are you screaming —— that?

7 Complete the following sentences, using an appropriate comparison:

(*a*) Don't do anything silly, ...

(*b*) It is cruel to treat a dog ......

(*c*) She is working for the exam ......

(*d*) Some artists, ... Shakespeare, Michelangelo or Beethoven reach heights ......

(*e*) After leaving school he took a job ......

(*f*) On hearing the news she felt ......

(*g*) Giving advice to her is ......

(*h*) This wall was built ......

(*i*) He served in the army ......

(*j*) Some students make amusing mistakes ......

8 Write sentences of your own, using an appropriate comparison, to refer or react to the following situations:

(*a*) A friend of yours has received bad news.

(*b*) You are asked how well a musical friend plays the piano.

(*c*) You are asked to give details of your career.

(*d*) You are asked to give examples of your favourite authors.

(*e*) Your dancing-partner asks your opinion of his/her skill.

(*f*) You are asked your opinion of a play you have seen.

(*g*) Describe the sensation of eating a peach.

(*h*) You are asked for a report on a conversation between two people who don't speak one another's language well.

9 Write an imaginary letter to a friend describing an unusual holiday, a village music festival, or an amateur dramatic production, introducing as many comparisons as you can. (*about* 150/180 *words*)

Suggested discussion topics

The attractions of foreign travel.

Modern music, both serious and popular.

Opera – an exotic and irrational entertainment.

Beauties of your country which a foreigner might miss.

It is occasionally possible in English to interfere with the normal subject–predicate word-order. It is rarely necessary, and always a little artificial to do so. The main cases where an inversion is regarded as conventionally necessary occur in certain types of conditional sentences and in certain cases where a restrictive adverbial phrase (usually a negative) is placed at the head of the sentence for purposes of emphasis. The examples given in this section should be noted, but, except for practice purposes, it is probably not advisable to copy them. This is not because they should be regarded as stylistically bad, but simply because the overseas student should increase his armoury of self-expression by precise use of forms, vocabulary and rhythm, not by rhetorical tricks.

PASSAGE 23*a*
Had his character been as firm as his intelligence was rapid, *had his protestations of saintliness not been marred* by the personal habits of a voluptuary, *had he been able* to adjust the requirements of his own Empire to that spirit of self-sacrifice which he demanded of others, then indeed he might have become the representative and even the leader of those hidden   5
forces which stirred in the first four decades of the nineteenth century. So soon, however, as the glamour of those startling spring weeks had begun to fade, it was recognised that the Tsar's personality was too disintegrated to carry conviction.
                    SIR HAROLD NICOLSON: *The Congress of Vienna*

Comment
The first sentence of this passage illustrates the use of the inverted form in REJECTED CONDITIONS (see §12). Note also the *might have* form of the verb in the main clause. A further point worth mentioning is that NO inversion is required after the subordinating temporal conjunction *as soon as* (here: *So soon as . . .*). The main clause (it was recognised . . . etc.) has the normal word-order.

    This type of inversion is also found in open conditions expressing doubt (*Were* he *to arrive* soon . . . and . . . *Should* you *see* him) when the conjunction *if* is omitted.

After a holiday from periodical literature, I am always staggered, when I get back to a well-stocked reading-room, by the inordinate snobbery of the English press. *In no other country do* so many newspapers *devote* so large a proportion of their space to a chronicle of the activities of the merely rich or the merely ennobled. *Nowhere else in Europe is* gossip- 5
writing a highly paid and creditable profession; *nowhere else would* such a headline as 'Peer's cousin in Car Smash' *be* even imaginable.

ALDOUS HUXLEY: *English Snobbery*

Comment

A number of adverbial expressions – all of them restrictive, and most of them negative in meaning – may only with caution be put at the head of the sentence. This is because they require the inversion of the normal subject–verb order. Chief among them are the three adverbs of frequency:

Rarely, seldom, and *never*;

the three adverbs of degree:

barely, hardly, and *scarcely*;

the adverb of place *nowhere*; the conjunctions *either* and *nor* when used separately; any adverbial of time, place or frequency beginning with *not* or *only* (e.g. *Only then; not often; only here*); and any verb object (transitive or prepositional) placed at the head of the sentence for emphasis, and prefaced by either of those two particles (e.g. *Not a word did she say: only to him did she divulge* her secret). THIS PROCEDURE IS HIGHLY ARTIFICIAL, AND SHOULD BE AVOIDED WHEREVER POSSIBLE. Don't forget that the phrase *any adverbial* includes phrases and clauses as well as ordinary adverbs (e.g.: *Only after the lesson did she discover* that she had lost her handbag; *Not until she had met him did she realise* how powerful his voice was).

QUESTION PAPER:

Comprehension

1 Give a word or phrase of similar meaning to:
   protestations (Passage 23*a, line* 2) disintegrated (23*a, line* 9)
   marred (23*a, line* 2) staggered (23*b, line* 1)
   voluptuary (23*a, line* 3) inordinate (23*b, line* 2)
   stirred (23*a, line* 6) gossip-writing (23*b, line* 5)
   glamour (23*a, line* 7)

2 By saying that the Tsar's character was *disintegrated*, Nicolson implies that

it was more than simply contradictory. What does he imply, and why might that be dangerous?

3 Do you agree with Huxley's condemnation of the 'inordinate snobbery' of the English press? Is it true that 'Nowhere else in Europe is gossip-writing a highly paid and creditable profession'? Are there any parallels to what he condemns in your own country?

Structures

4 Rearrange the layout of the italicised phrase or clause to increase the emphasis, making any necessary change in the word-order of the sentence.
 (*a*) *If he had been* less precipitate, he would not have made such a silly mistake.
 (*b*) *If you had considered* the matter more carefully, you would have noticed the flaws in his argument.
 (*c*) *If she had not posed* as a glamorous film-star, she would not have had her photograph in the gossip-column.
 (*d*) *If he were not* such an inordinate miser, he would have far more friends.
 (*e*) *If you should happen* to see her, tell her I shall be late.
 (*f*) *He didn't say a word*; he just stood and looked staggered.
 (*g*) You won't find gossip-writing as degrading as this *anywhere else*.
 (*h*) She had *barely* entered the room when a man proposed to her.
 (*i*) He is *not only* a selfish voluptuary, but an inordinate snob.
 (*j*) We *seldom* find that her protestations of innocence are genuine.

5 Write sentences of your own, using the word in brackets as the first word, to respond to or illustrate the following situations:
 (*a*) You have arrived in a strange town, and had your money stolen. (Barely . . .)
 (*b*) The police were both kind and efficient. (Not only . . .)
 (*c*) Such courtesy and efficiency were outside your previous experience. (Never . . .)
 (*d*) You would be surprised if you were treated so well anywhere else. (Nowhere else . . .)
 (*e*) You might have expected such treatment if you had been a diplomat, or a film-star. (Had I . . .)
 (*f*) This is surely a sign that the police are real gentlemen. (Only in a country . . .)
 (*g*) They didn't find your money, but everything else was wonderful. (Had they . . .)
 (*h*) But you were able to obtain funds from the consulate of your country, and you advise your friend to do the same if she has a similar experience. (Should you . . .)

6 Write a paragraph on *The Vices of the Modern Town*, using as many sentences as you can where an inversion of the normal word-order is necessary. (*about* 100/120 *words*)

Suggested discussion topics

The relationship between psychological abnormality and the lust for power.
The corrupting influence of modern mass-communications.
All men are snobs about something.
Noblesse oblige.

Subdivision II
Verb-nouns and
verb-adjectives

There are two things wrong with the gerund. The first is that it doesn't exist in many languages; the second, that it is identical in form with the present participle, and that it is sometimes difficult (though never necessary) to decide whether a given form ending in -*ing* is either the one or the other. In general, though, it is the standard noun derived from the verb in English, and the use of the infinitive for this purpose is rarer. It is the standard verb form used after all phrasal verbs in which the preposition or adverb adjunct really is part of the verb infinitive; in fact it and not the infinitive is always used after all prepositions except *to*. Certain verbs may be followed by either an infinitive or a gerund; others by a gerund only, others by an infinitive only. The passages in this section aim at showing how the gerund is used, both as the subject of a sentence or clause, or as the object or prepositional object.

PASSAGE 24*a*
The essence of the whole process is *learning* to conform to the conventions of the group in which the individual lives. When we ask a child TO NAME something, we are teaching him TO MAKE a response that ensures communication. We are also passing on to him our own *ways of observing*. We have various *means of rewarding* him when he is right, 5
punishing him when he is wrong. We can do it *by feeding* or *beating* him, but the first can only be infrequent and the second TENDS TO CUT OFF all connexion with him. We do it much more subtly *by establishing* first a special behaviour sequence, that of communication. The child's most important lesson is that *the fitting of stimuli* into a communicable form 10
produces 'satisfactory' results. It is DIFFICULT TO APPRECIATE how deeply this first *way of responding* controls all the others, which are later learned through it. Once this is established, it is not NECESSARY TO SET UP an elaborate apparatus of rewards and punishments TO TEACH each new association. *By giving* the signs of approval or disapproval we can 15
show the child instantly whether he has produced the right reactions or not. His whole brain system is trained so that it SEEKS TO ORGANISE all the sensory input into some communicable output – TO PUT it into words. From his earliest days *cutting off* means hunger and cold, whereas communication means satisfaction. The smile becomes the symbol of 20

completion and satisfaction and the cry that of disorder and pain. By association with these signs that communication has or has not been achieved, the names that are 'right' are built into the brain system; the child learns TO SELECT AND OBSERVE 'correctly'.

J. Z. YOUNG: Doubt and Certainty in Science

Comment

In addition to the gerunds in this passage, there are also quite a few infinitives; the first exercise the student might profitably attempt is that of replacing the gerunds by infinitives and *vice versa*, where this is possible. He should then try to work out what changes if any have occurred in the meaning of the sentence, and where the substitution is quite unthinkable, and for what reasons.

It is obviously quite impossible to substitute infinitives for gerunds in *line 6* (we can do it *by beating* him etc.), for example. Many students would, however, imagine that it is quite possible to substitute infinitives in *lines 4-5* (ways *of observing*; means *of rewarding*) and 12 (way *of responding*). They would fall into a common trap here. The construction after the word *way* is strangely inconsistent. The student will hear, for example:

That is *the only way to do this*.

Yet it would be manifestly wrong to substitute infinitives for gerunds in the examples with *way* quoted from the passage. It seems that the infinitive is used after the word *way* only when the context makes it clear that there is no alternative way mentioned. The construction after the noun *means* is clear, as *line 5* shows.

Students of some nationalities tend sometimes to misunderstand the use of the preposition *by* at the beginning of a clause, followed by a gerund. The example in *line 15* shows the commonest meaning in English. *By giving the signs of approval* etc., means not just *when we give* but *as a result of giving* them. Similarly *We can do it by feeding or beating him* is not temporal; the *by* implies 'using the process of' beating him, and thus has a meaning closely related to the other example quoted from the passage. The case of *by establishing first* etc. (*line 8*) may be justifiably considered as falling into either or both of these two categories.

PASSAGE 24*b*

I never *liked being in Parliament* and, as there are, TO JUDGE from the list of candidates, a lot of other people who do like it, it is only fair that they should have their try. THERE IS obviously MUCH TO BE SAID for the argument that a man who has *a prospect of holding* an office of responsibility has A DUTY TO REMAIN in Parliament whether he likes it or not,   5
but as there was *no chance of such office coming* my way, that argument did

not apply to me and frankly I do not think that a back bencher HAS
ENOUGH TO DO or ENOUGH RESPONSIBILITY TO JUSTIFY him *in
remaining* on the back benches for very long. That is ALL THAT I HAVE
TO SAY on the matter from the purely personal point of view.   10
    It is much EASIER TO SAY that there is something wrong with Parlia-
ment as it is today THAN TO SAY how it should be put right. Parliamen-
tary Government grew up in an aristocratic society and in a society in
which it was thought of the first importance that the Government should
not do too much. Parliament is essentially *an institution for preventing* the   15
Government *from doing things.*

CHRISTOPHER HOLLIS: Farewell to Westminster

Comment

This section gives a number of examples of verbs, nouns and adjectives
which may be followed by a gerund construction; there are also others
that require an infinitive. Some of them may be followed by either; in
some of these cases, the two constructions are interchangeable, but in
others not. For instance, in the first line, although the verb *to like* may be
followed by either a gerund or an infinitive, an infinitive could not be
substituted here. Being in Parliament is not a habit or a repeated process;
it is a continuous one, and while a gerund may be used after the verb *to
like* when speaking of a habit or custom, one does not normally use an
infinitive after it unless one is definitely talking of a habit or custom. And
with the negative (*don't like*) and the antonym (*dislike*), the gerund is
obligatory. The following list of verbs followed by a gerund does not
pretend to be complete, but the verbs in it are the commonest of their
kind. They may be listed under seven headings:

1 *Verbs indicating some emotional reaction:*
    to appreciate, to detest,* to dislike*, to enjoy,* to mind.
2 *Verbs indicating some form of avoidance of an action:*
    to avoid,* to escape,* to miss,* to postpone,* to prevent.*
3 *Verbs indicating some kind of intellectual consideration:*
    to consider, to recollect, to understand.
4 *Verbs indicating forgiveness:*
    to excuse*, to forgive,* to pardon.*
5 *Verbs indicating some form of danger:*
    to risk, to endanger,* to jeopardise.*
6 *Verbs indicating some form of work on a process:*
    to finish,* to practise.*
7 *Verbs of statement:*
    to mention, to deny.

NB: Verbs indicated with an asterisk are very rarely, if ever, used in
conjunction with an indirect statement (for Noun Clauses see §27).

The words *prospect, chance, opportunity* and *possibility* are tricky. Not only do they resemble other words of similar derivation in other languages and mean something different; they also require care when used with a dependent construction. *Chance* and *opportunity* may be used with an infinitive or with a gerund. *Prospect* and *possibility* are used with *of* and a gerund. *Responsibility*, too, is used with a gerund (the infinitive after *responsibility* in *line* 8 is coupled with the *enough*, not with the noun). *Duty* (*line* 5) is however quite naturally used with an infinitive, though when preceded by a definite article, *of* + the gerund is often more acceptable (He had *the duty of supervising* the loading of the ship).

PASSAGE 24c

Seeing his blunt whiskered head by the corks, the skipper ran to the boat for the rifle, which was lying with its muzzle in the bilge. Jarrk watched while the rifle was loaded and aimed, *expecting* what happened; a *cracking* thud in the water near him, a report that raised gulls and *wading* birds from tidemark *feeding* far up and down the estuary; and nothing else. The seal was *used to swimming down* when the rifle fired, and so he rolled under, and the marksman said this time he had hit the limmer. Some hopes, replied his mates, *watching* the water as they lay back, *boots sinking* in wet sand while the third man flacked the rope on the water in vain hope *of scaring* the seal away.

HENRY WILLIAMSON: *Solar the Salmon*

Comment

One of the tricky points about the verb form in *-ing* in English is that it may be an adjective – the present participle – or a noun – the gerund. Most of the examples in this passage are present participles. It is instructive to see how they are used. First of all, none of these is unattached: the noun to which each refers is clear and definite. In *line* 1 it is automatically assumed that the participle *seeing* refers to the subject of the main clause: *the skipper.* The same grammar point is true of the participles *expecting* and *watching* (*lines* 3 *and* 8 respectively). Very often, as here, the present participle used thus implies some form of causative relationship between the two verbs. This is so here: the word *seeing* might be paraphrased as 'When and because he saw . . .', the *expecting* as 'because he expected'. If the relationship is not causative, it is usually temporal, as with *watching* (= *While*, or *as they watched* . . .) and *with boots sinking* (= *during which time their boots were sinking*). Notice that here, where there is a sudden change of implied subject, the participle *follows* the noun it refers to.

Note that *used to* (= *accustomed to*) is followed by a gerund, not an infinitive (*line* 6), and that the noun (not the verb) *hope* is also followed by one (*line* 9).

QUESTION PAPER:

Comprehension

1 What does the author mean by the following phrases in Passage 24*a*?
  to make a response that ensures communication (*lines* 3–4)
  establishing a behaviour sequence (*lines* 8–9)
  an elaborate apparatus of rewards and punishments (*line* 14)
  the sensory input (*line* 18)
  built into the brain system (*line* 23)

2 Do you agree with Professor Young's contention that 'the essence of the whole process is learning to conform to the conventions of the group in which the individual lives'? (*The whole process* means the business of communicating with other people through language and behaviour.)

3 What does Hollis (Passage 24*b*) mean by:
  an office of responsibility (*lines* 4–5)
  a back bencher (*line* 7)
  an aristocratic society (*line* 13)
  essentially (*line* 15)

4 What is your opinion of Hollis's belief that 'Parliament is essentially an institution for preventing the Government from doing things'? What sort of things should it prevent the Government from doing, and what means can you think of that it might possess, under the British constitution, for doing so?

5 Give a word or phrase of similar meaning to:
  blunt (Passage 24*c*, *line* 1)   bilge (*line* 2)
  skipper (*line* 1)   a report (*line* 4)
  muzzle (*line* 2)

6 Use the following words in sentences showing that you understand the differences between them:
  (*a*) whiskered, bearded, moustached
  (*b*) thud, rumble, crack, boom, snap
  (*c*) to wade through, to skim over
  (The words in (*c*) may be used literally or figuratively.)

Structures

7 Substitute a word or phrase involving a verb form in *-ing* for the italicised words:
  (*a*) *When he saw me,* he waved to me.
  (*b*) *Because she was* intelligent, she understood the question.
  (*c*) *As they watched* the sunset, they were reminded of a painting by Turner.
  (*d*) She has great hopes *that she will marry* a millionaire.
  (*e*) We very much appreciate *the fact that you have washed the dishes* for us.
  (*f*) She mentioned *the fact that she had been to Rome.*

(g) There is little prospect *that he will be promoted.*

(h) This is a law *that helps to prevent smuggling.*

8   Develop the following sentences into a connected dialogue, using a suitable verb construction to complete them:

(a) It's about time you finished ......

(b) Will you forgive my ......?

(c) Please excuse his ......

(d) She was beginning to enjoy ......

(e) He is strong-minded, and detests ......

(f) The Directors do not appreciate ......

(g) Is it wise to risk ...... ?

(h) She has denied ......

(i) There is nothing to prevent your ......

(j) Do you mind their ...... ?

(k) He won't accept responsibility for ......

(l) There is no prospect of ......

(m) One day you'll get used to ......

(n) You can best achieve your aim by ......

(o) Catching the 4.44 train on Tuesday morning implies ......

9   Write sentences referring to or responding to the following situations:

(a) You arrive late at a lesson, and you haven't done your homework.

(b) Someone asks you what you think of a very unpleasant acquaintance.

(c) You are asked to invest a lot of money in a rather dubious enterprise.

(d) You are asked if you have ever played the game of cricket.

(e) Someone wants your help because her boy-friend wants to go swimming in a dangerous sea.

(f) A friend wants to know how to get to know some English people.

(g) How does a great tennis-player achieve his high standard?

(h) There is fog at the airport, and your plane is due to take off in three minutes.

10 Taking either Passage 24b or Passage 24c as a model, and using the same pattern of constructions for your sentences, write a paragraph describing your reactions to one particular subject at school which you either liked or detested.

Suggested discussion topics

The role of the back-bench M.P.

The best way of training children.

Blood and field sports.

§19 has already illustrated one of the most important uses of the infinitive in English. Because of the existence of the gerund, its function is both more limited and more flexible than in many other languages. It is very dangerous to seek simple parallels between English and other languages, for there are many cases where they differ sharply.

The infinitive is particularly useful in certain contexts as a kind of shorthand device. It may, for example, be used as a kind of shorthand temporal clause (he was *angry to find* he had lost his wallet); as a kind of shorthand relative clause (he is just *the man to ask*); or even as a kind of shorthand conditional clause (I should be *grateful to be relieved* of this job.)

PASSAGE 25*a*
Harold *persuaded Alec to let him drive them home*. The drinks hadn't cheered him up; they had depressed and fuddled him. Harold, who wasn't used to men with moods, thought that the best and kindest policy was *to ignore* Alec's. If he himself was out of spirits, *he hated anyone to comment on it*. It was a measure of self-protection dating from his schooldays,   5
when a long face was a sign of weakness and the whole pack would turn on him if they saw him looking sad. A cheerful countenance was the first line of defence. Most of Harold's men friends felt the same, and if they had seen one of their number looking quite suicidal, would never have dreamt of asking him the reason.   10
L. P. HARTLEY: *A Perfect Woman*

Comment
This first short excerpt gives two examples of the so-called ACCUSATIVE AND INFINITIVE construction, and one of the infinitive used as a kind of shorthand clause. It is interesting that the function of the two Accusative and Infinitive constructions is different. That in the first line is a kind of indirect command, and this is the normal way of expressing an indirect command in English. The second (*lines* 4–5: *he hated anyone to comment on it*) is common with certain verbs expressing an emotional attitude, principal among which are *to want, to like, to prefer, to desire,*

to hate and *can't bear*. Notice that the first two are NOT followed by a noun clause beginning with *that* as an alternative to this construction; this is possible with *to prefer* and *can't bear*.

Considered as a variant of an indirect command (calling it perhaps an indirect request), this construction may be used with a number of verbs, the chief of which are:

> *to advise, to allow, to ask, to beg, to cause, to challenge, to command, to dare, to encourage, to entreat, to force, to get, to implore, to instruct* (in the sense of *to give an order*), *to invite, to oblige, to order, to permit, to persuade, to press, to request, to tell, to tempt, to urge, to warn.*

The verbs in this list all have some idea of generating or forcing some kind of action.

In the case of the infinitive in *lines* 3-4 (the best and kindest policy was *to ignore* Alec's) the construction is a useful device for avoiding a clumsy relative clause involving an impersonal and vague antecedent: *the best . . . policy would be that of ignoring Alec's.* This is a common construction after the verb *to be*, and has parallels in a number of other languages. The narrative then continues:

PASSAGE 25*b*
During the visit Harold's own outlook had undergone a good many changes. It *was natural* to him *to feel critical* of another environment than his own; he suspected hostility at once; the herd instinct was very strong in him. In so far as he was a snob his snobbery only operated within his own social group; he didn't envy those above it, though he *tended to look   5 down* on those below it. Both seemed to him a little unreal, and as if they didn't know what life was about; and this was especially the case with Alec and his outfit, for Alec belonged to no group or social stratum, he *appeared to have* the freedom of several but *to be* indigenous to none.

Comment
One of the most confusing and irritating things about English is its inconsistency of construction when expressing the idea of habitual attitudes or tendencies. Why do we say 'She tends *to look down* on people'? or 'She has a tendency *to do* so', and yet: 'She has the habit *of doing* so'? With the two verbs *to seem* and *to appear*, the subsequent infinitive may be omitted if its complement is an adjective; Hartley might well have written in *line* 6 'Both seemed to him *to be* a little unreal.' The excerpt continues:

PASSAGE 25*c*
Harold disapproved of this, he was suspicious of any man who couldn't produce a dozen men who wore the same uniform as he did. Alec had

friends, of course, didn't Harold know it? And these friends were *prepared to do* a great deal for him. But the ties which bound him to them were emotional and personal, not social. The emotional and personal 5 sides of Alec's nature were, in Harold's view, much too highly developed. Nearly everything that Alec said to him during their expedition to the pub embarrassed him; he felt he was overhearing things he *was not meant to hear*, and that later Alec would be sorry he had said them.

Comment

A very common use of the infinitive is in context indicating a purpose, readiness, or intention to do something. This also covers certain adjectives with similar meanings frequently used as complements of the verb *to be*; the commonest are: *ready, eager, keen, willing, disposed, hesitant, inclined, reluctant, unwilling, disinclined, loth, free, fated* and *destined*. See also Final Clauses (§19, page 80).

The student will notice that a number of these adjectives are in fact past participles. This relates them to the verbs implying volition or intention that are used with an infinitive. Two of them occur in Passage 25c: *to prepare* and *to mean* (= *to intend*). Other important verbs of this kind are:

> *to decide, to hope, to intend, to offer, to prepare, to promise, to propose, to swear, to try* (when it means *to make the attempt*), *to undertake.*

All these verbs indicate a willingness to do something, carried often enough to a definite commitment to it, and sometimes to an actual attempt.

PASSAGE 25*d*

BESIDES BEING indecent, it was risky. How did Alec know that Harold wouldn't take advantage of these confidences? *To lay* all his cards on the table like that! *To expose* his whole being to another person's view! With one ear, Harold listened; with the other he *tried not to listen*. It all came, Harold told himself, FROM ALEC'S BEING educated privately; at 5 a public school he would have learnt reticence; he *would have learnt to conceal* his feelings until, under the salutary influence of self-discipline, he *would have ceased to have any* – any, that is, outside the married state, where it was still *permissible to indulge* them.

Comment

It is but a short step from past participles like *intended* and *meant* to those like *supposed* and then *permitted*. A number of verbs implying the concept of supposition are used with the accusative and infinitive, notably:

> *to assume, to suppose, to believe, to think, to consider, to understand, to feel, to presume, to guess.*

Their past participles, used adjectivally or in passive constructions, are of course followed by a straight infinitive with *to*. Strangely enough, the only outright adjective derived from a verb of this group used regularly in this way is *permissible*, in the last line of Passage 25*d*.

Another important group of verbs followed by dependent infinitives with *to* is that group indicating the effort or attempt to do something. There are two in Passage 25*d*: *to try* (*line* 4 – note the position of the negative) and *to learn* (*line* 6). The most important verbs in this group are:

> *to attempt, to endeavour, to learn, to try*

The nouns derived from these verbs are also followed by an infinitive.

Certain verbs implying the beginning, continuation, or completion of a process are also followed by an infinitive; one of them, *to cease*, is found in *line* 9 of Passage 25*d*. The others are:

> *to begin, to commence, to continue, to start.*

Students should be very careful about *to stop*. If this is followed by an infinitive, the infinitive is an infinitive of purpose (see Final Clauses, §19) and *not* a true complement of the verb *to stop* itself. The normal complement of *to stop* is a gerund (*Stop talking!* Please ask him to *stop shouting.*) She *stopped playing.* They should also note that all five of these verbs, as well as *to stop*, may be followed by a gerund.

The use of the infinitive as the subject of a sentence in English often has the idea of a kind of shocked surprise about it, particularly if there is no main verb. Thus, in *lines* 2 and 3, the infinitives *To lay . . .* and *To expose . . .* are a convenient shorthand for some such phrase as 'Fancy laying . . .'

PASSAGE 25*e*
She *tried not to worry* about this, but it blurred her image of herself as someone who didn't do that kind of thing. She felt she had invalidated her own judgement. Apart from moral questions, she *hesitated to give* her opinion on any problem: what *right* had she *to speak*? She felt that anything she said came from a tainted source, as if, *to borrow* a simile from   5
Harold's world, with which she was now so much more familiar, she had been a fraudulent financier *asked to give* his opinion on the value of an investment. Her parents had, according to their lights, maintained their respective standards of value. She had let hers down.

Comment
A number of adjectives and a handful of verbs implying fear or reluctance to do something are followed by an infinitive, such as *to hesitate* in this

passage. The two others most frequently encountered are *to fail* and *to shudder*. The main adjectives of this kind are *afraid, reluctant,* and *scared*.

Certain nouns indicating some form of requirement or obligation are followed by an infinitive, including *right* when it means privilege (*line* 4). The other commonest ones are:

> *need, duty, obligation, necessity, liability* and *responsibility.*

Thus the adjectives *needful, imperative, necessary, liable, apt, bound* and *essential* (among others) fall into this pattern.

In *lines* 5–6 there is an example of the infinitive used parenthetically as a kind of shorthand conditional phrase. It is frequently used thus, and also as an indicator of purpose (e.g. She told him she was going to London *to buy a new dress*). This last usage should be carefully remembered; it is archaic, to say the least, to use a noun clause containing a modal verb for this purpose in modern English, although the construction is certainly found in formal contexts (see §19). Even so, it can usually be avoided. Instead of saying: 'I am telling you this *that you* may not make this mistake', one might say: 'I am telling you this *to prevent* you making this mistake'. If a noun clause is used in a consecutive or final clause, students should remember that nowadays the conjunction-phrase *so that* is preferred to the simple *that*. Even so, the infinitive can nearly always be used in such contexts if the vocabulary is carefully selected.

All the examples in this section are taken from L. P. Hartley's *A Perfect Woman*, examples 25a–d from one consecutive passage in the book.

QUESTION PAPER:

Comprehension

1 Read Passages 25a–d together, and then describe what you imagine the two men Harold and Alec were like.

2 Give a word or phrase of similar meaning to:
fuddled (Passage 25a, *line* 2)	to overhear (25c, *line* 8)
a long face (25a, *line* 6)	to take advantage of (25d, *line* 2)
the whole pack (25a, *line* 6)	salutary (25d, *line* 7)
environment (25b, *line* 2)	to indulge (25d, *line* 9)
the herd instinct (25b, *line* 3)	blurred (25e, *line* 1)
social stratum (25b, *line* 8)	a tainted source (25e, *line* 5)
indigenous to none (25b, *line* 9)	according to their lights (25e, *line* 8)
ties (25c, *line* 4)	

3 Use the following words in sentences to show the difference in meaning between them:
   (*a*) blurred, fuddled, vague, incoherent

(*b*) pack, horde, mob, herd
(*c*) social stratum, class, environment, clique, body
(*d*) indigenous, native, inherent, intrinsic
(*e*) ties, bonds, yoke, link, union
(*f*) to overhear, to eavesdrop on, to get wind of
(*g*) salutary, sanitary, nutritious, wholesome.

4 Comment on Hartley's use of the following group words:
   pack, outfit, social stratum, herd.

Structures

5 Replace the phrase or clause in italics by a suitable construction involving the use of an infinitive:
   (*a*) *It is assumed that she left* the country under a false name.
   (*b*) It is believed that she was *with a strange man*.
   (*c*) *It is thought that she married* him last week.
   (*d*) She supposed *that he was* a millionaire.
   (*e*) He promised *that he would leave* her all his money.
   (*f*) He even undertook *the payment of* all her debts.
   (*g*) Her father intended *that she should* go on the stage.
   (*h*) Unfortunately, he didn't encourage her *in the learning of* her parts.
   (*i*) *It was her wish that she should* go to college.
   (*j*) But *it was also her wish that her father should* pay for her.
   (*k*) He *didn't feel very much like doing* this.
   (*l*) *It seems that she broke with her father* on this account.

6 Complete the following sentences with an appropriate infinitive construction:
   (*a*) You are under no obligation ......
   (*b*) When you start a car, it is imperative ......
   (*c*) That girl is apt ......
   (*d*) At six o'clock it began ......
   (*e*) It's taking that child a long time to learn ......
   (*f*) When his brother was killed in an accident, he swore ......
   (*g*) The directors of the firm are assumed ......
   (*h*) That politician is supposed ......
   (*i*) She is always disinclined ......
   (*j*) Are you ready ...... ?
   (*k*) We seem fated ......
   (*l*) The officer instructed the recruits ......
   (*m*) It's a lie! I challenge ......
   (*n*) Her mother encouraged ......
   (*o*) Try to persuade ......

7 Imagine that you are looking after a young child in a family. Write a dialogue between yourself and the parents, using the words given in brackets

with an appropriate infinitive construction, to illustrate or refer to the following situations:

(*a*) The parents require you to look after the child too much. (apt; responsibility).

(*b*) Previously, you have always accepted such responsibility. (undertake)

(*c*) You thought that the child would do as it was told. (assume)

(*d*) It hasn't always wanted to. (reluctant)

(*e*) But you had no great wish to punish it. (disposed)

(*f*) It became necessary, however, for you to do so. (obliged)

(*g*) One day you asked it very urgently if it would please stop pulling the cat's tail. (beg; entreat; urge)

(*h*) Finally you gave it a definite order to stop. (told)

(*i*) It wouldn't. (refuse)

(*j*) It asserted that you wouldn't have the courage to smack it. (challenge)

(*k*) You made up your mind that you would do so. (decide)

(*l*) You don't think that you ought to stay in your present post. (offer)

8 Write a letter to an employer, apologizing for some misbehaviour on your part, and suggesting ways in which you may make good the trouble that you have caused. Use as many suitable infinitive constructions as you can.

(*about* 150/180 *words*)

Suggested discussion topics

What is a gentleman?

All publicity is good; for we only conceal that of which we are ashamed.

Modern life undermines privacy, but encourages secretiveness.

The best ways of imposing discipline.

§26 *The uses of the past participle*

English speakers tend to use passives more often and more naturally than most other people, particularly when the interest in the sentence rests in the action performed rather than the person performing it. The passive is also often preferred when we know that some action has been performed, but we do not know who was responsible for it.

Since verb participles are adjectives, it is only a short step from a true passive sentence to one where a past participle is used as an adjectival predicate to the verb *to be*. This is what happens in the first sentence of the following passage:

PASSAGE 26*a*

The little 'green room' *was so well furnished* with writing tables and easy chairs that *there wasn't much floor space left* for the pacing movement that seemed to assist composition. Before long a typewriter *was carried out* into the garden-room, *warmed* to a temperature which set Rye panting with astonishment. Lamb House *was centrally heated* many years before   5 pipes and radiators *were known* over here except as tales of travellers from the United States. That garden-room had plenty of pacing-space, a long stretch from the fireplace at one end to a window at the other looking over the steep cobbled street. Henry James would occasionally glance through that window. He might even hail a passing friend or *be stirred* to a vigor- 10 ous outburst by the sight of a motor-car chugging up the hill. Those motors might be a magical marvel in the right hands, but how con-foundedly they added to the complications of life by gobbling up pro-tective distance.

THEODORA BOSANQUET: *As I Remember Henry James*

Comment

There are two points to notice here. One has already been mentioned in the introduction to this section; the other is that the two true passives (*line* 3: *the typewriter was carried out* and *line* 10: *He might . . . be stirred*) are used because it is immaterial *who* performed the action described; the things that matter are (1) who or what was affected by that action, and (2) the action itself *qua* action. Where the past participle of the passive verb reflects A STATE OF BEING rather than AN ACTION CARRIED OUT, its force is much more adjectival than verbal. This is the case in *lines* 5 (Lamb House *was centrally heated*) *and* 6 (radiators *were known*), and is clearly very often the case when the verb *to be* in the passive construction is in either the present simple or past simple tense.

In so much as there is a new cinema worth talking about, it is because a number of directors are very consciously thinking in terms of how screen language *can be made to work* for them. They *are more interested* in the way things look and feel and sound than in what they signify in general terms; *more interested* in mood than in narrative; *more concerned* with how people 5 behave and give themselves away in action than with how they might choose to see themselves. They are asking from their actors not the great neon-blazing star turns but performances which break through the hard professional surface: at the worst, an emotional strip-tease; at the best, a revelation. In players such as Jeanne Moreau and Monica Vitti, Jean- 10 Paul Belmondo and Marcello Mastroianni, they have acquired willing accomplices. Above all, they give us the sense of the film itself as a risky and unique creative adventure.

Any amount of nonsense *has been talked* during the last few years by directors whose main creative activity consists in taking over other 15 people's mannerisms. Entertainment-film clichés may afford restful and tranquilizing evidence that the conventions are still in working order. New-wave clichés are deadly because they come from directors trying to pass them off as new currency. But all this was *to be expected*. The cinema moves a few steps closer to the minority arts: its passion for allusion and 20 quotation, for instance, is not really very far distant from *the point reached* by poetry almost forty years ago; and its emphasis on the immediate *can* not too implausibly *be related* to action painting. And as it moves, so it acquires the affectations along with the advantages. Antonioni occupies the painter's traditional position: far enough back from his subject to 25 give us our sense of dramatic distance. Some of the young French directors *keep our noses pressed* up against it: we can distinguish a brilliant blob of colour here, some dashing brushwork there, but if we stand a few yards back all we can see is *a blurred image*, with *a signature scrawled* boldly across the corner. 30

PENELOPE HOUSTON: *The Contemporary Cinema*

Comment

When is a verb not a verb? Or, alternatively, when is an adjective not an adjective? The above passage gives some examples of participles, both present and past, in that limbo between their two areas of significance.

Disregarding the present participles, let us look at the past participles. Some of them (e.g. *made, line* 3; *talked, line* 14; *expected, line* 19; *related, line* 23) are simply the participle element in a straightforward passive tense or infinitive. Some (e.g. *interested, line* 5; *blurred, line* 29) are as good as ordinary attributive adjectives, and have almost completely lost their verb-force. It is the others which are of interest to us at present. The phrases in which they occur are:

> *the point reached by poetry (lines* 21–22)
> *keep our noses pressed up against it (line* 27)
> *a signature scrawled boldly across the corner (lines* 29–30)

The first thing to notice about them is a point of word-order. They are all used attributively, and they all have a predominantly adjectival force. Yet they all follow the noun to which they refer. There are two reasons for this. One is that although their significance is predominantly adjectival, they still retain a good deal of verbal force. The second is that though adjectives, they are not complete in meaning until the complementary adverbial phrases (by poetry; up against it; boldly across the corner) have completed the meaning of the phrase. While it is possible in English to place a whole string of different adjectives between an article and its noun, it is possible to do so with an adjectival phrase only if the rest of the phrase is an adverb of degree or frequency. This convention is relaxed only when the phrase consists of a well-worn cliché like 'never-to-be-forgotten' or a well-known quotation such as 'a plague on both your houses'. In the case of the phrase 'keep our noses pressed up against it' there is the additional factor that the noun *noses* is the direct object of the verb *to keep*, and it is very unusual in English to separate a verb from its direct object.

Subjects in passive sentences

Because it is possible to use the indirect object as the subject of a passive sentence in English, the tendency is to do so when the indirect object is a person and the direct object a thing in the active form. For example: *He was given a book* is much more natural English than *A book was given to him*. The convention is quite straightforward: if it is necessary to use a passive, try to ensure that the subject of the sentence is a person rather than a thing.

Comprehension

Passage 26*a*

1 Give a word or phrase of similar meaning to:
   panting (*line* 4)   chugging (*line* 11)
   cobbled (*line* 9)   gobbling (*line* 13)
   hail (*line* 10)

2 Use the following words in sentences of your own, showing that you know
   what they mean:
   to assist, to furnish, occasional, confounded

3 To what period does this passage refer? How do you know this?

Passage 26*b*

4 In what ways, according to the writer, has the attitude of film-directors to
   their job changed in recent years?

5 What do you think the following words or phrases mean?
   neon-blazing star turns (*line* 8)   a brilliant blob of colour (*lines* 27–28)
   emotional strip-tease (*line* 9)   dashing brushwork (*line* 28)
   action painting (*line* 23)   a blurred image (*line* 29)

6 Use the following words correctly in sentences of your own, showing that
   you know what they mean:
   unique (*line* 13)   allusion (*line* 20)
   deadly (*line* 18)   affectations (*line* 24)
   currency (*line* 19)   image (*line* 29)

7 Comment on the author's use of painting metaphors in the latter part of the
   second paragraph. Do you think it is well managed? What do you understand by the last sentence of the passage?

Structures

8 Put into the passive:
   (*a*) The sight of the soldiers stirred him.
   (*b*) People believe him to be eccentric.
   (*c*) They always talk a lot of nonsense about this.
   (*d*) But one must expect that sort of thing.
   (*e*) One might compare this to a late Beethoven quartet.
   (*f*) The author alludes to all sorts of calamities, but he doesn't describe any.
   (*g*) Someone had scrawled a signature across the painting.

9 Complete the following sentences, using a passive form of the verb given in
   brackets:
   (*a*) Justice must not only be done, it must (see) (do) ......
   (*b*) The police found the stolen goods on him and he (arrest) ......
   (*c*) The traffic is so dense that a law (pass) ......

(*d*) Isn't it about time that the brakes in your car (test) ......

(*e*) This forged money has (pass off) ......

(*f*) Tomorrow the new Chancellor will (install) ......

(*g*) The ceremony is now (broadcast) ......

(*h*) By tomorrow evening, six hundred copies (sell) ......

10 Write a paragraph describing a visit to a school, a farm, or a factory, emphasising what is done rather than who does it, and thus using verbs as often as you can in the passive form.　　　　　　(*about* 150 *words*)

Suggested discussion topics

The future of the cinema.

Modern trends in the arts.

We are slaves to speed, noise, and the machine.

Art is for the few, but it must be available for the many.

Subdivision III
The noun and
its appendages

§27 Noun clauses

If a clause fulfils the same function in a sentence as a noun might in the same position – for example, as the object or subject of a verb – we call it a Noun Clause. The principal type of noun clause in English is the indirect or reported speech type which may be used after a number of verbs, most of which the student will know well, as they often correspond to words in his own language. There is, however, one trap into which students often fall. English possesses a peculiar construction usually known as the accusative and infinitive (see above, §25) and also makes use of the gerund (see §24). It sometimes happens that where the student might use a noun clause for the expression of a certain concept in his own language, an Englishman might use one of these other constructions.

The purpose of this section is to show how noun clauses are used in writing of the 'internal monologue' kind, the sequence of the tenses in them, and the type of verb which may be followed by them.

PASSAGE 27*a*

He turned his thoughts to Pelican. It *looked pretty certain* now THAT THE POOR FELLOW WAS GOING TO TAKE THE RAP, but HE'D PRETTY NEAR BROUGHT his fellow directors ROUND to accepting the idea of offering that executive post, with a few shares to give the chap a bit of incentive. John WOULD BE SURE to crow over his disgraceful victory at 5 the party; and then, *Robin thought*, HE'D BE ABLE to announce Pelican's new appointment. Not that JOHN WOULD CARE so much, but IT WOULD BE a moral triumph. With this sense of moral glow upon him, Robin turned and asked the chauffeur after his wife, but he did not hear the answer because he suddenly remembered Elvira. Robin was always sud- 10 denly *remembering* the fact THAT HE HAD LOST HER, suffering a sense of void and defeat; nevertheless, though he hardly cared to admit it to himself, he felt a strange, new sense of ease in no longer having a divided life. The last few weeks of the *affaire*, with their accompaniment of scenes and tears, had proved very disagreeable. He had no talent for *Sturm und* 15 *Drang*. Not, *he reflected*, that his passion HAD BEEN less than other men's; HE HAD SUFFERED and WAS SUFFERING deeply, but *he supposed* HE WAS A BIT OF A FATALIST, or, without boasting, a little more adult in his adaptation to life. Timothy WOULD NEVER KNOW HOW MUCH HE OWED IN STABILITY TO his father's basically integrated character. 20 Once again he glowed and asked the somewhat surprised chauffeur after his wife.

ANGUS WILSON: Anglo-Saxon Attitudes

Comment

Most of this passage is an internal monologue, cast as reported speech. The remainder is direct narrative, in the simple past or past continuous (note the *was always . . . remembering*). It is worth noting that the clause *that he had lost her* (line 11) is just as much the object of the verb *was . . . remembering* as is the noun *the fact*. The sequence of tenses throughout conforms to what one would expect, the verbs introducing the noun clauses being all in the simple past tense or the past progressive. The last sentence but one even has a noun clause incapsulated within another (*lines* 19–20: Timothy *would never know* + *how much he owed*). Note that the past perfect in a noun clause of reported speech may stand for what would have been either a present perfect (*he had suffered* for 'I have suffered' and *he'd pretty near brought his fellow directors round* for 'I've pretty near brought . . .') or a simple past (*Not, he reflected, that his passion had been* for 'Not that my passion was').

Note on punctuation

It is a common mistake to place a comma before a noun clause. While this form of punctuation was current in earlier times, we tend today to treat a noun clause object of a verb as if it were a noun, and omit the comma. Commas are only included if there is a parenthetical phrase immediately preceding the noun clause itself, as in *lines* 7 *and* 19 above.

PASSAGE 27*b*

In the train, he began to sort the impressions he had acquired during the week-end, mentally making a hearty apology to Colonel Vesey's three communicative daughters for his mistrust of them. He could not have found more helpful assistants.

What *had* they *told* him? First, that Colonel Vesey *was* on bad terms 5 with Sir Harry. So much, indeed, he *would have guessed* from the story told by the old Somersetshire cleric; but *it was as well* to have it confirmed. The quarrel, *it appeared*, *was* so deep that *there was* practically no intercourse between the two houses except for that one visit of Exeter's on the afternoon of the murder – a remarkable coincidence, as Miss Rose 10 Vesey *had said*. But secondly, and far more important, Colonel Vesey himself *had been out*, and out in a car, on that very afternoon, and *had returned*, contrary to his habits, half an hour late without any explanation, and conveniently near the time when Sir Harry *had been killed*. In a car, there *would have been* plenty of time for him to shoot Sir Harry and make off. In that case, *Flint realised*, the 'man in the mask' *would* probably *have* to be exonerated. It *was* too unlikely that Sir Harry *would have collaborated* to that extent with his wife's old lover and his own enemy. Nor *was* it very likely that Colonel Vesey *was* Delrio. Flint *was* not very certain about the power of disguise; but he *felt* very doubtful whether the Colonel *could* ever *have achieved* a 'pale complexion'. Nor *had he* a cleft chin. But perhaps disguise *could manage* even that. Flint *did not know*.

G. D. H. & MARGARET COLE: The Murder at Crome House

Comment

Another internal monologue. Since the whole speculation refers to past events, and the narrative itself is in the past, there are numerous past perfects – and even one or two future-perfects-in-the-past. Notice that the verb *felt* (*line* 20) is the introductory verb for the noun clause in one sentence.

QUESTION PAPER:

Comprehension

1 What do the following colloquial phrases mean?
   to take the rap (Passage 27*a*, *line* 2)
   to crow over (27*a*, *line* 5)
   to ask after someone (27*a*, *line* 9)

2 What sort of a person do you think Robin (the *he* of Passage 27*a*) was? How much do you learn about him from the details of the passage?

3 Imagine that a friend has had some difficulty in understanding exactly what the situation is that Cole describes in Passage 27*b*. Explain in your own words:
   (*a*) what the background was,
   (*b*) the relationship between Colonel Vesey and Sir Harry,
   (*c*) how Inspector Flint had discovered what he did about the situation.

Structures

4 Link the following pairs of sentences together by turning the longer one into a noun clause dependent on the shorter:
   (*a*) I notice + you are wearing a new coat today.
   (*b*) She thinks + she is going to dine out this evening.
   (*c*) I fear + there is going to be a thunderstorm.
   (*d*) I doubt + the post has arrived yet.

(e) They noticed + you have lost your French accent.

(f) He felt + he will have to borrow some money from his father.

(g) They told her + 'You will have to get a new passport.'

(h) The bus-driver asked him + 'Have you gone crazy?'

(i) The committee considered + 'This is an impractical scheme.'

(j) The temperamental film-star screamed + 'I am fed up with this film; I have had enough; I shall go home tomorrow.'

5 Complete the following sentences with a suitable noun clause:

(a) I'm afraid it's true ......

(b) You can't deny ......

(c) Surely you aren't going to tell her ......?

(d) Did you notice ...... ?

(e) For Heaven's sake decide ......

(f) The postman saw ......

(g) The board of directors announced ......

(h) Can't you remember ......?

(i) I have always felt ......

(j) He thought ......

(k) When they considered ......

(l) After they had discussed ......

6 Write sentences of your own answering the following questions, beginning with the formula given in brackets:

(a) What did the customs officer ask you? (He asked . . .)

(b) What did you reply? (I told him . . .)

(c) Was there anything wrong? (Yes; he noticed . . .)

(d) How did he react to that? (He said . . .)

(e) Did you feel that he was being fair? (No; I considered . . .)

(f) Did you tell him so? (Yes; I protested . . .)

(g) And what did he say to that? (He replied . . .)

(h) So he really apologised to you? (In a way; he claimed . . .)

(i) And did you accept his statement? (Yes; he felt . . .)

(j) So all was well that ended well? (I suppose . . .)

7 Take passage 17b, on pages 73/4, and imagine that you are a newspaper correspondent reporting what Dr Vaughan Williams said. Begin your report: 'Dr Vaughan Williams assrted that . . .'

Suggested discussion topics

Capital punishment as a deterrent.

How to combat crime.

Modern morality.

It is not so much the actual technique of using relative pronouns in English that seems to worry students, as the punctuation. There are, however, some more serious difficulties, mostly involving the use of such pronouns as *what* and *whose* that usually require some attention.

PASSAGE 28*a*

Throughout a great part of Europe the First World War and its attendant revolutions passed from men's minds with surprising rapidity, and with them faded the extremes of the apocalyptic style. Symbolism re-established itself as the dominant convention of *the 'twenties, whose* greatest poets, Yeats, Rilke and Valéry, had already gone far towards 5 perfecting their styles before 1914. New *experiments and theories, which* had received some impetus in the war years, were for a while confined to a very small circle centred on Paris. Being the product of social tensions, they could not make much headway in the decade of false prosperity, but waited for the onset of the next crisis, the slump of 1929. *The years* 10 *that followed the armistice* were a period of aestheticism, *in which* it was even claimed in many quarters that the mission of art had in the present age received an unexampled extension, and that it was now in the artist's power to provide a substitute for religious experience. The divorce between the poet and the public was, nevertheless, almost universally 15 accepted on the plea that since he was compelled to explore territory in *advance of any that was ready* for general occupation, he must for the present, like any pioneer, remain out of touch with the mass of his future followers.

J. M. COHEN: *Poetry of This Age*

Comment

Relative clauses are described by several terms: defining and non-defining; restrictive and continuative, etc. There are two main types. Those which are essential to the noun or pronoun to which they refer, and whose omission would make that noun or pronoun ambiguous in sense, are here called IDENTIFYING clauses. The others, which merely provide additional information about an already sufficiently well identi-fied antecedent, are here called PARENTHETIC.

In Passage 28*a* there are two identifying clauses (*lines* 10–11: *the years that followed the armistice*; and *lines* 16–17: *territory in advance of any that was ready for general occupation*). It is clear that if these clauses are omitted, the sentences in which they stand undergo a radical change in meaning. In these two examples the author prefers the form *that* to *which*; this is a good example to follow. There is nothing stylistically superior in using *which* in such clauses; it is sheer snobbery to pretend that there is.

The parenthetic clauses (*lines* 6–7: *experiments and theories, which had received some impetus in the war years*; and *lines* 11–12: *a period of aestheticism, in which it was claimed* . . .) may quite easily be left out without altering the meaning of the words to which they respectively refer. That is why they are cordoned off from the rest of the sentence with commas.

The third parenthetic clause (*lines* 4-5: *the twenties, whose greatest poets* . . .) has the possessive *whose*. *Whose* and *of which* are not interchangeable. In this case, *whose* is preferred because there is a definite idea of Yeats, Rilke and Valéry BELONGING TO that period. It is not so much that they were a part of a larger collective whole body or mass, but that in some way they were rather a kind of personal possession of the age, responsible to it, and it responsible for them.

PASSAGE 28*b*

Gumbril senior occupied a tall, narrow-shouldered and rachitic house in a little obscure square not far from Paddington. There were five floors, and a basement with beetles, and nearly a hundred stairs, *which shook* when anyone ran too rudely down them. It was a prematurely old and decaying house in a decaying quarter. *The square in which it stood*   5
was steadily coming down in the world. The houses, *which* a few years ago *had all been occupied* by respectable families, were now split up into squalid little maisonettes, and from the neighbouring slums, *which* along with most other unpleasant things *the old bourgeois families* had been able to ignore, invading bands of children came to sport on the once sacred   10
pavements.

Mr Gumbril was almost the last survivor of the old inhabitants. He liked his house, and he liked his square. Social decadence had not affected *the fourteen plane trees which adorned its little garden,* and the gambols of the dirty children did not disturb the starlings, *who came*   15
evening by evening in summer-time, *to roost* in their branches.

ALDOUS HUXLEY: *Antic Hay*

Comment

This passage gives further examples of parenthetic relative clauses and needs little comment. Note, however, the use of the pronoun *who* (objective case *whom*) in *line* 15. Note also the identifying clause *The square in which it stood* (*line* 5). Had Huxley preferred to use the pronoun *that* in this case, the phrase would have run: 'The square *that* it stood in'. Remember also that if the relative pronoun in an identifying relative clause is the object or prepositional object of its clause, it may be omitted.

PASSAGE 28c

There is no doubt that a longing for a return to naturalism is often felt by a public not conscious of the artist's problem. Actually there are two publics. One, numerically the larger, thinks of the painter as the provider of *a commodity that it is seeking*; and *what this public seeks* is a confirmation of its own world, of its own bourgeois values. The other and smaller 5 public realizes that the great artist, *the artist who* in the end *is going to give it most satisfaction*, is looking beyond the present, trying to find a stepping-stone into the uncertain future. The more uncertain that future is – and it has never been so uncertain as it is today – the more desperate will be the plunge forward, and there will always be the risk 10 of disaster. But it can be nothing to the disaster TO BE EXPERIENCED by *those people who one day will find* that their world of conventional values has disappeared, and that they are left in a maddening chaos. Reality is not the four walls of *the room we are sitting in*, or *the trees and men we see* out of our window; it is a mental construction, a stability of vision, and 15 the next phase of human development may find such stability in *an art that is anti-organic, absolute, and ideal*. It has happened before in the history of the world and it may happen again.

SIR HERBERT READ: Contemporary British Art

Comment

This passage gives further examples of the identifying relative clause, two of which (*line* 14: *the room we are sitting in* and *the trees and men we see*) omit the relative pronoun altogether, as it is in an oblique relationship to its verb.[1] In *line* 11 there is an infinitive phrase which is a relative-clause equivalent: *the disaster to be experienced*. The reference is to the future. This cannot be used universally; it may be used, says Zandvoort (§33), to indicate contingency, possibility, or propriety. The example in this text is conditional, and thus contingent. Finally we have the clause *what this public seeks* as the subject of the verb *is* (*line* 4). Students should remember that in modern English, the relative pronouns *who*, *whom* *which*, and *that* are not used to introduce noun clauses standing as subjects of sentences or parts of sentences. Here, the pronoun *what* is the

---

[1] Such clauses are often called CONTACT clauses, and are particularly common in conversational English, though perfectly good literary English, as the passage shows. Note that the preposition *in*, which would precede the pronoun *which* if it were used here ('the room *in which we are sitting*') is placed at the end of the clause in a contact clause: the room *we are sitting in*. The same is of course true of all prepositions so used.

object of the verb *seeks*, and the entire clause containing both *what* and *seeks* is the subject of the verb + complement unit *is a confirmation of its own world*.

QUESTION PAPER:

Comprehension

1 In Passages 28*a* and 28*c*, the authors give their interpretations of various movements in art and society in recent years. Read the two passages one after the other, and interpret Passage 28*a* in the light of Passage 28*c*.

2 How far do you agree with Read's contention that 'reality is not the four walls of the room . . .; it is a mental construction . . .'?

3 Describe or define in your own words:
   symbolism, aestheticism (Passage 28*a*, *lines* 3, 11)
   a rachitic house (28*b*, *line* 1)
   squalid little maisonettes (28*b*, *line* 8)
   bourgeois values (28*c*, *line* 5)
   a stability of vision (28*c*, *line* 15)

4 Sir Herbert Read (Passage 28*c*) is scathing about conventional bourgeois values. To what extent are his own values and his own exposition of them conventional in this passage?

5 Give a word or phrase of similar meaning to:
   its attendant revolutions (Passage 28*a*, *lines* 1–2)
   the dominant convention (28*a*, *line* 4)
   impetus (28*a*, *line* 7)
   an unexampled extension (28*a*, *line* 13)
   prematurely old (28*b*, *line* 4)
   slums (28*b*, *line* 8)
   the once sacred pavements (28*b*, *lines* 10–11)
   gambols (28*b*, *line* 15)
   a stepping-stone into the uncertain future (28*c*, *lines* 7–8)
   the plunge forward (28*c*, *line* 10)
   anti-organic (28*c*, *line* 17)

6 What words or phrases in Passage 28*b* suggest that the writer was adopting a slightly satirical or ironic attitude to his subject? Suggest other, less satirical phrases he might have used, and examine why those he did use had an ironic flavour about them.

Structures

7 Join the two sentences of each pair together by making one into a relative clause. (Use contact clauses where possible.)
   (*a*) Mr Gumbril was the last survivor of the old inhabitants. He liked his house.

(*b*) The artist considered the painting as his best. He had just painted it.

(*c*) People forgot the First World War remarkably quickly. It was the most terrible war ever fought before 1939.

(*d*) Rilke, Yeats and Valéry were three poets. They are often called symbolists.

(*e*) Paris is famous as a centre of the arts. I have only visited Paris twice.

(*f*) The artist is a genius. You met him yesterday.

(*g*) The children were from the neighbouring slums. We spoke to them.

(*h*) The problem wants a drastic solution. We talked of it this morning.

(*i*) The house is not far from Paddington. The author was referring to it.

(*j*) The starlings roost in the plane-trees. Their noise disturbs my afternoon nap.

(*k*) Our teacher completely lost his self-control. It is a quality. He doesn't possess much of it.

(*l*) She said 'You are an idiot.' That was all.

8 Complete the sentences by adding a suitable relative clause:

(*a*) My landlady has a pet poodle ......

(*b*) This dog sleeps on a special cushion ......

(*c*) It has already ruined four pairs of my nylons ......

(*d*) The first time ......

(*e*) The next time ......

(*f*) If it does it again, ...

(*g*) I shall then have to leave my present digs ......

(*h*) Then I shall ask you to put me up, ...

9 Write sentences of your own, using an appropriate relative clause, to refer or react to the following situations:

(*a*) You have bought some very good handkerchiefs in a shop, and you want to know if they have any more.

(*b*) The reason you want them is that you wish to give some to a friend.

(*c*) This friend lives in America, and she is very rich.

(*d*) You envy her a little, as she has her own Rolls-Royce.

(*e*) Riches have not spoilt her character, however, and you like this.

(*f*) She is very cultured, and collects modern paintings.

(*g*) She speaks three languages well, and reads Valéry and Rilke.

(*h*) The shop-assistant tells you he once wrote a book on Valéry.

10 Write a paragraph describing an art-gallery or museum you have visited, making as much use as you can of relative clauses. (*about* 120/150 *words*)

Suggested discussion topics

The bourgeois achievement.

Society gets the art it deserves.

Poetry is dead; long live pop.

The modern political world is rather like Mr Gumbril's house: rachitic, prematurely old and decaying, and split up into squalid little national maisonettes.

§29 The impersonal pronoun it with a noun or adjective predicate

Students often find it difficult to decide when to use *there is* or *there are* at the beginning of a clause, and when to use *it is*. They also often find it difficult to know quite what they should do if they want to connect an adjective with a clause predicatively. So students of certain nationalities produce sentences like *Good is, if you follow my example*, where the English usage is: *It is good if you follow my example*. The passages in this section give examples of preparatory *it is*, and of the contrast between *it is* and *there is* respectively.

PASSAGE 29*a*

It has often been said, and *it is still sometimes repeated* by good students of Cervantes, that his main object in writing 'Don Quixote' was to put an end to the influence of the romances of chivalry. *It is true that* these romances were the fashionable reading of his age, that many of them were trash, and that some of them were pernicious trash. *It is true* also that the   5
very scheme of his book lends itself to a scathing exposure of their weaknesses, and that the moral is pointed in the scene of the Inquisition of the Books, where the priest, the barber, the housekeeper, and the niece destroy the greater part of his library by fire. But *how came it* that Cervantes knew the romances so well, and dwelt on some of their incidents   10
in such loving detail? Moreover, *it is worth noting that* not a few of them are excluded by name from the general condemnation.

SIR WALTER RALEIGH: *Don Quixote*

Comment

Basically, the difference between *it* and *there* is that *it* is a pronoun, and *there* is an adverb. If this fact is remembered, many of the difficulties with the expressions *it is* and *there is* disappear. It seems to be a convention of English to avoid noun clauses (unless they are reported questions) as subjects of sentences if possible. This is particularly the case if the verb happens to be in the passive. So while in the last sentence it is just possible to write a solid, clumsy sentence with 'That not a few of them are excluded by name . . .' as its subject, it is greatly preferable to make *It* the subject, and put the noun clause in apposition to it. And it would be stylistically unforgivable to recast the first sentence as follows:

> 'That Cervantes' main object in writing "Don Quixote" was to put an end to the influences of the romance of chivalry has often been said and is still sometimes repeated by good students of the great writer.'

But, alas, it would be possible English. Students must always try, then, to avoid making noun clauses the subject of sentences if they begin with *that*.

PASSAGE 29*b*

Many difficulties have to be overcome before human beings can live more or less peaceably in associations and before associations can co-exist without devastating conflicts. *It was, and still is, comforting to believe* that these difficulties could all be overcome if only the intrinsic or essential nature of associations were properly understood. When this is 5 accepted, *it is easy to proceed further* and to say that true enlightenment will be achieved when we discover the true meanings of the words 'State', 'authority', 'right', and the rest. To avoid apparent logical troubles *it is often held* that enquiry should be directed to discovering the concepts or ideas for which these words stand, but this supposed distinction 10 between words and concepts is not important for our present purpose.

There have always been widespread doubts as to the efficacy of this essentialist assumption even in the minds of many of those who have made use of it. Beginning with the Sophist Thrasymachus, whose views on politics are reported or parodied in the first book of the *Republic*, 15 *there has been* a persistent positivist opposition which has maintained that the recommended procedure of searching for the essential meaning of 'justice' and similar words is futile. It does nothing to help in the solution of any practical political problem. For this we need an accurate description of what actually happens, or tends to happen, in human associa- 20 tions. *There is no sense* in asking what ought to happen, or what would happen, under imaginary ideal conditions, and disputes on such points are purely verbal and a waste of time.

T. D. WELDON: *The Vocabulary of Politics*

Comment

Since *it* is a pronoun, one important difference between *it is* and *there is* arises straight away. You cannot follow *there is* by an adjectival complement, whereas you can follow *it is* by one. So: *it is comforting* (*line* 3), *it is easy* (*line* 6), and even *it is held* (*lines* 8–9 – the past participle of an impersonal passive construction being an adjective anyway). Similarly, one cannot follow *there is* by an indirect statement. *There is* posits the

EXISTENCE of a thing or situation; *it is* differentiates that thing or situation. So in *line* 16 of Passage 29*b*, it would be perfectly possible to substitute *it has been* for *there has been* as the verb for *a persistent positivist opposition*, but the meaning of the sentence would then be: 'the *positivist* opposition (not any other of the various oppositions) is the one that has maintained . . .' As it stands, the sentence merely draws attention to the existence of that opposition; it does not differentiate it from other types of opposition. So, taking these two sentences:

There is truth that matters

and

It is truth that matters,

and completing them by adding what they imply but do not state, the result is

There is truth that matters – (and truth that doesn't matter)

and

It is truth that matters – (not justice, or love, or social convenience or any other abstraction.)

In other words, the first sentence means:

Truth that matters exists,

and the second:

Truth matters.

QUESTION PAPER:

Comprehension

1 Define the following literary terms:
   a novel, a romance, a comedy, a drama

2 Give a word or phrase of similar meaning to:
   his main object (Passage 29*a*, *line* 2)
   fashionable reading (29*a*, *line* 4)
   pernicious trash (29*a*, *line* 5)
   a scathing exposure (29*a*, *line* 6)
   dwelt on some of their incidents (29*a*, *line* 10)

3 What is the difference in meaning between:
   (*a*) chivalry, courtesy, quixotry, politeness;
   (*b*) trash, drivel, gibberish;
   (*c*) pernicious, mischievous, malignant, baleful;

(*d*) scathing, virulent, damaging, abusive;

(*e*) exposure, exposition, exhibition.

4 Dr Weldon sets out two lines of approach to philosophic definitions in Passage 29*b*. He calls one 'essentialist' and the other 'positivist'. What do you understand by these terms as he uses them, and which do you think he favours?

5 Give a word or phrase of similar meaning to:
intrinsic (Passage 29*b*, *line* 4)
concepts (29*b*, *line* 9)
efficacy (29*b*, *line* 12)
parodied (29*b*, *line* 15)
purely verbal (29*b*, *line* 23)

6 Explain the difference between:

(*a*) His meaning is clear *and* His opinion is clear.

(*b*) He achieved his goal *and* He reached his goal.

(*c*) That's not politics *and* That's not politic.

(*d*) He maintained a large household *and* He retained a large household.

(*e*) The procedure was very complex *and* The process was very complex.

Structures

7 Fill in the gaps with a suitable variant of *It is* or *There is*:

(*a*) —— a man at the door waiting to see you.

(*b*) —— a good idea to sleep after a heavy meal.

(*c*) —— considerable criticism of your suggestion.

(*d*) —— rather ignorant and ill-informed criticism.

(*e*) —— a fact that most men are larger and heavier than most women.

(*f*) —— a concert at the Festival Hall tomorrow evening.

(*g*) —— worth going to hear, as Oistrakh is playing.

(*h*) —— no sense in waiting for her; she's always late.

(*i*) —— often believed that the English are reserved.

(*j*) —— many writers of chivalric romances before Cervantes wrote *Don Quixote*.

8 Complete the following sentences with a suitable clause beginning with *It is* or *There is*:

(*a*) Can you let me know soon how many ...... ?

(*b*) Someone told me ...... to get used to English money.

(*c*) ...... no doubt that ......

(*d*) ...... absurd to think that ......

(*e*) ...... over eight million inhabitants ......

(*f*) ...... time to go; we've been here three hours, ...

(*g*) ...... time to go; try and get tickets ......

9 Compose sentences of your own, beginning with the phrase in brackets, to illustrate or refer to the following situations:

(*a*) A friend has asked you to come on a bicycle tour with him. (It is . . .)

(*b*) You have been to a political meeting, and are asked what it was like. (There . . .)

(*c*) Someone asks your opinion of a strange fellow-student. (It is . . .)

(*d*) You are asked to lend your watch to someone. (There is . . .)

(*e*) The police ask you if you have noticed anything unusual in your neighbourhood recently. (There . . .)

(*f*) You meet a friend you have not seen for many years. (It is . . .)

10 Describe your classroom to someone who has never seen it. (150/180 *words*)

Suggested discussion topics

How far do you agree with Dr Weldon's last sentence in Passage 29*b*?

What is it that makes some writers internationally famous, whereas others are admired only in their own country?

There is no such thing as a moral or an immoral book. Books are well written, or badly written.

The last of the scholastics was Karl Marx.

It sometimes happens that students find it difficult to know how to arrange a series of adjectives, all used attributively to the same noun. This section gives examples of the attributive use of adjectives, and reminds the student that in some cases, attributive adjectives are placed after the noun they refer to (see above, §§21 and 26).

> PASSAGE 30*a*
> In a *steamer chair*, under a *manuka tree* that grew in the middle of the *front grass patch*, Linda Burnell dreamed the morning away. She did nothing. She looked up at the *dark, close, dry leaves* of the manuka, at the chinks of blue between, and now and again a *tiny yellowish flower* dropped on her. Pretty – yes, if you held one of those flowers on the palm of your 5 hand and looked at it closely, it was an *exquisite small thing*. Each *pale yellow petal* shone as if each was the *careful work* of *a loving hand*. The *tiny tongue* in the centre gave it the shape of a bell. And when you turned it over the outside was a *deep bronze colour*. But as soon as they flowered, they fell and were scattered. You brushed them off your frock as you 10 talked; the *horrid little things* got caught in one's hair. Why, then, flower at all? Who takes the trouble – or the joy – to make all these things that are wasted, wasted. . . . It was uncanny.
>
> > KATHERINE MANSFIELD: *At the Bay*

Comment

The first thing worth noting here is that English, unlike many other languages, makes more use of nouns as attributive adjectives than of adjectives as nouns. Thus in this passage notice *steamer chair, front grass patch*, and possibly *bronze colour*. The relationship between the two nouns may be purely descriptive, as in these cases, or it may be functional (*door-bell; camera-case; book-case*). If it is functional, the adjective and the noun tend to be hyphened together, and the stress falls on the first word only.

There can be the same distinction when the first of the two words is an ordinary adjective or a verb form in -*ing*. There is a world of difference between *a dancing teacher* (descriptive) and *a dancing-teacher* (one who teaches dancing), or *blackbird* – between a *black bird* (descriptive) and a *blackbird* (English term for *Turdus merula*).

The second thing is that the order of adjectives is not purely arbitrary. Generally speaking, those adjectives that are most strongly associated with the noun come closest to it. This means that adjectives of colour (e.g. here *yellow, bronze, yellowish*) will be closest to the noun, adjectives describing the *kind* of colour (*deep, pale, dim, drab*, etc.) thus preceding them as quasi-adverbs of degree. This is a self-evident convention. It follows naturally that adjectives of size or shape – or, if one is describing a vehicle or aircraft, of speed – should likewise precede rather than follow adjectives of colour, and that generally speaking, adjectives denoting qualities should precede those of size or shape (e.g. *horrid little* things, *line* 11; *exquisite small* thing, *line* 6).

Adjectives denoting age or sex are naturally closely associated with the nouns they qualify, and should be placed *after* those of size or shape, but *before* those of colour. This second convention might perhaps be relaxed if the adjective of colour is so closely associated with the noun as to be almost part of its definition (e.g. *black cat: tabby cat: tortoiseshell cat: golden retriever*). Adjectives of nationality are very closely associated with their nouns, of course, and stand closest of all to them.

PASSAGE 30*b*

The *early afternoon sun* entered the room where sunshine seemed naturally to belong. The *bare walls* of this room had been painted *pale yellow last year*, and the yellow had actually proved to be exactly as they wanted it. A *mellow wicker bird-cage*, which must have once brought a canary from Madeira, hung above the *stiff-chintzed window-seat*. The   5
cage contained a *rag bird* of *silky feathers* and *glass-bead eyes*, and Jane had always feared that *some shortsighted person* might think they really kept a bird in a cage. *A large bunch* of helicrysum *of all colours* hung head downwards elsewhere; the *brass fender and scuttle* were like *amateur suns*. When the *true sunshine* entered the room, it magically touched to com-   10
pletion all that had been like *latent sun* already.

VIOLA MEYNELL: *The Pain in the Neck*

Comment

In addition to features already mentioned in the comment on Passage 30*a*, there are here two additional points concerning attributive adjectivals. Firstly, there is the use of 'artificial' past participles from non-existent verbs. An example here is *stiff-chintzed* (*line* 5). While it would be untrue to say that the verb *to chintz* does not exist, one may well argue that the artificial past participle comes from a noun rather than any verb. This is a common usage in English (cf. the *fat-legged* table, the *red-roofed* house, the *square-nosed* punt; and the artificial participle is often hyphened, as in the three examples just quoted, to a descriptive adjective of some kind. The meaning of such adjectives is clear, and some have become so associated with a particular adjective (e.g. *shortsighted*, *line* 7) as to have lost the hyphen completely.

Secondly, there are some adjectival attributes following their nouns here: a rag bird *of silky feathers and glass-bead eyes* (*line* 6); helicrysum *of all colours* (line 8). Note that attributive adjectival phrases including a prepositional expression of some kind normally follow their noun rather than precede it in English, unlike some other languages. Note also the fact that the adjective attribute of *painted* (*line* 2) is so closely connected with the noun it refers to and the verb governing that noun that it precedes the adverbial of time *last year*. (Cp. §§20 and 21.)

QUESTION PAPER:

Comprehension

1 Give a word or phrase of similar meaning to:
   chink (Passage 30*a*, *line* 4) mellow (30*b*, *line* 4)
   uncanny (30*a*, *line* 13) latent (30*b*, *line* 11)

2 If you were asked to say what was the main difference in approach between the two writers in these passages, what would you say it was?

3 Is there anything about the style and manner of these passages which suggests to you that the writers were women?

4 Comment on the use of the following terms in Passage 30*b*:
   mellow wicker bird-cage (*line* 4)
   stiff-chintzed window-seat (*line* 5)
   amateur suns (*line* 9)

5 What do the two passages tell you about the characters, Linda Burnell (Passage 30*a*) and Jane Skeat (Passage 30*b*), mentioned in them?

Structures

6 Put the adjectivals attributively to the noun they refer to in a suitable order: As we approached the (old, brown, little) cottage, we noticed a (heavy, large, leather) suitcase standing on the (whitewashed, stone) doorstep. It looked as if our (expected, Irish) guests had already arrived. We turned into the (tree-lined, cool) drive, strolled along under the (squat, oak, covered with ivy, green) trees. Just as we were about to enter by the (with faded curtains, cracked, back) door, a (red, cheerful) face appeared at the (upstairs, tiny, open) window. It was Uncle Pat.

7 Improve the following sentences by adding suitable adjectives where possible:
   (a) That girl is a waitress.
   (b) That student is a man.
   (c) The trees were in the park.
   (d) The dog slept on the mat.
   (e) There was a parrot perched on the sailor's shoulder.
   (f) The car broke down on the road in the afternoon.
   (g) The girl's uncle sat in the sun reading a book.
   (h) A bunch of flowers lay on the table, and a vase stood beside them.

8 Describe the various speakers at a very strange public meeting you have recently attended.   (*about* 180 *words*)

Suggested discussion topics

   Women as artists.

   The souls of women are so small,
   That some believe they've none at all.
                    (*Samuel Butler*)

   England is the paradise of women, the purgatory of men, and the hell of horses. (*John Florio*)

Nouns that stand for things normally recognisable by their shape or fixed duration are considered as *countables* in English, and it is rarely difficult to decide when to use an article with them. It is the so-called *uncountables*, nouns denoting abstractions, or things which are recognised as a mass rather than a shape (*sugar, concrete, gas, sand, water,* etc.) or natural forces (*gravity, electricity, lightning*), which confuse students. This section shows how such nouns are used without an article, and in what contexts an article is necessary.

PASSAGE 31*a*

The endless continuity of *time* is appalling; arbitrarily, therefore, men parcel up *the flux* into sections. It is always and everywhere horribly the same; they impose imaginary differentiations and plant little landmarks of their own devising. *The current* flows implacably on, forthright and irreversible; in their imagination, they distort it into *a circular* or at least *a spiral* 5 *movement* with periodical returns to *an identity*. *Time* is unbearable. To make it bearable, men transform it into something that has the qualities of *space.* For we feel at home in *space* – at any rate, in *the comfortable little space that belongs to this planet* and in which we have our daily being. But *in time*, in *the undifferentiated flux* OF *perpetual perishing*, we can never 10 feel at home. *Time*, therefore, must be transformed, so far as our capacities for *make-believe* will allow of it, into *space.*

How shall *time* be spatialised? *Nature* gives the first hint. The heavenly bodies march about the sky, and their marching is *time made visible.* The seasons recur, *night* and *day* recur, *hunger* and *desire* and *sleep* recur. It 15 seems natural, therefore, to conceive of *time* as a series of circles – *little round day, large round month, huge round year.* On this natural system of *spatialisation* men have grafted all kinds of arbitrary systems of their own. The rim *of the year* is studded with periodical festivals which serve to break up and differentiate the flux – to emphasise, by their regular recur- 20 rence, the essentially circular nature of *the movement* of *spatialised time.*

ALDOUS HUXLEY: *Beyond the Mexique Bay*

Comment

In a passage entirely devoted to the discussion of aspects of the uncountables time and space, it is natural that the two nouns appear in most cases without an article. Zandvoort (§328 *et seq.*) says that abstract nouns take no article unless applied to a special case. Such a case occurs in *lines* 8-9: *the comfortable little space/that belongs to this planet.* The article would be just as necessary if we omitted the two adjectives *comfortable* and *little.* It is the identifying relative clause that makes the article necessary, because it restricts the meaning of the word *space* to that of a PARTICULAR space. Similarly, whereas *Nature (line 13)* is used as a personified general abstraction, and becomes a proper noun, *the essentially circular nature (line 21)* is qualified by the phrase *of the movement,* and the word *movement* itself is a PARTICULAR movement – that of spatialised time.

Adjectives of quality or description do not make it necessary to put an article before any uncountable noun they qualify. So we have *perpetual perishing (line 10), spatialised time (line 13),* and even *time made visible (line 14).* We even find countable nouns, such as *day, month, year* used (*line 17*) as uncountable abstractions, and therefore without an article. Similarly (*lines 14–15*) we find *the seasons* (countable), but *day, night, hunger, desire, sleep.* These are all regarded as states or conditions of existence, and therefore as uncountable abstractions.

PASSAGE 31*b*
The Gothic spirit is not merely vertical; it leaps and soars like a rocket. Its essence lies in its power to suggest, not *the final perfection of classic reason,* like a Greek temple, but a dynamic search for *the unattainable.* The secondary arts of *sculpture* and *stained glass* which it fostered so easily, seem to grow organically out of it rather than to be imposed on it.   5
Like a living plant, a Gothic building can enrich itself from its own roots, throwing out *foliage,* tendrils and flowers without losing its central unity. And *that same leaping, nervous energy* on which the whole of a Gothic structure is based, communicates itself to every part of the building but particularly to those portions of it which, however firmly they   10
may be embedded in *the design of the whole,* can at least be thought of as belonging to the separate category of *sculpture.*
ERIC NEWTON: *European Painting and Sculpture*

Comment
Some nouns may be countable or uncountable, like the words *design* and *spirit. Gothic spirit* (without an article) would be a somewhat less aesthetic term than *The Gothic spirit!* (Medieval whisky, perhaps?) *Sculpture, stained glass* and *foliage* are concrete uncountables – what Jespersen calls mass-words. Most commodities (*salt, sugar, concrete, sand, cement, wine, whisky,* etc.) and most aesthetic designations (*painting, sculpture, music,*

etc.) which are purely formal or definitions, fall into this category. (See also Passage 13a for examples of this.) But note: *good weather*, but *the weather was good*. However, one important English usage is often misunderstood. This is the use of adjectives as nouns. This happens rather more rarely in English than in many other languages, but it occurs twice here; in *line 3*(*the unattainable*), and *line 11* (*the whole*). The usage normally occurs as a collective referring to a group of people (*the rich*, *the poor*, *the old*, *the dead*) but is also found when the adjectives refer to an abstract quality of some kind, as here (*the unattainable*).

QUESTION PAPER:

Comprehension

1 Give a word or phrase of similar meaning to:

Passage 31a	Passage 31b
men parcel up the flux (*lines* 1–2)	essence (*line* 2)
implacably (*line* 4)	fostered (*line* 4)
undifferentiated (*line* 10)	imposed (upon) (*line* 5)
make-believe (*line* 12)	tendrils (*line* 7)
grafted (*line* 18)	embedded in (*line* 11)
arbitrary (*line* 18)	design (*line* 11)

2 What does Huxley mean when he says that 'time is unbearable'? What examples can you give of his two time-divisions: the natural systems and the arbitrary ones?

3 What do you think of Newton's contrast between classic art and Gothic art? Can you think of any examples of Gothic art which are not dynamic or organic in the sense in which he uses these terms?

4 Read Passage 14a, and compare MacNeile Dixon's argument there with Huxley's here.

Structures

5 Insert the article where necessary:
   (a) —— weather was so bad that we lost all —— sense of —— direction.
   (b) —— wine, —— women, and —— song are his motto.
   (c) —— stained glass in King's College Chapel, Cambridge, is very beautiful.
   (d) —— water is all right for washing in, but I prefer —— whisky for drinking.
   (e) —— music of Mozart is usually called —— classical music, whereas —— music of Wagner is —— romantic music.
   (f) I ordered half a ton of —— sand, and —— idiots have sent me half a ton of —— salt.

(g) —— sand at Daytona Beach, in America, is famous for —— motor-racing.

(h) —— Matterhorn, —— Eiger, and —— Mont Blanc are three of —— most famous peaks in —— Alps.

(i) —— Time and —— Tide wait for no man.

(j) When —— tide is in, —— water from the sea comes right up to —— causeway.

6 Complete the following sentences, using a noun complement:

(a) That girl prefers pop music to ......

(b) The London of today is quite different from ......

(c) Reconciling the wants of the individual to the demands of society is ......

(d) Her chief recreations are ......

(e) To make a currant cake, you need ......

(f) Reinforced concrete, much used in modern building, is made from ......

(g) He is very fond of abstract subjects like ......

(h) Which do you prefer to drink ...... or ...... ?

(i) In order to look beautiful nowadays, a girl needs ......

(j) Something will have to be done about ......

7 Imagine that you have to fill in a rather odd questionnaire when applying for a job. Answer the following questions, each with a complete sentence:

(a) What three characteristics do you think a leader most needs?

(b) What are your three favourite spare-time activities?

(c) Which of the fine arts do you think is the most relaxing to man?

(d) Which two subjects did you detest most at school?

(e) What is the highest mountain in your country?

(f) If you met an English stranger, what would you talk to him about?

(g) What widespread human habit do you dislike most?

(h) What disease would you least like to die of?

8 Write a paragraph based on Passage 31b, and of a similar length, about the music of your favourite composer, the style of your favourite painter, or the work of your favourite writer.

Suggested discussion topics

Modern architecture.

He that will not apply new remedies must expect new evils; for time is the greatest innovator. (*Bacon*)

A building I should like to knock down.

Popular festivals and their meaning.

Students quite often have difficulties about the indefinite pronouns, such as *something*, *anything*, *everything* and *nothing*, and the adjectives related to them. This section gives examples of their use.

PASSAGE 32

By itself, the ringing of a bell means *nothing*. But in certain recognised contexts, it may mean things as different as 'time for school!', '*somebody* at the door!', 'come to church!', 'that's the end of the lesson', or 'come here please, waitress!' We might well wonder how it is that the same noise can mean so many different things; but of course the answer is easy. 5 The noise occurs in recognised contexts: in times and places and circumstances when we know that it can only mean one thing.

Thus not only can *almost anything* be used as a sign, but *almost any sign* can be used to communicate several different things. *Everything* depends on our agreement about, and our understanding of, the ways in 10 which we use signs. Let us apply this to verbal signs, or words. First, *any* convenient collection of letters can be used as a word. We can communicate just as well by using 'father', 'pater', 'Vater', 'père', 'Daddy', 'Pop', or *anything else*: provided we are understood, it makes no difference. Secondly, the same collection of letters can be used to communicate 15 quite *different* things. The word 'port' can mean a special sort of wine, the opposite of starboard, a harbour, and various *other* things: the word 'bat' can mean either the sort of thing you play cricket with, or the sort of thing you find in belfries.

JOHN WILSON: *Language and the Pursuit of Truth*

Comment

Nothing, being quite exclusive in meaning, rarely offers any problems to the overseas student. *Anything*, *something* and *everything*, and the various other groups, *anywhere*, *anyone*, etc. seem to be the ones that cause trouble. Attention has also been drawn in this passage to the two adjectives *other* and *different*, which also cause some problems of a rather similar nature, although they do not by any stretch of the imagination come into the same semantic group.

Any and *every* are in a sense opposites. *Every* is inclusive; *any* is selective. This can be seen if we attach an identifying relative clause (see also §28) to an expression with either of them. Compare:

anything he says is nonsense

with

everything he says is nonsense

and it will be noticed straight away that although the message conveyed differs little, in the first sentence there is a definite idea of *picking and choosing from among the things he says*, whereas in the other, there is not. So where the idea of choice is present, it is far more likely that some expression with *any* will be correct than one with *every*. A common mistake is to say: 'You can do *everything you like*' or '*everything you want to*', etc., whereas *anything* would be more idiomatic.

This is not to say that such verbs as *to like, to need, to desire*, etc. are never followed by an expression with *every*. But it does mean that the element of *selection* is always present when *any* is used with an affirmative verb. The choice is implicit, if not expressed. (See, e.g., *almost anything* – line 6; *any convenient collection* – line 12; *anything else* – line 14.)

Other and *different*, as used here, clearly do not mean the same. *Various other things* (*line 17*) means various things *in addition to* those already mentioned; *different things* means things which are not identical. Obviously their meanings will overlap on occasion, but basically this is the difference between them.

Some implies a selected but unspecified quantity, example or number of examples of a thing, person or commodity. Thus, in *lines 2–3*, there is '*somebody* at the door', an individual, not identified, but definite. '*Somebody* will tell you' and '*anybody* will tell you' are different in that the former implies 'it *isn't everybody* that can, but *it is possible* to find a person who can', whereas the latter implies 'it doesn't matter who you ask, that person can tell you'.

QUESTION PAPER:

Comprehension

1 The author gives a number of examples of uses of words like *port* and *bat* with different meanings. What do we call this feature of English? Use the following words, taken from the passage, as nouns, then as verbs, and then as adjectives, in separate sentences, bringing out any differences in meaning: mean, well, place, sign, harbour.

2 What particular features of English do you think would be difficult for a

fellow-student from your own country to understand, and how would you set about trying to explain them to him?

3 What features of English do you consider to be advantages for the overseas learner studying the language?

Structures

4 Fill in the blanks with an appropriate pronoun or adjective form of *some, any, every*, or *nothing*:

(*a*) Does —— nowadays believe that the world is flat?

(*b*) There is —— wrong with this camera; —— of the pictures I have taken with my last three films has come out.

(*c*) Perhaps there is —— wrong with the way you hold it. —— people don't hold the camera still, and then —— in the picture is blurred.

(*d*) I don't know —— about the technical side of it; —— I have learnt about taking pictures has been from experience.

(*e*) —— that the books tell you is much use, anyway. You can try —— textbook you like, and —— one will tell you —— quite different.

(*f*) I quite agree. —— of them tell you —— things; —— another; but they —— tell you contradictory things. The last two I read contradicted one another on —— single subject.

(*g*) Well, anyway; give it to me, and I'll see if I can do —— about it.

(*h*) Will it cost me ——? I presume —— will send me a bill. You can't get —— for —— nowadays, can you?

(*i*) It won't cost —— very much. And even if it did, I'm sure you'd manage to find enough money ——.

(*j*) Yes; we enjoy —— more than taking —— snapshots —— day. —— would call us typical tourists to look at us, but —— in this country is so interesting, and —— ever stares at you.

5 Complete the following sentences, using an appropriate expression with *some, any, every*, or *nothing*:

(*a*) Where's my notebook? ......

(*b*) Heavens! What a mess! There are ......

(*c*) You don't look very well; is ...... ?

(*d*) There's the door-bell; go and see ......

(*e*) That chap's extremely careless; ......

(*f*) The situation is very complex, but never mind, we'll ......

(*g*) When we got to the concert-hall, ...

(*h*) Ten minutes later, the place was deserted; ......

(*i*) My hostess is very kind; she lets me ......

(*j*) It was a disastrous meeting; almost ......

(*k*) Did you want ...... ?

(*l*) Well; that's that; there's ......

6 Write a newspaper report of a public ceremony which went wrong in every detail, although it was an important occasion and the weather started off fine.

(*about* 200 *words*)

Suggested discussion topics

It's not the artist's duty to communicate, but to express himself.
The advantages and disadvantages of a synthetic international language.
Problems of communication in an alien society.

Subdivision IV
Link-words
[prepositions and
conjunctions]

INTRODUCTORY NOTES

Prepositions and conjunctions often require considerable thought. The trouble with both is that they express a relationship, rather than an idea or an action, and thus their meaning is coloured by the two other speech items they relate to one another. This means, particularly in the case of prepositions, that while they may start with a clear meaning when used in expressions of time, place, or direction, they tend to develop extended figurative uses which seem to the overseas student to have no possible connection with the basic meaning. This is particularly the case when the two prepositions used with adjectives obviously opposite in meaning happen to be different. Why *dependent on*, but *independent of*, for example? Again, two adjectives whose meanings correspond fairly closely may require a different preposition – and thus sometimes a different dependent verb construction – such as 'able *to do*' something, but 'capable *of doing*' it.

Conjunctions, too, often cause difficulties in this way. How many German or Italian students, for example, are tempted to say 'Also in England' when they mean 'Even in England'? Every teacher will be able to think of a fair number of such cases. There is always a tendency simply to take the commonest meaning of a preposition (*of* 'equals' *de*; *with* 'equals' *med*; *before* 'equals' *vor*, and so on) and apply it indiscriminately in English where the meaning in the student's own language would be figurative or metaphorically idiomatic.

This section is intended to give a number of examples of extended and figurative uses of common prepositions, particularly when they are used as complements to verbs and adjectives; it also gives examples of the normal uses of co-ordinating and subordinating conjunctions which are fairly frequently misused by overseas students.

§33 Common prepositions of place and direction

Not just a section, but a whole volume would be required to deal adequately with English prepositional usages. It is not possible to cover them fully, but only to try to give examples of some of the commonest literal and idiomatic uses in the following sections. The student's task is not made any easier by the transfer of function from one meaning of the same word to another, which is so common a feature of English. Thus *before* may be a preposition, and adverb, or a conjunction. Certain conjunctions, indeed, may be described as 'prepositions with a noun-clause instead of a noun for their object', and the distinction between preposition and adverbs is often tenuous. But it is hoped that this part of the course is useful as a remedial or refresher.

PASSAGE 33a

In a dream, not listening and not even *looking at* the rickshaw-boy any more, she remembered how, *in London, at the steamship agency,* she had quite *by accident* met Paterson *on a day* before the war. Two people overhearing each other *inquiring for* passages *to the same remote river town on the Irrawaddy* could only *laugh in surprise at each other* before they began 5 speaking. It was a happy beginning; she was nineteen and her schooling *in England* was over. Paterson was twenty-three and had *to her* the appearance of a conqueror. She remembered Burma: the little town, the port, the steamers *coming up from Rangoon,* the hibiscus and the heat, the dust and the exquisite white pagodas, the glaring dazzling plain *with its tender* 10 *distant mountains,* the delicate sad monastic bells and the jacaranda trees. It was *part of* the ecstasy to *describe* it all *to Paterson.*

H. E. BATES: *The Jacaranda Tree*

Comment

There is little that is unexpected here; the prepositions of place and direction are used in a perfectly orthodox manner. The uses of *at* in extended expressions – *look at (line* 1) and *laugh at (line* 5) – should be known to any advanced student. Notice, however, *in surprise* preferred to *with surprise* in *line* 5, and *by accident* (but *on purpose*) in *line* 3.

A track leading *to the place* went *over flat fields between dry stone walls*
that in summer were *yellow with stonecrop* and lichen, and *at the end* stood
the square grey house. He had lived there all his life, about thirty-five
years, but he could not remember anyone ever painting it. Not that it
mattered. Nobody ever came *up there.* A big walnut tree stood *in the farm-* 5
yard, by a stone barn, and a few damson trees *along the banks* of a pond.
Every autumn most of the damsons and walnuts were blown off *by the*
wind and fell *into the water,* and the long uncut grass and the tall coffee-
brown docks. It was seven or eight miles *into market* and *by the time* you
got the damsons gathered or the walnuts splashed and loaded them *up into* 10
the back of the Morris, and *by the time* you counted petrol and time and
the auctioneer's fee and everything else, it was hardly worth the trouble.
Besides this he could not read or write very well. He had always been able
to read print a little, but not written words. He had to *take* figures, like
many other things, *on trust.* All this was because he had never been *to* 15
school very much. *In winter* the weather was often too bad *for the three-*
mile journey; in summer there were crops to be hoed and harvested and his
father needed him more.

H. E. BATES: The Little Farm

Comment
The meaning of most of the prepositions of space and direction in this
passage is self-evident, but students sometimes confuse *between* and
among. Between certainly implies some form of restriction or boundary,
as here, and gives the idea of two limits, within which the restricted or
enclosed item exists. *By* has the idea of *close to, next to* of place, and *not*
later than of time. When followed by a gerund, it has the force of *as a*
result of (*By asking* her to come, you caused a lot of trouble). *Besides*
(= *in addition to*) should not be confused with *beside* (= *next to*). Notice
in winter and *in summer* (no articles), and the expression *to take something*
on trust.

They rested and watched *in relays* all the rest of the afternoon and *on into*
the evening. The heat began to go down a little with the sun, *about six*
o'clock, but all afternoon the bare cornland was white with heat *below the*
shimmering blue-green vines on the far slope of the valley. As he tried un-
successfully to sleep *under the trees* he watched the sky *splintered above* 5
him into sharp blue lace by the needles of the pines, and as he lay *on the*
edge of the wood, taking his *turn at watching,* he occasionally saw the distant telegraph poles quivering *on the blue-white horizon* in the taut heat of
full afternoon. Once he went along *to the far edge* of the wood and lay
watching the farmhouse *a mile or two away,* a block of bare whitewash 10
among its low cubes of newly harvested corn and a clump of high grey

poplars, but no one came *out of it*, and the folds of the valley, *beyond the vineyards*, remained empty *in the sun*.

H. E. BATES: Fair Stood the Wind for France

Comment

Further common prepositions of place, time and direction. Again most of the meanings are self-evident. *Below* and *beneath* and *under* often confuse students. *Below* means *lower than*, or *down stream* from; *under* often implies *covered by* or *less than*; *beneath* is less easy to deal with, and is much more a preposition quite simply of place than the others, which have more extended uses. *Among* as used here implies *in the midst of* rather than *flanked by*.

Because the corresponding preposition to *in* may be both locative and directional in some languages, students tend to forget that *in* is nearly always a preposition of *place*, and *into* of actual or implied *direction*.

Note also *beyond*, which means *on the far side of*, and thus implies that the thing mentioned is out of reach. So, in a figurative sense, notice also expressions like *beyond my understanding* or, quite simply, *beyond me*.

Away is an adverbial postposition, and always follows its object, as here: *a mile or two away*.

QUESTION PAPER:

Preposition drills

1 Replace the blank with a suitable preposition:
   (a) We walked —— the fields to the barn.
   (b) —— the barn and the house was a large field.
   (c) —— the apple-trees in the field stood a horse.
   (d) The farm extended several hundred yards —— the road.
   (e) —— the end of the road was a signpost.
   (f) —— the signpost were painted the words 'To Nowhere'.
   (g) Nowhere was the name of the next village, three miles ——.
   (h) —— the time we had arrived —— the barn, it began to rain.
   (i) We took cover —— the leaky barn roof.
   (j) —— the floor of the barn was some hay.
   (k) —— this hay we found a petrol-tin.
   (l) —— this, there were some walnuts, a tin of damsons, and an old lace curtain.
   (m) We began to speculate where these things had come ——.
   (n) —— the time we had decided that they belonged —— smugglers, the rain stopped.
   (o) While we were waiting, we ate eight walnuts —— us.
   (p) As it was a very cold day, we were blue —— cold when we left the barn.

2 Complete the following sentences with a suitable prepositional expression:
   (a) The track led us ......
   (b) There was a mountain stream ......
   (c) It was always very cold here, even ......
   (d) There were a few trees growing ......
   (e) We had been told about them ......
   (f) There we were ......
   (g) The nearest town was ......
   (h) The mountains were purple ......
   (i) Our dog jumped ......
   (j) Then my friend fell ......
   (k) This all happened quite ......
   (l) So we laughed ......

3 Use the following prepositional expressions in sentences of your own, bringing out clearly the difference in meaning between them:
      on the river *and* in the river
      below the town *and* under the town
      beside the car *and* besides the car
      at eight o'clock *and* by eight o'clock
      over the fields *and* above the fields
      in the room *and* into the room
      between the houses *and* among the houses
      along the bridge *and* beyond the bridge.

4 Write a description of the view from your bedroom window, using as many suitable prepositional expressions as you can.   (*about 75/100 words*)

5 Describe a day's routine in your life. Make use of the following prepositions with expressions of *time*:
      by, in, on, at, between.

Comprehension

6 Make a list of words (e.g. *glaring, dazzling*) implying some form of uncomfortably bright light, and use them in sentences to bring out the differences in meaning.

7 The italicised words, used literally in the texts, are used figuratively in the sentences below. Paraphrase the sentences, and show what the words in italics mean.
   (a) He leads a *monastic* existence.
   (b) In the *heat* of the moment, she slapped him.
   (c) She's a *grass* widow at the moment.
   (d) He's *stone* deaf.
   (e) We have a good *crop* of students this year.
   (f) They *sloped* off, muttering angrily.
   (g) He belongs to one of those political *splinter* groups.
   (h) They had wine *laced* with gin – horrible!

Suggested discussion topics

The most beautiful city I know.
'Breaking the ice'.
Our society is over-urbanised.

Prepositions of time, though not always easy, need not be regarded as very confusing. Occasionally students find it difficult to know when to use *since* and *during*, and some students confuse *in* and *on* and *at* in time-expressions. This section attempts to give idiomatic examples of common prepositions of time used in a normal context.

PASSAGE 34*a*

I take it that *at forty*, one has not lost hope that the best is still to be; that one day you may still achieve whatever it is, happiness, a holiday *at Skegness*, a room of one's own, a child, a canary, a grande passion, a long-playing gramophone, the peace of God or bird songs *at eventide*. Perhaps *in a few years* one will have to admit the unlikelihood ... etc. But 5
for the moment, hope there still is, plus a new found courage: the 'now-or-never' of mid-afternoon. After all, these things are no more unattainable now than *at twenty* whatever is said about baldness or middle-aged spread.

PHILIP HOPE-WALLACE: *Half-Way House*

Comment

The three prepositions *at, in,* and *for* are involved here. Notice that *at* refers to the precise moment of time, and the exact geographical location – the 'spot on the map'. So one uses it of ages in life (*at twenty, at forty*), of precise moments of the day (*at noon, at eventide*) and for correlations of time and distance: speeds (*at 60 miles an hour*), or rates of measurement (*at sixpence a pound*) and percentages (*at ten per cent*).

In refers less to the moment as such than to the moment enclosed within a period. So here, we have *in a few years*. It can of course also refer to the 'enclosed period' itself: He will finish *in ten minutes*. But again, the moment of finishing is important here; the period is marked off by a reference to a particular moment.

For implies duration. *For the moment*, in *line 6* is an example of this. When the period of time is not bounded by a definite, stated beginning or end, use *for*: 'he worked *for five hours*'.

PASSAGE 34*b*

While he was speaking Kate had remained kneeling at the grate with the poker in her hand, but *when he stopped* she made a move to rise quickly. Her stiff new mourning skirt got in the way, however, and the cold and damp at the graveside had brought about an unexpected return of, rheumatism, and so *as she went* to rise up quickly, she listed forward with 5 the jerky movement of a camel. It couldn't be certain whether Lally was laughing at Matthew's words, or at the camelish appearance of Kate. Kate, however, was the first to take offence. But she attributed the laughing to Matthew's words.

MARY LAVIN: The Will

Comment

Time-relationships are of course expressed, not only by means of pre-position-and-noun combinations, but also by means of conjunction-and-verb ones. Here there are instances of three of the principal time-conjunctions used in close context. *While* indicates that two actions were going on at the same time, and that at least one of them lasts a certain time. *When* is the loosest of the three; it can imply that the two actions linked together are happening together, or that one precedes the other in time, as here (He stopped, *and then* she made a move . . .). *As*, like *while*, implies that the two actions related to one another were contemporaneous, but it also implies that both were short, and, quite often, that one is connected to the other not only by a time-relationship, but also by one of consequence. Remember that *as* may often be a near-synonym of *because*.

Note also the expressions with at: *at the grate*, *laughing at*, *at the graveside*; and the use of the past perfect and past continuous tenses (see §§1–10 for tenses).

PASSAGE 34c

Throughout the twenties the number of unemployed in Britain never dropped below the million mark and the sight of seedy men wearing scraps of uniform, tramps surging into the casual wards of country towns *evening after evening*, thin, worried-looking women and obviously underfed children became so common that they caused no more emotion 5 than the beggars do in Egypt. Nor was the blight confined to cities. Agriculture had been declining *ever since 1870*, but the war had temporarily halted this and things looked actually rosy *in 1920*, when farmers were offered government protection from the vicissitudes of foreign agriculture. 10

RONALD BLYTHE: The Age of Illusion

Comment

Two prepositions which sometimes cause trouble occur in this passage: *throughout* and *since*. *Throughout* and *during* are different from *for*, although both are used to refer to a period of time. With *for*, one knows only the length of the period (see above, Passage 34a Comment). With *during* and *throughout*, on the other hand, it is necessary to know the placing of the period within its time context. It is not any particular period, specified only by its length (*for six weeks, for nine years, for two minutes*, etc.) but a period of which one knows the beginning and the end, as here: *throughout the twenties*, which began in 1920 and ended in 1930.

Since, however, is always used in relation to a *point of time*. How, though, can 1870 be a point of time? The point of time in question is either the *first* moment of 1870 or the *last*. But it is the point at which the described action begins. Hence the past perfect (NB it is a past perfect progressive) that relates the point of time 1870 to the described present (i.e. 1920) in the text.

Note also the frequentative *evening after evening* (cp. also *evening by evening*, which is similar in meaning, but cumulative as well as frequentative: e.g. *day by day* she learnt more – *day after day* she studies her books); and the preposition *in* in the expression *in* 1920.

QUESTION PAPER:

Preposition drills

1 Replace the blank with a suitable preposition:
   (*a*) She has been learning English —— six years.
   (*b*) I shall be leaving —— three days.
   (*c*) —— the week of the festival, he was very gay.
   (*d*) —— the history of England, there has been a gradual growth of democracy.
   (*e*) She stayed at the hotel —— a fortnight.
   (*f*) —— the age of twenty-two, she got married.
   (*g*) I've done enough work —— the moment.
   (*h*) We travelled —— seventy miles an hour all the way.
   (*i*) I have had this car —— 1963.
   (*j*) Day —— day her English improves.
   (*k*) Day —— day he does the same old routine job.
   (*l*) —— eventide the sunsets are often very lovely.
   (*m*) —— 1974 he will be seventy years old.
   (*n*) —— Friday we shall return home.
   (*o*) —— his holiday he met a very pretty girl.
   (*p*) —— his holiday he practised his golf.
   (*q*) —— a moment she will be ready.
   (*r*) They had been waiting —— twenty minutes.

(s) They had been waiting —— morning.

(t) There will be an interval —— the end of the concerto.

2 Complete the sentence with a suitable prepositional phrase:

(a) We have been waiting here ......

(b) She will become a doctor ......

(c) She regularly attends lectures ......

(d) He will celebrate his 100th birthday ......

(e) He married again ......

(f) If you care to wait, ...

(g) That's quite enough discussion of that point ......

(h) When did I buy that tennis-racket? I think it was ......

(i) We are going to visit my parents ......

(j) In England you get the vote ......

(k) Why is that sports-car ......?

(l) You are a very lazy student; you have paid no attention ......

(m) When do you want to go? ......

(n) She is hoping to stay in the Lake District ......

(o) That shop has been for sale ......

3 Write sentences of your own, using a suitable prepositional phrase or adverbial clause of time, to illustrate or refer to the following situations:

(a) A friend expresses surprise at an elderly uncle's vitality.

(b) Someone asks you when you hope to buy a car.

(c) An acquaintance suggests that you join a party to see a film you have already seen six times.

(d) You are rather bored because you have been doing the same job of work for too long.

(e) You are asked your holiday plans.

(f) Someone describes your country as an insignificant, corrupt oligarchy.

(g) You are playing the piano to a friend, who asks you how long you have been learning.

(h) You express annoyance at a stranger's behaviour, which has completely ruined a visit to the theatre for you.

(i) A friend expresses surprise that you have arrived so early in town after leaving home so late.

(j) Someone asks what you think will happen to your country at the next election, and when it will be.

4 Replace the adverbial expressions in italics by prepositional phrases:

While my sister was on holiday in Spain, she met a most interesting young man. *When he was sixteen years old* he had joined an expedition to Central America. Then, *while several weeks elapsed*, he and his party had been shut off from the outside world. *As the days succeeded one another* their food supply had diminished, and they had actually not eaten *while they had been* up a remote river *for 48 hours*. *From the time that he got back* from the jungle expedition, he had worked as a docker, a farmer, a student, and now he was a doctor. My sister was quite captivated by his charm, and hopes to marry him *when six months have passed from now.*

5   Write a *curriculum vitae* (if necessary, fictitious) in answer to an advertisement requiring an intelligent, experienced secretary for a firm's export department.   (*about* 150/180 *words*)

Comprehension

6   What do the following expressions mean:
     the now-or-never of mid-afternoon (Passage 34*a*, *lines* 6–7)
     middle-aged spread (34*a*, *line* 8)
     she listed forward (34*b*, *line* 5)
     to take offence (34*b*, *line* 8)
     seedy men wearing scraps of uniform (34*c*, *lines* 2–3)
     things looked actually rosy (34*c*, *line* 8)
     the vicissitudes of foreign agriculture (34*c*, *lines* 9–10)

7   How would you sum up Hope-Wallace's reactions to having reached the age of forty? Does he regret it?

8   What do you think is the context of Passage 34*b*? Why do you imagine the characters behave as they do?

9   What, in your opinion, are the best ways of helping the economy of a country or an industry when there is a slump?

Suggested discussion topics

     The happiest days of one's life.
     Relations – a tedious pack of people who haven't the slightest idea how to live or when to die.
     Modern economic problems and possible solutions to them.

Most prepositions can be used in expressions describing reactions, and
many of them are used quite consistently for this purpose in English.
The student need not concern himself here with their semi-adverbial
senses in e.g. phrasal verbs, although this is an aspect of preposition work
which no student can neglect. The passages in this section have been
chosen in an attempt to show how the purely literal space-time connota-
tion of prepositions can be gradually extended and how the quasi-
figurative usage falls into a fairly consistent pattern.

PASSAGE 35*a*

One gets *used to anything*: that is what one hears *on many lips* these days,
though everybody, I suppose, remembers the sense of *shock he felt at the
·first bombed house* he saw. *I think of one* in Woburn Square neatly *sliced in
half. With its sideways exposure* it looked like a Swiss chalet: there were a
pair of ski-ing sticks hanging *in the attic*, and *in another room* a grand piano   5
cocked one leg over the abyss. The combination of music and ski-ing made
one *think of the Sanger family* and Constant Nymphs *dying pathetically of
private sorrow to popular applause. In the bathroom* the geyser looked odd
and twisted *seen from the wrong side*, and the kitchen impossibly *crowded
with furniture* until one realised one had been given a kind of mouse-eye   10
view *from behind the stove* and the dresser – all the space where people
used to move about *with toast* and tea-pots was *out of sight*. But
after quite a short time one ceased to *look* twice *at* the intimate *exposure of
interior furnishings*, and waking *on a cement floor among strangers*, one no
longer thinks what an odd life this is. 'One gets *used to anything*.'   15
GRAHAM GREENE: *Preparation for Violence*

Comment

This passage contains a number of prepositions of space, time and
direction that have already been discussed; but it also contains some
cases where they are used, not to illustrate a time or space relationship,
but a less literal one. The literal usages need not be considered further.

PASSAGE 35*b*

In my time, I have seen a great change in acting, but I doubt if the change is *for the better* as some people, who are *bemused with* the notion that the latest thing is the best, suppose. I *belonged to* a family which liked, even loved, the theatre, although it had no other *connection with it* than that of *paying for* admission, and *in consequence of* this fact, I was frequently taken 5 to see plays *at an age* when other boys if they went *to the theatre at all*, went *to a pantomime* or a circus once or twice a year. I had seen a great variety of plays, *ranging from* Shakespeare's *to* George R. Sims', before I was sixteen, and I had seen Irving, Ellen Terry, Forbes-Robertson, Wilson Barrett, and, once, Sarah Bernhardt, often enough to make those 10 who are the same age as myself suspect that I must be much older than I am. I am one of the few critics of my age who really know what penny-gaffs are like, for I have sat *entranced in* a score of them.

ST JOHN ERVINE: Acting in My Time

Comment

The preposition *for* often implies some kind of exchange or development (we exchanged our pounds *for* dollars; we swopped our tickets *for* less expensive ones). So you have a change *for* the better.

With is more often used to link an adjective or participle signifying an emotional reaction and a *personal* object (I was angry *with them;* pleased *with her;* bored *with their company*); it is found rather less frequently as here: *bemused with the notion* (*line* 2). Note also *connection with* (*line* 4). This is a fairly easy extension of the more literal meaning.

Students very frequently get the following wrong:

'to *pay for* something' (where many languages have a transitive verb).

The verb *to pay* is used transitively, but not when it means *to exchange money for goods or services*. Note also 'to go *to* the theatre', etc. (NOT *in*). A common use of *in* is with participles like *absorbed*, but in *line* 13 *entranced in* is probably locative, not figurative.

QUESTION PAPER:

Preposition drills

1   Replace the blank with a suitable preposition:
    (*a*) We shall get used —— hearing English.
    (*b*) Have you paid —— the tickets?
    (*c*) What you said has no connection —— the discussion.
    (*d*) There has been a distinct change —— the better in your work.
    (*e*) He felt a distinct regret —— leaving London.
    (*f*) His brother died —— pneumonia last year.
    (*g*) The station was crowded —— people.
    (*h*) Look —— her! —— her absurd hat she looks like a camel.

(i) Does this bicycle belong —— you?

(j) When did you last go —— school?

(k) Her knowledge of literature ranges —— Chaucer —— Eliot.

(l) Are you angry —— him?

(m) London has changed a lot —— the worse —— my time.

(n) Her pockets are crammed —— sweets.

(o) They were furious —— the customs officer —— confiscating their whisky.

2 Complete the following sentences with a suitable prepositional expression:

(a) The weather is changing ......

(b) That car looks quite ridiculous ......

(c) We can go out tonight; let's go ......

(d) She's very devout; she goes ......

(e) There are too many people in this restaurant; it's ......

(f) Stop complaining; there's no need to be ......

(g) No; although my name is Churchill, I have ......

(h) Whose watch is this? It ......

(i) Hang that coat up ......

(j) Did you think ......?

(k) She's very ill; in fact ......

(l) The knife was so sharp that ......

3 Write an imaginary entry in a holiday diary, describing a typical day, what you did and where you went. (*about* 100 *words*)

Comprehension

4 What is the difference between these sentences:

(a) She is used to scrubbing the floor.

(b) She used to scrub the floor.

(c) She will get used to scrubbing the floor.

(d) She is used to scrub the floor.

5 Explain the following references:

With its sideways exposure it looked like a Swiss chalet (Passage 35*a*, *line* 4)

a grand piano cocked one leg over the abyss (35*a*, *lines* 5–6)

a kind of mouse-eye view (35*a*, *lines* 10–11)

one ceased to look twice at ...... (35*a*, *line* 13)

a pantomime (35*b*, *line* 7)

a pennygaff (35*b*, *lines* 10–13)

6 What do you understand by the following kinds of play?

a tragedy; a comedy; a farce; a kitchen-sink drama; a musical comedy; a burlesque.

7 What is the difference between:

a critic, a critique *and* a criticism,

a circus, a circuit *and* a circle,

a slice, a lump, a chunk *and* a hunk,
a stove, an oven *and* a geyser.
furniture, tools, equipment *and* utensils.

Suggested discussion topics

Bread and circuses – the motto of modern life.

The future of the live theatre.

'One gets used to anything – even nuclear war, concentration camps and political or racial persecution.'

§36 *Figurative uses of prepositions of time, place and direction*

The following section develops further what the last section started, and some of the usages here will necessarily overlap with what has already been illustrated there. However, in this section the intention has been to select passages which include cases of prepositions of direction as well as those of space and time, used figuratively rather than literally, but not so remotely from their basic meaning as to baffle the overseas student into believing that there is no connection with that basic meaning.

PASSAGE 36a

While he lay there Forrester sat *with his arms across his knees, thinking of what Carrington* said. The sun was beginning to drop fiercely down *to-wards the edge* of the valley, and *from the horizon* the broad purple band of evening haze, pink *at the edges,* like a fire itself, *was growing* upwards, already *turning* the western sky *from the whitish-blue of the day's heat to   5 tender green. In a little over half an hour* it would be dark. As he *thought of it,* he *gave up the thought of rescue: at first* only temporarily, *until the morning,* and then permanently. Almost as an experiment he began to *calculate from the speed* of the Dakota and *from its time of arrival* how far it could possibly be, southwards, to the river valley. *In a straight line* he   10 reckoned that it could not be more than twenty miles; but he knew that the line would not be straight and he began *to think of it* as thirty miles. Then it *occurred to him* that they could *travel by night;* he remembered that the moon would be up *by nine.*

H. E. BATES: *The Purple Plain*

Comment

The main points here are the use of the prepositions *from* and *to* and *of.* It is not difficult to see why one says 'turning *from . . . to*' (*line* 4). The inchoative verbs (*to turn, to grow*) implying a change of state are used this way (see §21). Notice, however, that the other two principal inchoatives, *to get* and *to become,* do not have a prepositional complement, but a *direct object,* and cannot be used in this way. A slightly wider extension of the meaning of *from* gives us to *calculate from* (*line* 9). Its use with expressions of time is easy to understand, and there is no particular difficulty in seeing why, if it is possible to calculate *from* a speed, one may also calculate *from a time of arrival* (*line* 9).

There is also the use of *to*. As a preposition of direction, its meaning is clear. The difference between *to* and *towards* is simply that *to* generally implies the arrival at the eventual destination as well as the movement in its direction, whereas *towards* implies the direction but not the arrival as well. Note, however, *it occurred to him* (*line* 13).

There are certain cases where a verb with an indirect object may not be used without the preposition. Many advanced students occasionally forget this. The commonest and most important of these are:

to seem (it seems *to me*; NOT it seems me)
to say (he said *to me*); to describe; to reply
to suggest (he suggested *to her* that they should go)
to propose (like *to suggest*)
to appear (like *to occur*)
to explain (they explained *the rules to her*)

Remember that *to suggest*, *to propose* and *to explain* are transitive verbs and that it is perfectly possible for their direct object to be a *person* (e.g. I cannot explain *that girl*; *I propose Mr Smith* as our delegate; *Don't suggest him* as leader, for Heaven's sake).

The preposition after *to think* in its normal usage is *of*. (When it is part of a phrasal verb pattern, of course, there are other possibilities, such as *to think over*, etc., but those are of no concern here.) Rather fewer verbs are used with an *of* complement in English than with, say, *de* in French or *von* in German, but there are a fair number of them, and the student should watch out for them. Notice particularly: *to accuse of*, *to convince of*, *to convict of* (and remember what *convict* means!), *to deprive of*, *to make of*, *to relieve of*, *to suspect of*, *to rob of* (but *to steal* FROM), *to die of* (and thus *to perish of*, *to starve of*, but *to suffer* FROM). Certain other verbs may occasionally be used with *of*, too (e.g. Who would have believed that *of him*? This, however, is rather different, because the prepositional expression is not an immediate part of the verb complement, but depends on the direct object).

Note also *over* (*line* 6) meaning 'more than' with a definite extent of time or size.

PASSAGE 36*b*

Buck was young *for a foreman*, being only *about thirty*, but his capacity could be *gauged by* that quaint air of *wisdom beyond his age* which is also to be seen in a good young dog. He was slightly *above middle height, with curly sandy hair* and a pleasant Scotch face *on a beautiful body*. He was slim but not thin, hard but not stiff, supple but not sinuous. His small   5 feet lifted themselves lightly in their heavy boots. His fustians, ungaitered, but tied *below the knee* like those of his men, *took on* a grace *of their own from the grace* of his figure. Their soft golden-brown was so exactly *suited to* the woods that it might have been provided by Nature *by way of* protective colouring.

10

CONSTANCE HOLME: *The Last Inch*

Comment

The prepositions *beyond*, *above* and *below* need no comment here. The only comment required on *about* concerns its use as an adverb. It is normally used as an adverb only when it means 'in the immediate locality' (There is a lot of 'flu *about* at the moment).

The use of *for* is easy to understand, and difficult to paraphrase. This particular use of it is common, is vaguely concessive, and implies 'when one remembers that (he is)'.

Note the use of *by* (common with verbs like *to judge*, *to estimate*, *to calculate*, *to measure*) indicating the scale or criterion of judgment involved. Whether or not the phrase *by way of* is an extension of this, is difficult to say, but the phrase is worth remembering.

On one's own and *of one's own* frequently confuse students. The former implies absence of company or assistance ('She lives *on her own*'; 'Did you do this exercise *on your own?*'). The latter implies some form of possession, involvement, even uniqueness.

Note also that whereas the verb *to suit* is transitive ('that didn't *suit him*; he wanted more'), the past participle used adjectivally requires the preposition *to* (*line* 9).

QUESTION PAPER:

Preposition drills

1 Insert a suitable preposition:
   (*a*) I don't know what to think —— your behaviour.
   (*b*) It seems —— me that you have been rather silly.
   (*c*) Perhaps he can explain —— me why he was late.
   (*d*) I suspect that student —— cheating.
   (*e*) But probably he is suffering —— a headache.
   (*f*) Don't accuse him —— anything.
   (*g*) It occurred —— him that you might be interested —— this book.
   (*h*) I estimate —— the figures you have given me that we shall succeed —— our undertaking.
   (*i*) —— eight o'clock, we shall be finished.
   (*j*) Then we can rest —— the morning.

2 Complete the following sentences, using a prepositional expression:

    (*a*) Have you anything to propose ...... ?

    (*b*) Did he suggest the same ...... ?

    (*c*) She was so upset; she felt she would die ......

    (*d*) Children should never be starved ......

    (*e*) May I relieve you ...... ?

    (*f*) Such strange behaviour is not in keeping with his character; who would have believed ...... ?

    (*g*) When will it occur ...... ?

    (*h*) The accused was convicted ......

    (*i*) Would you mind explaining this sentence ...... ?

    (*j*) Did you calculate our speed ...... ?

3 Write sentences referring to the following situations, using a suitable prepositional expression:

    (*a*) You are not sure how to use a new duplicating-machine.

    (*b*) A young friend has been appointed to a very responsible post.

    (*c*) Someone whom you have not seen for many years asks after your elderly uncle.

    (*d*) You have just had what you think is a splendid idea.

    (*e*) You are asked what the crime is that the accused is supposed to have committed in a court case.

    (*f*) You offer to help an elderly lady carrying a heavy bag.

    (*g*) Someone aks you why you look so pale.

    (*h*) A friend asks what you think of his holiday plans.

4 Write an account of a demonstration by a salesman of a new type of vacuum-cleaner. Use the following verbs, with appropriate prepositional expressions: to appear, to seem, to demonstrate, to explain, to calculate, to think, to suspect, to suit. (*about* 180 *words*)

Comprehension

5 Explain the following references in Passage 36*b*:

    that quaint air of wisdom (*line* 2)

    slim but not thin, hard but not stiff, supple but not sinuous (*line* 5)

    protective colouring (*line* 10)

6 Why do you think Carrington and Forrester in Passage 36*a* found themselves in that situation? What had happened beforehand?

7 Write a short physical description, modelled on Passage 36*b*, of a friend of yours.

Suggested discussion topics

    What makes a hero?

    How does one get to know people properly?

Because so many nouns, verbs and adjectives may be used figuratively, so the prepositions which complement them may also acquire figurative uses. These are not as inconsistent as they might seem at first sight, though there are enough difficulties to discourage anyone who attempts to reduce the figurative uses of English prepositions to a system. It is not so difficult to understand, for example, why the preposition *on*, which seems basically to mean *above and supported by*, should be used with verbs like *to rely*, *to depend* or *to devolve*, where the idea of *support* is implicit in the meaning of the verb. But what about *to insist*? Why *on* – and if so, why not *to desist on*, instead of the correct *to desist from*? And why is *to resist* transitive, requiring no prepositional complement at all?

The passage here and those in §38 illustrate some fairly common idiomatic prepositional usages. They cannot possibly cover them all, but consideration of these examples may help the student avoid certain common mistakes.

PASSAGE 37

So Mrs Moore had all she wished; she escaped the trial, the marriage, and the hot weather; she would *return to* England *in comfort and distinction*, and see her other children. But she accepted her good luck *without enthusiasm*. She had *come to* that state where the *horror of the universe* and its smallness are both visible *at the same time* – the *twilight of the double* 5
vision in which so many elderly people are *involved*. If this world is not *to our taste*, well, *at all events* there is Heaven, Hell, Annihilation – *one or other of* those large things, that large scenic *background of* stars, fires, blue or black air. All heroic endeavour, and all that is known as art, assumes that there is such a background, just as all practical endeavour, 10
when the world is *to our taste*, assumes that the world is all. But *in the twilight of the double vision*, a spiritual muddledom is *set up for which* no high-sounding words can be found; we can neither act nor *refrain from* action, we can neither ignore nor respect Infinity. Mrs Moore had always *inclined to* resignation. 15

E. M. FORSTER: *A Passage to India*

Comment

The first preposition in this passage is *to*, which is used first of all literally: 'she would return *to* England'. Here, it is obviously directional, and it retains a vestige of its directional sense in '*She had come to that state*'. In the phrase *to our taste*, it means *according to*, or *on the basis of*. This use is quite common – one also says: *to my mind, to my horror, to my knowledge, to my belief, to my liking, to my shame*. Notice also that Mrs Moore was *inclined to* resignation. This again has a vestige of the directional meaning about it, and so one says that someone has a *tendency to* something, or is *impervious to* it. This goes further – you are good, kind, unkind, cruel, respectful etc. *to* someone. And of course do not forget those old stumbling-blocks *to explain to, to say to, to seem to*, all of which catch students out.

There is little difficulty with the preposition *in* as it is used here (*in comfort; involved in*). Note however, that one *believes, trusts* and *is lacking* or *deficient in* something – a usage that is commonly forgotten. There is also a difference between *in the end* (meaning *finally, eventually*) and *at the end*, which is much less figurative, and refers to a definite point of time (cf. '*at* the same time', in *line 5* of Passage 37).

The idiomatic phrase *at all events* means *in any case*. The commonest idiomatic uses of *at* as a complement are probably those indicating some kind of skill (or lack of it): *good at, skilful at, bad at*, etc., and those concerning an emotional reaction to a situation (*annoyed at, irritated at, concerned at, furious at* etc.) Notice, however, that *at* is preferred only for SITUATIONS or EVENTS arousing emotion; one is annoyed *with* a person, for example.

From, as used here, is frequently found with verbs implying some form of escape or avoidance; one *dissuades* someone *from* a course of action, *releases* someone *from* captivity, *disengages* or *disentangles* something *from* something. But don't forget 'to deprive *of*'.

The use of *of* and *for* here are not noteworthy, but students should remember that certain adjectives like *tired, ashamed, proud, typical, afraid, sick*, etc., are used with a complementary *of*.

QUESTION PAPER:

Preposition drills

1 Replace the blank with a suitable preposition:
  (*a*) It is kind —— you to ask me.
  (*b*) This country is now independent —— Britain.
  (*c*) I am ashamed —— you.

(*d*) Don't be afraid —— him.
(*e*) She has been deprived —— any chance in life.
(*f*) This is not —— my taste.
(*g*) She is impervious —— all criticism.
(*h*) —— my certain knowledge she is at least sixty.
(*i*) Kindly explain this —— the customs officer.
(*j*) She is inclined —— mysticism.
(*k*) She is good —— tennis.
(*l*) Why are you so annoyed —— the results?
(*m*) She is very rich; —— all events, she claims to be.
(*n*) The government is concerned —— the food shortage.
(*o*) I am disappointed —— your answer.
(*p*) We shall dissuade him —— his foolhardy plan.
(*q*) It's about time he was released —— captivity.
(*r*) They managed to disengage the balloon —— the tree.
(*s*) One cannot disentangle truth —— fiction in her story.
(*t*) Please refrain —— smoking.
(*u*) Do you believe —— God?
(*v*) That student is lacking —— intelligence.
(*w*) Persevere, and you'll manage it —— the end.
(*x*) Trust —— me; I'll help you.
(*y*) She has got involved —— some kind of conspiracy.

2 Complete the following sentences with a suitable prepositional expression:
(*a*) She has always been good ......
(*b*) She would be all right if she weren't so disrespectful ......
(*c*) Do you think this whisky is deficient ......?
(*d*) That dishonest girl is very skilful ......
(*e*) Can you release that dog ...... ?
(*f*) They say that that child is deprived ......
(*g*) She was terrified ......
(*h*) The student was indignant ......
(*i*) Such people will never believe ......
(*j*) I asked him to explain ......

3 Compose sentences of your own, using the words suggested, to illustrate or refer to the following situations:
(*a*) A friend has been cheated by a swindler. (Trust)
(*b*) Someone asks you to join the committee of a club. (Involved)
(*c*) You are asked what a certain acquaintance is like. (Inclined)
(*d*) You don't want your friends to hear the bad language used by some of the company. (Refrain)
(*e*) A kitten has been playing with your knitting. (Disentangle)
(*f*) You are asked to play in an orchestra. (Good)
(*g*) Someone has broken an important undertaking to you. (Furious)
(*h*) You express your admiration at someone's coolness in a dangerous situation. (Impervious)

4 Write an assessment of a policeman's character (*about* 100 *words*), making use of the following participles or adjectives + a prepositional complement: skilful, deficient, ashamed, irritated, involved, deprived, impervious, concerned, dissuaded, released.

Comprehension

5 What does the author mean by:
    the twilight of the double vision (*lines* 5–6 & 11)
    blue or black air (*line* 9)
    a spiritual muddledom (*line* 12)
    high-sounding words (*line* 14)

6 What do you think of the point of view expressed by Forster in the fourth and fifth sentences of the passage? ('If this world ... assumes that the world is all')?

7 Why should the universe seem both horrific and small at the same time?

8 What do you think Mrs Moore was like, judging from this passage?

Suggested discussion topic

    Why are we here?

§38 *Extensions of meaning*
with common prepositions – 2

This section is a continuation of §37.

PASSAGE 38*a*

As he took the aircraft from the strip to its dispersal point at the far end, he felt the heat concentrate violently in the cabin. It became terrific in the few minutes when he taxied in, his two ground crew boys running *by the wings*, naked to the waist, so *dark with sun* that they were almost as dark as the Burmese boys still *filling in with loads* of rubble the bomb craters 5
of the road running between the strip and the town. *By the time* he brought the aircraft to a stop and cut its engines he was *drenched with sweat*, and as he climbed down on to the dust the final rush of heat and light rebounding off the glassy particles of dust smashed across his eyes, dazzling him *with such violence* that he could not see. 10

H. E. BATES: *The Purple Plain*

Comment

The usages in the first sentence of this passage have already been mentioned; in the later sentences there are certain uses of *with* which occasionally cause trouble. It is very common in English to find this preposition used after a verb or adjective that signifies some form of symptomatic visible or audible reaction, usually emotional (e.g. She *blushed with shame*; she is *green with envy*; her eyes *blazed with anger*; he went *blue with cold*). So in this case you have *dark with sun*.

This usage is an extension of the common meaning of *with*: *as a result of*. This occurs in *line 10*: *dazzling him with such violence*. So you have: hitting him *with such force*; filling him *with such pride*; speaking *with such emotion*. And so it is no surprise to find that the character in the passage was *drenched with sweat* (cf. *dry with heat*; *damp with fear*, which are extensions of this 'symptomatic' use).

Note also the use of *by* as a preposition of place and time.

PASSAGE 38*b*

In looking at any object, for example a house or a person, I *concentrate* my gaze *on* what I choose as the central point and focus it clearly, allowing

the rest of the object to form a blur – of which however I apprehend the
extent and general colouring. If after studying the central point I am still
interested in the object, I *look for* other *points of interest*: thus, after long 5
acquaintance with a person I know his single features *by heart*, but cannot
recompose his face *from memory*. I must always have seen *in the same
partial way*, because when *thinking of* the house where I spent my childhood, I remember the shapes of particular bricks *in the wall*, the angle of
the slate roof, but cannot recompose the general façade. *In ordinary* 10
conversation I *concentrate my gaze on* both eyes of the person addressing
me; *in difficult conversation* I tend to *concentrate it on his right eye*, and if the
strain persists abnormally, I lose focus and he *recedes into the distance*, so
that I see him whole, but small. I have, however, a perfect memory-sense
by touch: I can remember the shape of any body or inanimate object I have 15
once touched, and if I were asked to reconstruct the dimensions of a house
in which I have lived for some years, I should imagine myself walking
through it *in the half-dark*, and know just how the rooms stood *in
relation to* one another, their size, the position of their furniture, and so on.

ROBERT GRAVES: How Poets See

Comment

The two main idiomatic points here are *interest(ed)* IN and *to concentrate*
ON, along with which remember *from memory* and *by heart, by touch,
by sight*.

A smaller, but important point is the use of *in* with a collective or
group word, especially after superlatives, when one element or aspect of
the collective is singled out for mention (see above *line* 9: particular
bricks *in the wall* – not OF). Thus one says: the best student *in the class*.
OF is preferred when the collective is replaced by a plural ('The best
student *of the three*').

QUESTION PAPER:

Preposition drills

1 Replace the blank with a suitable preposition:
   (*a*) She arrived at the party black ——— coal-dust.
   (*b*) She then filled her glass ——— neat whisky.
   (*c*) ——— the time her hostess had noticed her, she was concentrating ——— a
   young journalist.
   (*d*) In fact, he seemed very interested ——— her.
   (*e*) He knew her ——— sight, but he couldn't remember her name ———
   memory.
   (*f*) She was the prettiest girl ——— the room, but there were other points
   ——— interest, too.

(g) After a short acquaintance —— her, the journalist asked her to marry him.

(h) They have now been happily married —— some years.

(i) She still goes ——·behaving —— the same way when she goes —— parties.

(j) But if too many male guests show an interest —— her, she quickly tells them her husband is the best boxer —— the country.

2   Complete the following sentences with a suitable prepositional expression:

(a) You poor thing! You are shivering . . . . . .

(b) Come in, and fill your glasses . . . . . .

(c) You must learn to concentrate . . . . . .

(d) The funniness of the story struck him . . . . . .

(e) Are you interested . . . . . . ?

(f) His daughter's achievement filled him . . . . . .

(g) That is the silliest exercise . . . . . .

(h) Do you know any Shakespeare sonnets . . . . . . ?

(i) Yes, and I can recite the whole of 'To be or not to be' . . . . . .

(j) You must have been studying Shakespeare . . . . . .

3   Compose sentences of your own relating to or reacting to the following situations, using a suitable prepositional expression in each:

(a) What are your chief hobbies?

(b) Is any one of them your favourite at the moment?

(c) Have you got a good memory?

(d) Would you recognise your Prime Minister if you saw him?

(e) What would you do if you were at a party and a friend mentioned that his glass was empty?

(f) Supposing someone gave you a luxury yacht, how would you feel?

(g) What is your opinion of Shakespeare?

(h) How long have you been studying English?

4   Write a character study of the ideal boy (girl) friend, using as many prepositional expressions as you can.   (*about* 150 *words*)

Comprehension

5   Describe your own reactions to a visual stimulus, contrasting or comparing them with those of Robert Graves.

6   The following words are related to words in the text of Passage 38*b*. They have rather different meanings, however. Find the words they are related to, and use them and the words given below in sentences, bringing out the differences in meaning:

objective, apprehensive, recessive

7   The following words from Passage 38*b* have colloquial meanings related to, but different from their literal ones. Use each word in contrasted pairs of sentences, one with its literal, one with its colloquial meaning:

angle, slate, brick

(Use *angle* and *slate* as verbs.)

Suggested discussion topics

Which of the senses would you hate losing most?

Genius – 99 per cent perspiration and 1 per cent inspiration.

The business of a poet . . . is to examine, not the individual but the species.
  (*Dr Johnson*)

Part 2

SENTENCES IN PARAGRAPHS

INTRODUCTION

The first part of this course tried to show how certain modern English writers use certain grammatical and syntactical devices – structures. The next part, which is much shorter, attempts to show how writers (in many cases the same ones) build up paragraphs, relate words to one another within the sentence and sentences to one another within the paragraph. It is hoped that the examples given will also show that to write effectively a student does not so much need a large vocabulary as one of which he is in full command. While a large vocabulary is an immeasurable asset to anyone, using it indiscriminately or imprecisely wastes it. And if the ideas expressed are carelessly or wrongly organised within the sentence or paragraph, what might have been an advantage will degenerate from a waste into a menace. It is also hoped that the following passages may help the student develop his repertoire of self-expression and subtlety of understanding, so that he will grasp how sound, rhythm, meaning and choice of structure all contribute to a clean and supple style, and how ignorance of sound, clumsiness of rhythm, or ambiguity of structure make the style and with it the meaning not only muddy and ineffectual, but also ugly and unattractive.

§39 *Factual description*

The passages in this section are straightforward descriptive paragraphs taken from narrative works. The first is a vivid description of a sequence of actions; the second, a static description of a small town in nineteenth-century Ireland. The student will notice the almost complete absence of subordinate clauses from both passages. In the first, this adds to the graphic effect of the movement in the passage. In the second, the comparative looseness of the sentence construction is admirably suited to the evocative informality of the description.

PASSAGE 39*a*

The black cloud had crossed the sky, a blob of dark against the stars. The night was quiet again.

Tom stepped into the water and felt the bottom drop from under his feet. He threshed the two strokes across the ditch and pulled himself heavily up the other bank. His clothes clung to him. He moved and 5 made a slopping noise; his shoes squished. Then he sat down, took off his shoes and emptied them. He wrung the bottoms of his trousers, took off his coat and squeezed the water from it.

Along the highway he saw the dancing beams of the flashlights, searching the ditches. Tom put on his shoes and moved cautiously across the 10 stubble field. The squishing noise no longer came from his shoes. He went by instinct toward the other side of the stubble field, and at last he came to the road. Very cautiously he approached the square of houses.

Once a guard, thinking he heard a noise, called: 'Who's there?'

Tom dropped and froze to the ground, and the flashlight beam passed 15 over him. He crept silently to the door of the Joad house. The door squalled on its hinges. And Ma's voice, calm and steady and wide awake:

'What's that?'

JOHN STEINBECK: *The Grapes of Wrath*

QUESTIONS:

1 What circumstances do you think led up to the events described in this passage? On what evidence in the passage do you base your answer?

2 Explain the following words or phrases:
a blob of dark
He threshed the two strokes across the ditch
a slopping noise
his shoes squished
the stubble field
Tom froze to the ground
The door squalled on its hinges.

3 What difference would it have made to the atmosphere of the passage if
Steinbeck had made the following substitutions of words:
calm for *quiet* (*line* 2)   *slithered* for *crept* (*line* 16)
floundered for *threshed* (*line* 4)   *screeched* for *squalled* (*line* 17)
slunk for *moved cautiously* (*line* 10)

4 Write short paragraphs of your own, using the following words in an
appropriate context:
(*a*) to creak, to twang, to clank, to clink, to clang, to squeak, to screech, to
jangle
(*b*) to skulk, to swagger, to mince, to strut, to lurch, to lollop, to totter, to
toddle, to plod, to trudge, to stump, to creep
(*c*) still, serene, stagnant, unruffled, quiescent, stationary
(*d*) blob, patch, strip, stripe, expanse

5 Reconstruct the paragraph, combining as many of the simple sentences as
you feel reasonable into compound sentences with subordinate clauses. Now
compare the two versions. How does the effect of your passage differ from
Steinbeck's?

PASSAGE 39*b*

Castlebar had preserved the appearance of a feudal town. Though the
castle had vanished, on its site fortifications still frowned above steep and
narrow streets, the houses were beautiful and ancient, built, with enormous solidity, of cut grey stone, adorned with cornices, stone-wreathed
windows and carved doorways. In the late eighteenth century a Mall had   5
been added to the town, with formal walks under rows of trees, but the
streets tailed off abruptly into mud cabins, curlews wheeled and cried in
the centre of the town, and the walkers in the Mall had bare feet. After
1798 what remained of the castle and Castlebar House had been turned
into a barracks for the English garrison, and an unpretentious square   10
villa in the demesne called sometimes the Lawn and sometimes the Summer House, became the Irish residence of the Earls of Lucan, and was
officially described as Castlebar House.
                          CECIL WOODHAM-SMITH: *The Reason Why*

QUESTIONS:

1 Explain why you think the author used the following words in the passage:
    frowned (*line* 2)   unpretentious (*line* 10)
    stone-wreathed (*line* 4)   villa (*line* 11)
    tailed off (*line* 7)

2 What is the difference between:
    feudal and *feuding*
    ancient and *old*
    adorned with and *decorated with*
    mall, avenue, alley and *lane*
    abruptly, brusquely, briefly and *shortly*
    bare and *naked*
    Summer House and *summer-house*
    officially and *officiously*

3 What is the significance of the following details in the description?
    curlews wheeled and cried in the centre of the town (*lines* 7–8)
    the walkers in the Mall had bare feet (*line* 8)
    what remained of the castle (*line* 9)

4 From close examination of the details of the passage, what do you infer were the relations between the English inhabitants of Castlebar and the Irish?

5 Write a description of a small town in your own country, making similar use of significant details to create the right atmosphere. (*about* 150 *words*)

PASSAGE 39c

The Canon dressed and, waving the remonstrances of his housekeeper aside, left the house. Before him was a climb that would take at least three hours, over some of the roughest ground in the country. He walked up to the top of the village street and struck off up a boreen that went for a bit and then petered out as if discouraged. After that he had to make do 5 with the narrow rocky footpath when he could see it or stumble a while over the tangled scrub and sharp stones till he found it again. The unwonted exercise made his heart pound and his head swim, and his clothes stuck damply to him: darkness fell before he was half-way up and although he had a torch the way in front was so strange and featureless he 10 thought he should never arrive at his goal. His feet pained him from continually stubbing against the bits of rock: in spite of the long dry spell the mountain was soaking, and as the way is with Irish mountains, the higher he went the wetter it grew, until he found the water gurgling about his ankles and seeping over the top of his boots; and more than once he 15 missed his footing and measured his length on the prickly ground.

        HONOR TRACY: *The Straight and Narrow Path*

QUESTIONS:

1 What do you learn about the Canon's character and habits from this passage?

2 Why do you think the author uses the following phrases?
petered out as if discouraged (*line* 5)
he had to make do with the narrow rocky footpath (*lines* 5–6)
as the way is with Irish mountains (*line* 13)
he measured his length (*line* 16)

3 Make sentences of your own, using the following words in an appropriate context. Try if possible to use the words in *e*, *f* and *g* figuratively.
(*a*) remonstrance, retort, protest, complaint
(*b*) peter out, hang fire, tail off, stop short
(*c*) tangled, dishevelled, rumpled, deranged, bedraggled
(*d*) damp, dank, clammy, moist, soggy, muggy, watery
(*e*) gurgle, ripple, babble, tinkle, murmur, mutter
(*f*) seep, percolate, emanate, emerge, dribble, ooze, exude
(*g*) prickly, spiky, thorny, barbed, bristling

4 Compare the author's description of the Canon's walk with Steinbeck's of Tom Joad's flight in Passage 39*a*. What similarities, and what differences do you note in (*a*) vocabulary, (*b*) method of relating what happened to its effect on the central character, and (*c*) aim in writing the passage? With which of the two characters do you feel more sympathy, and why?

5 Do you find any points of similarity between Miss Woodham-Smith's attitude to Ireland in Passage 39*b* and Miss Tracy's in Passage 39*c*?

6 Write a description (*about* 150 *words*) of an uncomfortable journey, from either memory or imagination, making yourself the central figure. Model your approach on that of either Mr Steinbeck (Passage 39*a*) or Miss Tracy (Passage 39*c*).

§40 Inferential factual description

The passages in this section are also descriptive, but the description goes far beyond the simple highlighting of significant details that occurred in the §39 passages. In one case the detailed actions themselves are placed purposefully in their context, each illustrating a fleeting emotional attitude; in the other the scene itself has a symbolic significance. This means that the external details picked out symbolise an inner state or quality, just as in Passage 40a the actions described are intended to show the attitude of the main character to others in the narration.

PASSAGE 40a

Mrs Tanner stood in the porch watching the hired car disappear down the drive taking her son to the London train – first short lap of his long journey overseas. She waved once or twice; but it was not Jeremy's face that turned to smile at her, only Naomi's, so she bent her heavy body ostentatiously to examine the loose paving in the front steps. Her sudden   5
attention to the cracked paving would make clear her deliberate rejection of the smile, for her daughter-in-law knew well enough that the dilapidation of the house was one of the things that least concerned her. It was surely enough that she shared this war-time rural isolation with Naomi, had allowed her to go alone with Jeremy for his embarkation; she had   10
earned a right to a single act of rudeness to this stranger brought in by marriage. In any case Naomi was well aware of the mutual indifference upon which their friendly relationship rested.

ANGUS WILSON: *A Sad Fall*

QUESTIONS:

1 How do Mrs Tanner's actions illustrate her relationship to her daughter-in-law?

2 Why do you think her son was making a long journey overseas? What details in the passage support your deduction?

3 What sort of a house do you think Mrs Tanner was living in? What details in the passage give you this impression?

4 What do the following words or phrases add to the effect of the passage?
   the hired car (*line* 1)
   only Naomi's (*line* 4)
   she bent her heavy body ostentatiously (*lines* 4–5)
   dilapidation (*lines* 7–8)
   It was surely enough (*lines* 8–9)
   she had earned a right to a single act of rudeness (*lines* 10–11)
   this stranger brought in by marriage (*lines* 11–12)
   the mutual indifference upon which their friendly relationship rested
   (*lines* 12–13)

5 Use the following pairs of words in contrasted sentences to show that you
   understand the difference in meaning between them:
   (*a*) *lap* and *circuit*
   (*b*) *overseas* and *abroad*
   (*c*) *ostentatiously* and *ostensibly*
   (*d*) *paving* and *pavement*
   (*e*) *to share* and *to divide*
   (*f*) *mutual* and *reciprocal*
   (*g*) *to rest* and *to remain*

6 Write a description of a departure or leave-taking, trying to highlight small
   significant actions by those concerned in the way Angus Wilson does in this
   passage.   (*about* 150 *words*)

PASSAGE 40*b*

Strange things happened at midday. The glittering sea rose up, moved
apart in planes of blatant impossibility; the coral reef and the few,
stunted palms that clung to the more elevated parts would float up into the
sky, would quiver, be plucked apart, run like rain-drops on a wire or be
repeated as in an odd succession of mirrors. Sometimes land loomed where   5
there was no land and flicked out like a bubble as the children watched.
Piggy discounted all this learnedly as a 'mirage'; and since no boy could
reach even the reef over the stretch of water where the snapping sharks
waited, they grew accustomed to these mysteries and ignored them, just
as they ignored the miraculous, throbbing stars. At midday the illusions   10
merged into the sky and there the sun gazed down like an angry eye.
Then, at the end of the afternoon, the mirage subsided and the horizon
became level and blue and clipped as the sun declined. That was another
time of comparative coolness but menaced by the coming of the dark.
When the sun sank, darkness dropped on the island like an extinguisher   15
and soon the shelters were full of restlessness, under the remote stars.
                    WILLIAM GOLDING: *Lord of the Flies*

QUESTIONS:

1   Comment on the author's use of the following words or phrases in this passage:

blatant impossibility (*line* 2)
be plucked apart (*line* 4)
flicked out like a bubble (*line* 6)
throbbing stars (*line* 10)
the horizon became ... clipped (*lines* 12–13)
darkness dropped on the island (*line* 15)

2   Examine the similes used by the author in this passage. Do you consider them appropriate?

3   Explain the differences in meaning between:
   (*a*) *stunted, small, puny* and *squat*
   (*b*) *to quiver, to shiver, to quake* and *to writhe*
   (*c*) *to pluck, to strip, to wrench*
   (*d*) *to ignore, to overlook, to neglect* and *to omit*
   (*e*) *to throb, to flutter, to tingle* and *to wince*
   (*f*) *remote, isolated, lonely, distant* and *inaccessible*
   Which of the words of similar but different meaning might Golding have used in the passage instead of the one he did without materially altering its effect?

4   The opening sentence of this passage is 'Strange things happened at midday.' Do you think the author's description of them is effective and convincing? What factors in the passage do you either admire or dislike? Why?

5   What can you deduce from the passage about the circumstances of the characters mentioned?

6   Describe a sunrise or a sunset as effectively as you can, making use of atmospheric vocabulary and similes as Golding does in this passage.

(*about* 80/100 *words*)

The four passages in this section have been chosen to indicate how four straightforward descriptions of people may create quite a different effect in the reader's mind according to the vocabulary used. Passage 41*a* is an orthodox exposition of character through a description of a person's behaviour; 41*b* is a visual description of a character's outward appearance, the details and images carefully chosen to produce a particular effect; 41*c* is a deliberate attempt to ridicule by exaggeration; and 41*d* evokes character rather than describing it. What they all have in common is a satirical flavour.

PASSAGE 41*a*

Mr Samgrass was a genealogist and a legitimist; he loved dispossessed royalty and knew the exact validity of the claims of the pretenders to many thrones; he was not a man of religious habit, but he knew more than most Catholics about their Church; he had friends in the Vatican and could talk at length of policy and appointments, saying which contempor- 5 ary ecclesiastics were in good favour, which in bad, what recent theolog- ical hypothesis was suspect, and how this or that Jesuit or Dominican had skated on thin ice or sailed near the wind in his Lenten discourses; he had everything except the Faith, and later liked to attend benediction in the chapel of Brideshead and see the ladies of the family with their 10 necks arched in devotion under their black laced mantillas; he loved for- gotten scandals in high life, and was an expert in putative parentage; he claimed to love the past, but I always felt that he thought all the splendid company, living or dead, with whom he associated slightly absurd; it was Mr Samgrass who was real, the rest were an insubstantial pageant. 15 He was the Victorian tourist, solid and patronising, for whose amuse- ment these foreign things were paraded. And there was something a little too brisk about his literary manners; I suspected the existence of a con- cealed typewriter somewhere in his panelled rooms.

EVELYN WAUGH: *Brideshead Revisited*

QUESTIONS:

1 What does the author mean by the following expressions:
   a genealogist
   a legitimist
   he loved dispossessed royalty
   to skate on thin ice
   to sail near the wind
   he was an expert in putative parentage
   the Victorian tourist, solid and patronising
   panelled rooms

2 Does the author show his feelings about people like Mr Samgrass? If so, how, and what are those feelings?

3 How much do we learn from the passage about Mr Samgrass's appearance? What aspects of Mr Samgrass's character really interest the author?

4 What details of Mr Samgrass's behaviour does the author single out in order to define his character? How does his choice of detail and his description through use of vocabulary influence the reader's feelings about Mr Samgrass?

5 Is Mr Samgrass the kind of person you would like to meet? Give your reasons.

6 Using this passage as a model, write a description of a clergyman, schoolmaster, public official, army officer, or bank manager whose character resembles Mr Samgrass's.

PASSAGE 41*b*

Noticing this I missed what Elizabeth said next, which I was sorry for when I saw the man she was now wanting Jean and me to meet. His mouth, which had all the mobility of a partly-collapsed inner-tube, was incompletely encircled by a brownish grime of stubble; his greying hair came horizontally out of his scalp and projected in two stiff, inorganic 5 shelves over his ears; his eyes, long and heavily-lidded, glared a little. He was wearing a formal dark suit, which evidently caused him rancour, and his hands, like the hands of all the men I'd met that evening, were shaking. More important than any of this, I knew him: name, Gareth Probert; occupation, poetry-writing office-worker. 10

'We're rather proud of this man just now,' Elizabeth told Jean and me. After explaining who he was, she went on straight away to give a mixture of fact and conjecture about a book of poems Probert might be going to have published. The central or connecting theme of this work, it turned out, was an adolescent's discovery of the meaning of Wales. Quite 15 soon Elizabeth was lavishing on its author flattery so gross and prolonged that I was afraid he mightn't like it. He seemed to like it.

KINGSLEY AMIS: *That Uncertain Feeling*

QUESTIONS:

1 Give a word or phrase of similar meaning to:
   grime (*line* 4)   rancour (*line* 7)
   stubble (*line* 4)   conjecture (*line* 13)
   glared (*line* 6)   to lavish (*line* 16)

2 How does the author manage to convey his disrespect for the character he is describing?

3 What impression do you get of the character's personality from the external details mentioned of his appearance?

4 Have you ever met anyone whose character resembled that of Gareth Probert? If so, describe meeting him or her in two paragraphs modelled on the above passage.

5 What do we learn about the narrator from this passage?

6 What tricks of style in this passage turn an accurate visual description of a credible human being into a satire on a certain type of *poseur*?

PASSAGE 41C
Ten men of revolting appearance were approaching from the drive. They were low of brow, crafty of eye, and crooked of limb. They advanced huddled together with the loping tread of wolves, peering about them furtively as they came, as though in constant terror of ambush; they slavered at their mouths, which hung loosely over their receding chins,   5
while each clutched under his ape-like arm a burden of curious and unaccountable shape. On seeing the Doctor they halted and edged back, those behind squinting and moulting over their companions' shoulders.
                         EVELYN WAUGH: *Decline and Fall*

QUESTIONS:

1 How does the author's choice of vocabulary describing the movements of the characters reinforce the impression he wants to give of their inner nature?

2 What do you think these men were going to do? And what do you think the 'burden of curious and unaccountable shape' was?

3 Use the following words or phrases from the passage in sentences of your own, showing that you know their meaning:
   revolting   furtively
   crafty   to slaver
   huddled together   to clutch
   loping   to squint
   to peer about

4 Passage 41a and this passage are by the same author. Do you find anything in this passage which would indicate that they are?

5 Describe a village band arriving to play at a local festival
(a) straightforwardly,
(b) ironically.

PASSAGE 41d

With this incongruity in his mind, he walked about till he came to a great bronze panel on which were sculptured in high relief representations of the different kinds of men who had served in the last war. There were soldiers laden with the panoply of battle, so thickly thewed and tall that they could without stumbling carry rifle and three hundred cartridges, a great pack, a steel helmet, and a cartload of Picardy mud; there were sailors, severe of gaze to watch for periscope and reef and mine, and wrapped in oilskins against the bitterness of the North Sea; there were subalterns whose youth was grim, not gay; young airmen who had lived like hawks and poets and paladins and died the quick death of dragon-flies; there were solid stubborn ploughmen transformed by discipline to grandeur; there were nurses of gentle gallantry and grave beauty – and leading them in their unplanned path to the laurel-grove a piper marched – O glory and grace of the McCrimmons! – whose pibroch like an evening wave lipped all the gleaming bronze.

Standing before the strong heroism of these figures Magnus began to think of living men, and imagined a panel that should represent, not his countrymen who had died, but his countrymen who still existed. Piety, reverence, and glory ran from his mind, and so violent was their outgoing that the inrush of contrary emotions was savage, and he filled his imagined frieze with the ignoblest spawning of the time: weaklings, fools, and knaves; dullards, fat profiteers, and starving dole men; the chatterers, the rushers to and fro, the self-doubters and the self-satisfied; with snivelling piety and supercilious unbelief; with empty heads and full bellies; with ossified Tories and rattle-brained Socialists; with pimping prettiness and ugliness too mean to hide itself; with cowardice, hypocrisy, greed, stupidity, and all the other ailments and emblems and deformities that satirists, from the earliest time, have discovered to be the characteristic features of humanity.

ERIC LINKLATER: *Magnus Merriman*

QUESTIONS:

1 Examine carefully all the abstract nouns and adjectives and verb participles used as adjectives in this passage. Find out the meaning of those you do not know, and explain why you think the author used the following:

spawning (*line* 21)   supercilious (*line* 24)

snivelling (*lines* 23–24)   ossified (*line* 25)
What words might he have used instead of these?

2 How does the author use contrast, and particularly antithesis, to contribute to the effect of his passage?

3 Describe any public memorial you know
(*a*) in the manner of the first paragraph
(*b*) in the manner of the second.

This passage is a sensitive and vivid description of a simple natural phenomenon – a butterfly feeding. But the butterfly, in the context of the novel from which the passage is taken, evokes feelings symbolic of deeper issues that are cruelly appropriate to the two lovers who are observing it. Thus the paragraph starts off by being a purely visual description in terms of colour and detail; the development becomes almost a miniature allegory, and is doubly symbolic. In the first place the symbolism is objective, but because the symbolic interpretation laid by the author on the butterfly's action is what it is, the butterfly becomes symbolic of the two lovers themselves; *its* 'tireless concupiscence' reflects *their* tireless concupiscence; *its* 'aimed and accurate greed' reflects *theirs*. So the structure of the paragraph hinges on the fourth sentence, and the vocabulary changes from the objective vocabulary of form and visual quality to the abstract vocabulary of emotion, desire, and action.

PASSAGE 42

New from the chrysalis, bright and still untattered, a swallowtail had settled on one of the clusters of mauve flowers. The pale yellow wings, with their black markings, their eyes of blue and crimson, were fully outstretched in the sunlight. Their forward edges had the curve of a sabre, and from the tips the line slanted elegantly backwards towards the two 5
projecting tails of the lower wings. The whole butterfly seemed the symbol, the hieroglyph of gay and airy speed. The spread wings were tremulous as though from an uncontrollable excess of life, of passionate energy. Rapidly, ravenously, but with an extraordinary precision of purposeful movement, the creature plunged its uncoiled proboscis into 10
the tiny trumpet-shaped flowers that composed the cluster. A quick motion of the head and thorax, and the probe had been thrust home, to be withdrawn a moment later and plunged as swiftly and unerringly between the lips of another and yet another flower, until all the blooms within striking distance had been explored and it was necessary to hasten 15
on towards a yet unrifled part of the cluster. Again, again, to the very quick of the expectant flowers, deep to the sheathed and hidden sources of that hot intoxicating sweetness! Again, again, with what tireless concupiscence, what an intense passion of aimed and accurate greed!

ALDOUS HUXLEY: *Eyeless in Gaza*

QUESTIONS:

1 Examine the adverbs in this passage, and note which verbs Huxley used them with. How many of them seem to you to be unexpected ones in their context?

2 Explain what the author means by the following terms:
still untattered (*line* 1)
cluster (*line* 2)
the curve of a sabre (*line* 4)
hieroglyph (*line* 7)
gay and airy speed (*line* 7)
the probe had been thrust home (*line* 12)
unerringly (*line* 13)
within striking distance (*line* 15)
a yet unrifled part (*line* 16)
the sheathed and hidden sources (*line* 17)
tireless concupiscence (*lines* 18–19)
aimed and accurate greed (*line* 19)

3 Find examples in the passage of:
alliteration,
rhetorical repetition,
projection of emotion on to things incapable of feeling it.
What effect is the author trying to create by using these tricks of style?

4 What effect would the substitution of the following words have on the passage?
(*a*) *clumps* for *clusters* (*line* 2)
(*b*) *urbanely* for *elegantly* (*line* 5)
(*c*) *trivial* for *airy* (*line* 7)
(*d*) *convulsive* for *tremulous* (*line* 8)
(*e*) *dipped* for *plunged* (*line* 10)
(*f*) *inserted* for *thrust home* (*line* 12)
(*g*) *infallibly* for *unerringly* (*line* 13)
(*h*) *unransacked* for *unrifled* (*line* 16)
(*i*) *watchful* for *expectant* (*line* 17)
(*j*) *inebriating* for *intoxicating* (*line* 18)

5 Think of two or three natural phenomena, the observation of which might evoke some kind of emotive symbolism in the spectator. Now write a paragraph, modelled structurally on Huxley's, depicting *one* of them.

(about 150 words)

(Examples: a thunderstorm, a waterfall, a bird's flight, etc.)

§43 *The development of the argument within the paragraph*

The paragraphs in this section illustrate the various ways of developing an argument from the first sentence. This is often a weakness of students' writing; they tend to imagine that a paragraph consists of a string of loosely related facts or ideas, images or examples, and make no real attempt to bring them together into a coherent entity. All these passages are taken from essays on more or less general philosophical, scientific or social issues; the examples given in them serve only to illustrate a general point in the argument. The student should note carefully how slight differences in style and approach differentiate them from one another, although all three are built up similarly.

PASSAGE 43*a*

All men are snobs about something. One is almost tempted to add: There is nothing about which men cannot feel snobbish. But this would doubtless be an exaggeration. There are certain disfiguring and mortal diseases about which there has probably never been any snobbery. I cannot imagine, for example, that there are any leprosy snobs. More pictur- 5
esque diseases, even when they are dangerous, and less dangerous diseases, particularly when they are the diseases of the rich, can be and very frequently are a source of snobbish self-importance. I have met several adolescent consumption-snobs, who thought that it would be romantic to fade away in the flower of youth, like Keats or Marie Bashkirtseff. Alas, 10
the final stages of the consumptive fading are generally a good deal less romantic than these ingenuous young tubercle-snobs seem to imagine. To any who has actually witnessed these final stages, the complacent poeticisings of these adolescents must seem as exasperating as they are profoundly pathetic. In the case of those commoner disease-snobs, whose 15
claim to distinction is that they suffer from one of the maladies of the rich, exasperation is not tempered by very much sympathy. People who possess sufficient leisure, sufficient wealth, not to mention sufficient health, to go travelling from spa to spa, from doctor to fashionable doctor, in search of cures from problematical diseases (which, in so far 20
as they exist at all, probably have their source in overeating) cannot expect us to be very lavish in our solicitude and pity.

ALDOUS HUXLEY: *Selected Snobberies*

QUESTIONS:

1 Examine the structure of this paragraph, paying particular attention to the rhythm and construction of the sentences, the transition from general statement to particular example, and noting how and when the author uses vocabulary, rhythm, and variation in order to inject irony into his argument.

2 Does anything about the paragraph seem to you to indicate that the author himself is something of a snob?

3 Write two further paragraphs to the one quoted, continuing the passage as you think the author might have developed his theme. The three paragraphs together should constitute a complete short essay, and should be of similar length to one another.

4 Write one paragraph, built up on exactly the same pattern, on any *one* of the following subjects:

Laziness	The English Sunday
Old Cars	Popular Fashions
Insects	

5 Give a word or phrase of similar meaning to:

disfiguring (*line* 3)	exasperating (*line* 14)
adolescent (*line* 9)	leisure (*line* 18)
the flower of youth (*line* 10)	spa (*line* 19)
complacent (*line* 13)	solicitude (*line* 22)

6 Explain the difference in meaning between:
(a) *mortal, fatal, lethal* and *deadly*
(b) *sound, sane* and *healthy*
(c) *pitying, pathetic* and *sympathetic*
(d) *wealth, riches* and *opulence*

PASSAGE 43*b*

Each animal has some special ways of conducting its life. The cow and sheep have special stomachs that digest grass. The tiger has its teeth, the elephant its trunk and its teeth, and so on. What then are the special characteristics of modern man? Surely the chief one is that of co-operation between individuals. Man's large brain is used to develop an intricate 5 social system, based mainly on communication by words. Man has many other special features, such as good eyes for getting information, and good hands for doing intricate things. But it is chiefly co-operation that enables him to obtain a living for more than 2,000,000,000 human beings scattered over nearly all regions of the earth. Sophocles expressed it long ago 10 in a few words when he said: 'Of all the wonders none is more wonderful than man – who has learned the arts of speech, of windswift thought, and of living in neighbourliness.' These are indeed the matters that must chiefly engage the serious student of man. Of course on this subject of human co-operation a vast mass of knowledge has been collected by 15 generations of anthropologists, psychologists, sociologists, and others. But there is, even yet, no coherent body of knowledge about the biology of man that sets him in his proper place in the living world. Biologists are only now beginning to study what may be called the higher attributes of man, his language, his social behaviour, his religion, and his science. We 20 may find valuable new ideas by applying the biological method to the very highest of our activities and correlating these with the study of the organ that mediates them – the brain.

J. Z. YOUNG: Doubt and Certainty in Science

QUESTIONS:

1 What features in the exposition of this paragraph suggest to you that although it deals with an advanced subject, it was intended to be understood by a non-expert audience?

2 This paragraph is more loosely constructed than Passage 43a. Which sentences, if any, could be cut from it *in their entirety* without weakening the argument? What do these dispensable sentences add to the paragraph?

3 Write sentences of your own which the author might have inserted in the following places to develop various lines of his argument further.
(*a*) After 'good hands for doing intricate things' (*lines* 8–9)
(*b*) after 'engage the serious student of man' (*line* 14)
Why do you think the author did not proceed further along those lines in his actual text?

4 Give a word or phrase of similar meaning to:
intricate (*line* 8)
engage (*line* 14)
no coherent body of knowledge (*line* 17)
correlating (*line* 22)

5 Do you agree with Professor Young's assertion that the chief characteristic of modern man 'is that of co-operation between individuals'? What other characteristics might he have emphasised as being the result of his possessing a large brain?

6 Use the following groups of words in contrasted sentences to show that you understand their differences in meaning:
(*a*) co-operation, collusion
(*b*) intricate, complicated, complex
(*c*) chiefly, mostly, generally
(*d*) coherent, united, integrated, integral

PASSAGE 43c
The growth and decay of a living organism is a real creation and a real perishing. You can say if you like that there is only a rearrangement of

pre-existing and imperishable parts. This may be true, but its truth is trivial when applied to living things, though useful within its own sphere in physics. The physicist in order to simplify his problems uses an ana- 5 lytic method; he considers successively smaller and smaller parts of the objects he studies until he comes down to the smallest parts of all. If the larger objects are random collections of the smaller ones, the method gives you all the information you can reasonably expect. But if a large object is an ordered collection of the parts, information about the parts in 10 isolation can never tell you everything about the whole collection except in the relatively uninteresting case where the order of the whole is merely a repetition of an order inherent in the parts. All the parts of a jigsaw puzzle laid out on a table can be said to contain the picture poten- tially, but you will not be able to see the picture until they are arranged 15 in order, so that it is accurate to say that the picture exists only when they are arranged in order, and not when they are put away in the box. There is here on a small scale real creation and perishing.

A. D. RITCHIE: *The Biological Approach to Philosophy*

QUESTIONS:

1 How does the illustration chosen – that of the jigsaw puzzle – illustrate the point that Professor Ritchie is trying to make with it?
2 What does he mean by *real creation*?
3 Is it possible to cut out any of the sentences in this paragraph without spoiling the progression of the argument? If so, which?
4 Describe the steps by which Professor Ritchie builds up his argument in this passage.

§44 *Beginning and ending an essay*

Many students find it difficult to begin an essay. In this section, the question paper comes first, as it deals with this topic. The texts, which are included as simple examples of final paragraphs from various essays, appear without comment or question. Students (and tutors) may feel encouraged to devise their own ways of studying and practising what may be learnt from them, according to their needs.

QUESTIONS:

1 The following sentences are taken from the beginnings of a number of essays. First of all, decide what subject the essay is about; then sketch out and write a paragraph developing the first sentence.
   (*a*) The problem of education is in the forefront of public attention at the present time, and the Government, like the country, has been seriously preoccupied with it.
   (*b*) It is obvious that there is a great deal of difference between being international and being cosmopolitan.
   (*c*) It is surely discreditable, under the age of thirty, not to be shy.
   (*d*) As I write, highly civilised human beings are flying overhead, trying to kill me.
   (*e*) There were six of them, the best and bravest of the hero's companions.
2 Take any one of the following sentences, and use it to begin the opening paragraph of an essay on *one* of the topics suggested. Make your paragraph about 100 words long.

SENTENCES:
   (*a*) Every time I arrive in England, whether by plane or boat, it is raining.
   (*b*) It is always difficult to understand why male politicians assume that women are unpractical.
   (*c*) It has been said that the characteristic sound of summer is the hum of insects, as the characteristic sound of spring is the singing of birds.
   (*d*) The world would be poor without the antics of clergymen.

TITLES
National Customs; Climate and Character; A Woman's Place is the Home;

Picnics; Professionalism; It is Better to Travel Hopefully than to Arrive; Modern Morality.

3   Write three different suitable opening sentences to an essay on any *one* of the following topics. One should be in the manner of a serious quasi-philosophic dissertation, one in the style of a conversational piece of belle-lettristic writing, and one in the style of a polemical attack. Then sketch out and continue *one* of your examples until you have a complete opening paragraph.

Street-lighting; Foreign Travel; The English Week-end; Prejudices; The Benefits of Idleness; Getting Up; Detective Stories.

Final paragraph from essays

PASSAGE 44*a*
Perhaps shyness is a purely Anglo-Saxon failing. I doubt whether even the tenderest of the Roman poets, whether Vergil even, was shy. Horace, as we know, was one large lump of bounce. Nor was Dante shy – disagreeable was Dante, but never shy. Ah, yes, – there is Racine. He at least was so shy that he ran away and hid himself at Port-Royal. But   5
then Racine, as M. Lemaître has remarked, stands apart. Yes, I think shyness is an Anglo-Saxon quality. And as such it should be honoured as a bond between the English-speaking nations.

HAROLD NICOLSON: *A Defence of Shyness*

PASSAGE 44*b*
Dickens is a baffling figure. There are moments when it seems that his chief purpose in writing was to put a spoke in the wheel of our literary aesthetics. We manage to include everybody but him; and we are inclined in our salad days to resent the existence of anybody who enters the scheme. That is why people tried to get rid of him by declaring that he   5
was not an artist. It was an odd way of predicating non-existence. Now it is going out of fashion, I suppose because it did not have the desired effect of annihilating Dickens; and also perhaps because simple people asked why the books of a man who was not an artist should have this curious trick of immortality. There was, alas, no answer. So we are begin-   10
ning to discover that Dickens *was* an artist, but, of course, only in parts. When we have discovered which are the parts we shall breathe again.

J. MIDDLETON MURRY: *Dickens*

PASSAGE 44*c*
He was the greatest teaching Editor I have ever known. He took as much pains with his writers as he did with the copy that was sent to Manchester nightly on the private wire. After a few months of the Bone treatment I was beginning to understand what criticism really meant.

Exactly thirty-three years ago, in late November, when the lamplight 5
along the Embankment was spilling gently into the river mist, the *Manchester Guardian* gave me a regular column called 'The Week on the Screen'. And that, my sincer[1] friend, is the way I became a film critic.

C. A. LEJEUNE: *The Shaping of a Critic*

[1] Sic! This paragraph is from a piece in *Time and Tide* (1955), and begins with a reference to a letter from a schoolboy who wrote to ask Miss Lejeune how she became a critic. He signed himself 'Yours sincerly'.

Part 3

SELF-EXPRESSION IN
A WIDER CONTEXT

Most students are required to write essays from a fairly early stage in their studies, and probably most teachers feel that the balance of aims in an essay should vary according to the linguistic level of the student. When one is learning a musical instrument, a good deal of time is spent in the early stages playing simple little tunes one knows almost by heart anyway, and this helps one acquire facility in understanding note-values, while at the same time requiring at any rate a little self-expression to be put into the performance of a tune whose musical meaning is already understood. At the same time scales and technical studies must be practised in order to master certain co-ordinative and muscular skills which will be needed, and which will become second nature later on. The musical value of these studies is usually infinitesimal. But – and here the analogy between learning an instrument and learning a language breaks down – one is rarely required to compose any music for one's instrument, showing that the underlying skills *and* theory have been mastered. That is reserved for the music student who intends to make a career of his art.

One may liken the technical studies to grammar or structure drills; one may liken the gradual development of comprehension exercises to the learning of one's 'pieces'. The process of writing an essay demands not only linguistic skill, but also the desire and ability to say something personal within the framework of a given form, *and to suit the form chosen to the type of material* presented. It is in this last respect that nearly all students come a cropper at some time. Harmony between what has to be said and the form in which it is cast is exceptionally rare.

Much of the trouble experienced by most students appears to arise from the fact that the conscious organisation of the material begins at far too early a stage in the actual writing of the essay; most students begin to plan their essay long before they have really searched their mind for ideas, and all too often the plan itself is of a completely stereotyped nature, suitable to some subjects, but utterly useless for others. A platitudinous definition is followed by a barren abstract argument about the true nature of the subject, with commonplace pros and cons, and the whole is rounded off by a facile and predictable conclusion.

The mastery of form is all too often neglected, simply because it is all too rarely recognised as a necessary skill to be learned. And it is a skill that can be learned. Sir Edward Elgar taught himself the craft of writing movements in sonata form by taking the opening *allegro* of Mozart's G Minor Symphony, analysing its structure, noting the proportions between exposition, development, restatement and coda, further subdividing the exposition into first and second subject, bridge passage, etc., carefully noting the modulations in the development section, how long the composer remained in any given key, and so on. He then wrote a movement based on exactly those proportions and relationships. It is quite possible that even if originality of thought cannot be acquired, mastery of form can, by a similar procedure in the study of essay-writing technique.

Paradoxically enough, it is form on the larger scale that is the easiest to acquire. This is why it has been asserted that most students began to plan their essay at far too early a stage in the writing of it. It is the minutiae of form – those details corresponding to developmental key-changes, the relative proportions between first subject, bridge passage, second subject, codetta, and cadential passage – which bother most students. And it is probable that they bother them because the students haven't really understood how they may develop their material.

The first thing to ensure is that the subjects set fall within the personal experience of the student; this is particularly so with students at inter-mediate level. It sounds a platitude – it *is* a platitude – but all the same, one does not place a subject within a student's range of experience simply by giving him a kind of blanket topic which it would require the wit of Bacon and the vocabulary of Shakespeare to encompass within 400 words – which is taken to be the normal length of an intermediate to advanced practice essay. Many students, confronted with a particular topic, groan that they know nothing about it. Yet a quarter of an hour with a pen in the student's hand, simply setting down the stream of ideas as they flow into his head – *whether or not they are immediately relevant to the essay topic* – will nearly always produce at least one, and usually two or three thoughts on the theme which are completely original *because they fall within the sphere of experience of the student himself and of no one else*. At the intermediate stage, then, subjects should be chosen which offer the student a chance to set down immediate and personal experiences of an unusual kind.

It is also at this stage, however, that the student must begin to master for-mal essay construction, and must therefore learn the most suitable method of developing what may well be an entirely personal opening sentence. This is why there were in the previous section a number of examples of paragraphs built up in different ways, setting the students exercises in imitating or parodying the form and style of those paragraphs, selecting what it is hoped is suitable material for the treatment and form of paragraph suggested. The principal danger in the 'personal-experience' approach is of course that the student will produce a set of jolly little anecdotes vaguely connected with the theme, but not an essay.

So to come to the second factor: the student must learn to arrange his concrete experiences so that each anecdote becomes quasi-symbolic; it acts as a single definite example of a general proposition. This is where the gap occurs between immediate personal experience, which most students, given practice, can usually express interestingly and fluently, and the setting of that experience into a general pattern of thought. The problem here, then, is to set subjects which allow the student to generalise from personal and immediate experiences without becoming on the one hand platitudinous, and on the other frivolous or bombastic. One successful method of doing this is to ask students to write their own continuation or conclusion to a given paragraph from, or incomplete version of, an essay written by some master of the form, or, if the essay chosen for study is a light-hearted one, to write an additional paragraph which might without difficulty be inserted in the middle without spoiling the shape of the original.

Once this technique has been mastered, the student may go one stage further. Just as the budding piano virtuoso aims at mastering the *Appassionata* or one of Liszt's transcendental studies, so the advanced student should be able to attempt what we may call a 'virtuoso' essay. The virtuosity may consist either in the masterly handling of an unpromising subject, or the brilliant display of linguistic skill when dealing with a trivial one. Only the most exceptional students can display it in writing profound and strikingly original disquisitions on well-worn themes, and if they are as original as that, it is unlikely that any teacher will have much to teach them about the construction of an essay; their very originality will create new forms for their thought.

The first approach may surely be practised by making the student write essays where he is required to be a kind of devil's advocate. The main danger in this is of course that there is a tendency to facetiousness, once he knows that what he is saying will not be taken seriously anyway. The gap between wit and facetiousness is so small that it is not always kept open even by native writers. It may be argued that it is dangerous to attempt to make overseas students write rather self-consciously witty essays. But why not? It is surely no more absurd then expecting them to write seriously on some world-shattering theme which they all too often have neither the knowledge nor the vocabulary to cope with adequately.

(There is a world of difference between *discussing* such a theme in class, when each student present can contribute to the flow of ideas and the teacher can help out with vocabulary difficulties, and *writing* on such a theme in an essay, alone, isolated from dictionary, class-mates and tutor alike.) And the attempt to write in a new manner eventually helps to expand not only their means of expression, but their outlook.

The problem of transforming facetiousness into wit is really rather a matter of getting the student to understand and appreciate shades of meaning in vocabulary, and of approaching themes with generally accepted ideas in an iconoclastic way. A good two-fifths of Wilde's epigrams, for example, are the result of an absurd inversion of a commonplace:

'I can sympathise with anything except suffering'.
'I can resist anything except temptation'.
'The gods bestowed on Max the gift of perpetual old age'.
'He hasn't an enemy in the world, and none of his friends like him'.
'I suppose I shall have to die beyond my means'.

Other types of epigram, being the result of unexpected and telling juxtaposition of words of similar rhythmic balance and internal assonance (unspeakable – uneatable) are possible only to the quick-witted, but the careful study of detailed choice of vocabulary and sentence rhythm can yield a lot to the conscientious student. Once he has learned to appreciate it, he should want to learn to understand *how* the effect is created. And he will notice that in the best cases, either the exuberance (e.g. Linklater) or the brevity (Wilde; Shaw) enhance the effect of the thought.

Sullivan is once reputed to have told Dame Ethel Smythe when she showed him a composition: 'An artist has to make a penny do the work of a shilling, and here you go chucking away sovereigns.' This is the converse of the student's inability to produce succinctness – his inability to develop promising ideas. All too often students produce quite penetrating and shrewd observations in their essays, abandon them without development, and rush on to another, usually far less interesting theme. Again, the conscious planning stage takes place too early. The striking ideas can, and of course should, be developed. How one writer does this, using wit, rhythm and irony to develop a trite, bald statement, we have already tried to show in Passage 43*a*. It should not be beyond the wit of the intelligent advanced student or his teacher to note and analyse similar material elsewhere, and to imitate the manner to the best of his ability. There is no copyright on good phrases, and even if the student feels uneasy about 'lifting' a telling phrase from a writer, he may always acknowledge his debt by mentioning who coined the phrase. And there is certainly no copyright on good methods. You cannot take out a patent on paragraph structure. It is hoped the examples in the previous section of the course have helped to show what can be done in the way of development of material.

What is clear from most of the chosen examples is that few of them start with a definition. But nearly all of them start with a plain, colourless matter-of-fact statement. And nearly all of them expand that statement methodically and colourfully, the details of the expansion being chosen with care, so that they are not merely arresting, but also typical. So direct description and imagery complement one another.

Most students pay far too little attention to the effect that rhythm may have on their sentence and paragraph structure – the placing of subordinate clauses in relation to the main clause, and indeed the rhythm of various near-synonyms which affects the balance of the sentence. The introduction of one simple bisyllable – *doubtless* – into the third sentence of Passage 43a coloured the whole of the rest of the sentence by turning a plain factual exposition into an ironic, not to say sarcastic, exposure of human failings. But at least as important as this was the placing of the word *doubtless* in the sentence. Try placing it in any of the other accepted positions and see how the balance of the sentence, and its ironic flavour, are disturbed.

The entire aim of learning either structures or vocabulary is to permit clear and precise expression of the writer's thoughts. One of the most spectacular military disasters in Britain's history was apparently caused by an ambiguity in the wording of Lord Raglan's order to Lord Lucan at Balaclava, which resulted in the Light Brigade's famous charge. One of the best ways of making students aware of the importance of precision in vocabulary is the 'Blank Dictation', where certain key words are left out, and the students required to supply their own suggestions as to what the omissions might be. The more precise in meaning and striking in flavour the words omitted, the more likely the students are to appreciate the discrepancy between their own choice and the original.

The study of vocabulary is a severe discipline in itself, and if properly attempted, will take up a large proportion of the advanced student's time. At this level it is just not enough to give an explanation of each word, and then see the student write down a more or less appropriate translation in his own language. One suggestion is that the vocabulary section of the student's notes should have not two, but five columns, arranged as follows:

NEW WORD | CONTEXT IN WHICH FOUND | DEFINITION |
TRANSLATION | NEAR-SYNONYMS

It follows from this that the student will require, not merely a good bilingual dictionary, but also a reputable English one (*The Advanced Learner's*, for example), and Roget's *Thesaurus*. We have always found that it is vitally necessary for the student to remember the context in which any new word was first found; certainly the phrase or clause, and even occasionally the entire sentence, and, if possible, to note further occurrences of the same word when encountered later, also in context.

The phasing of vocabulary-learning, and of the types of word learned and used, can be easily and usefully geared to the development of the type of theme set and essay required. At the earliest stages most vocabulary is of a visual or aural kind, standing for what is perceived readily and frequently through the senses. The next stage involves the examination and analysis of what has been perceived through the senses; this in turn involves the student in an attempt to define precisely something that he knows he has experienced, but lacks the ability to analyse, describe, and convey to others. He is at this stage inclined to use words or phrases like 'I enjoyed it', 'It was nice', and so on. Very often he can set out the details of what appealed to him but cannot say exactly what appeal they made. So what is an emotive or intuitive grasp of his reactions needs to be communicated. This process can only be assisted by the development of his emotive vocabulary. Beyond this comes the stage when he can define and abstract what he has seen, heard, felt or reacted to, compare it with other valid and describable experiences, and reflect on and draw conclusions from the comparisons. The essay should test him in his ability to perform all these six processes, and his vocabulary at any stage in his study of the language should be matched to the subject-range placed at his disposal. Obviously, the more advanced the student, the more likely the subject will be to fall into the last category.

Ending an essay is always the most difficult thing of all. It is difficult enough for an English-speaking person, and so a solution is offered. Occasionally, a circular essay, closing with the same sentence as it began, is effective, but normally, the final paragraph should merely draw together the main points made, and, if possible, close the work with a bang – not a grand amen, but a simple and emphatic dominant-tonic cadence. The solution is given by offering a list of possible essay subjects that it is thought conform to the principles set out above. The list contains seventy-five specimen subjects; twenty-five are considered to be suitable for intermediate students, twenty-five for intermediate-advanced, and twenty-five for advanced ones.

Some possible essay topics [*intermediate*]
1 Window-shopping.
2 A person I shall never forget.
3 My favourite character in history.
4 The art of writing letters.
5 An ideal house.
6 Animals in captivity.
7 Desert Island Discs.
8 A visit to the theatre.
9 After the ball was over.
10 Old cars.
11 The person I should least like to be.
12 The pleasures of Winter.
13 A book I shall never read again.
14 Going to a party.
15 An ideal politician.
16 Keeping up with the Joneses.
17 A crime I should like to commit.
18 A photo-album.
19 Spring, the sweet spring, is the year's pleasant king.
20 When good Americans die, they go to Paris. (*Wilde*)
21 Twenty years of romance make a woman look like a ruin; but twenty years of marriage make her look something like a public building. (*Wilde*)
22 England is the most class-ridden country under the sun. (*Orwell*)
23 To a poet, nothing can be useless. (*Johnson*)
24 If a thing's worth doing, it's worth doing badly. (*Gustav Holst*)
25 A novel is a mirror walking along a main road. (*Stendahl*)

Some possible essay topics [*intermediate to advanced*]
1 England, the snail that's shod with lightning.
2 Are we all born mad?
3 Morality is a matter of social convenience, not of absolute authority.
4 The English take their pleasures sadly.
5 Necessity knows no law.
6 Speech was given to man to disguise his thoughts.
7 Man is man and master of his fate. (*Tennyson*)
8 A king may make a nobleman, but he cannot make a gentleman. (*Burke*)
9 You can never plan the future by the past. (*Burke*)
10 Spare the rod and spoil the child.
11 Life is one long process of getting tired. (*Samuel Butler*)
12 Men will wrangle for religion; write for it; fight for it; anything but – live for it. (*Charles Colton*)
13 Organized waste is the basis of modern prosperity. (*Aldous Huxley*)
14 Beauty is in the eye of the beholder.
15 Superstition is the religion of feeble minds. (*Burke*)

16 All men are equal, but some are more equal than others.

17 The price of liberty is eternal vigilance.

18 Democracy substitutes election by the incompetent many for appointment by the corrupt few. (*Shaw*)

19 Literature flourishes best when it is half a trade and half an art. (*W. R. Inge*)

20 An honest God is the noblest work of man. (*R. G. Ingersoll*)

21 The trouble with modern commercial life is that it doesn't believe in principle; it only believes in interest.

22 The world is too much with us. (*Wordsworth*)

23 A pity beyond all telling is hid in the heart of love. (*Yeats*)

24 Scratch the Christian and you find the pagan – spoiled. (*Israel Zangwill*)

25 All things are artificial; for Nature is the art of God. (*Sir Thomas Browne*)

Some possible essay topics [advanced]

1 Our society is in truth an anti-society, since the exercise of power for its own sake is its prime, and ultimately its sole, function.

2 It is a pity that man cannot at the same time be impressive and truthful. (*E. M. Forster*)

3 A society with plenty of snobberies is like a dog with plenty of fleas; it is unlikely to become comatose. (*Aldous Huxley*)

4 The truth is rarely pure and never simple. (*Oscar Wilde*)

5 Life is an incurable disease. (*Abraham Cowley*)

6 It is much safer to obey than rule. (*St Thomas à Kempis*)

7 Be good, sweet maid, and let who will be clever. (*Kingsley*)

8 There is no scandal like rags, nor any crime so shameful as poverty. (*Farquhar*)

9 Education makes people easy to lead, but difficult to drive; easy to govern, but impossible to enslave.

10 There is no road or ready way to virtue. (*Sir Thomas Browne*)

11 Love ceases to be a pleasure when it ceases to be a secret. (*Aphra Behn*)

12 Women run to extremes; they are either better or worse than men. (*la Bruyère*)

13 Dictators ride to and fro upon tigers from which they dare not dismount. (*Churchill*)

14 No man can serve two masters. (*St Matthew* 6: 24)

15 Envy and wrath shorten the life. (*Ecclesiasticus* 30: 24)

16 He who can, does; he who cannot, teaches. (*Shaw*)

17 There is only one religion, though there are a hundred versions of it. (*Shaw*)

18 A little sincerity is a dangerous thing, and a great deal of it is absolutely fatal. (*Wilde*)

19 Poverty is no disgrace to a man, but it is confoundedly inconvenient. (*Sidney Smith*)

20 Beauty is truth, truth beauty. (*Keats*)

21 Security is mortals' chiefest enemy. (*Shakespeare*)

22 Man's a ribald; man's a rake; man is Nature's sole mistake. (*Gilbert*)

23 If one judges love by the majority of its effects, it is more like hatred than friendship. (*la Rochefoucauld*)

24 We may give advice, but we can never prompt behaviour. (*la Rochefoucauld*)

25 The secret of the arts is to correct Nature. (*Voltaire*)

It is quite useless for any student to be able to write a flawless essay if he is incapable of expressing himself accurately in spoken discussion on a serious topic. By the time he is in an advanced class, self-expression should be so spontaneous that the spoken word is as readily usable as the written. In advanced classes of mature interests, it should be possible for students themselves to run the discussion.

But the old-fashioned 'conversation' approach simply will not do. It is a self-indulgence on the part of student and teacher alike simply to chat merrily away (such chatter usually degenerates anyway into a dialogue between one student and the teacher – or, worse still, into a garrulous monologue *by* the teacher). But it is equally frustrating to spontaneous expression if the teacher holds up the discussion to correct every mistake of self-expression made by a student, even in the gentlest and most tactful manner. Either the discussion will cease to flow, or the correction will pass by unnoticed because the student is so interested in *what* is being said that he is not interested in *how* it is said.

Ideally, the discussion should allow the students self-expression on a topic that ought to interest them, should bring them to realise where the gaps lie in their structural or vocabulary repertoire, should offer them a chance to pit their minds against one another in argument, and should give them an opportunity to remove other people's misconceptions about their own country or people and to reconsider their own perhaps mistaken ideas about a subject or attitude. To do this it is clear that the teacher should choose not only the topic itself carefully, but also the aspects of the topic that will prove most fruitful for discussion in a particular class. He should also be well aware of the structures and vocabulary that will present difficulty during the period, and prepare exercises for practising them. This means that the preparation of the discussion is a far more serious matter than is often realised. While many discussions do arise spontaneously out of the work done or the texts worked over, a prepared discussion can often cover more linguistic ground in forty-five minutes than a formal course can in a week, simply because if the students express themselves fluently, they will also make mistakes spontaneously, *and the mistakes will always form a pattern.* And the pattern will naturally reflect the students' needs. And just as it is far quicker to say something than to write it, so the tempo of practice will be more intensive.

Yet what is to be done with the strong, silent student who will not say anything? The following procedure, which has been found reasonably successful over a period of years, may help to meet his needs too.

First of all, the teacher's work must be done thoroughly *before* anyone utters a word, and his presence during the discussion itself should be as unobtrusive as possible. Indeed, as already stated, he should if possible not even take the chair. His job is to listen carefully to what the students have to say, and to listen with two things in mind:

(1) What mistakes are the students making in the actual English? These should be *immediately* and carefully noted, classified, and matched with practice exercises for later correction. The remedial exercises may be given either the same day or on the following day, *and should be followed up after a suitable interval.*

(2) What misconceptions, either factual or 'philosophical' (i.e. logical, aesthetic, ethical, etc.), is the chairman allowing to pass. Is the discussion getting away from the point? If so, does this matter, or should it be tactfully redirected back to the central theme?

Clearly the tape-recorder is a valuable – indeed almost an essential – aid here. Its inhibiting effect is soon lost as the discussion gets under way. Afterwards the teacher should play the discussion through, marking the cases of false emphasis, wrong interpretation of vocabulary, or wrong structures, either for future reference, or for later playback as illustrations to his remedial work.

The preparation of the discussion may be divided under two heads: (1) preparation of the theme; and (2) preparation of the vocabulary and/or structural work. The former is reasonably straightforward, though not always easy; the latter tricky. One can never predict with certainty what a student will say about a given topic.

The preparation of the theme involves planning the outline of what is in effect a forty-five minute lecture, given spontaneously by the class as a group, covering varying aspects of the theme, and progressing by the counterpointing of one opinion by a contrasting or contradictory one. Thus the teacher's guiding-points, the headings around which the discussion must revolve, should be controversial – if not indeed provocative – and should imply more than they state. There is no harm in their being ambiguous; the literal-minded student will probably draw attention to it if they are, and the more imaginative one will re-interpret them in his own way, often a way strikingly and fruitfully different from that intended by the teacher.

The first sub-heading should clearly be introductory, and the last in the nature of a summary of the topic. In a discussion intended to last three-quarters of an hour, the most suitable number of sub-headings is probably about five. They should be given to the class on the day pre-ceding the discussion itself, and the class should be required to spend at least part of its homework formulating its ideas about different aspects of the topic. It happens very rarely indeed that no single one of the sub-headings is of any interest at all even to the most reticent student.

Hand-in-hand with this goes the preparation of the vocabulary re-quired. This will vary, naturally, according to the topic. It may consist in the presentation and assimilation of technical terms (e.g. when discuss-ing a performance of a play, such words as *lighting, backcloth, posture, diction*, etc.) or it may include clarification of confusing terms (e.g. the difference between *divorce, separation* and *annulment*, or *space, room* and *place*). With experience, the teacher can usually warn the students of the more obvious pitfalls.

Structural preparation is much more difficult. Even so, certain subjects (*If I were a millionaire*; *What has gone wrong with the United Nations?*; *Why do so many people reject modern art?*) can be arranged so that the topic, or better still, the sub-headings, will, by their very phrasing, induce the students to express themselves in certain structures. Again, the teacher's job should be to remind the students beforehand of the pitfalls – but *not* to correct their mistakes during the discussion if he can possibly avoid doing so.

The amount and the kind of preparation that should be made by the students themselves must of course be carefully controlled by the teacher. Obviously a planned discussion which consists of a series of set speeches read from paper, or from notes, in a monotone, with false word-grouping, is useless. It lacks spontaneity, and it is usually incomprehensible. Even so, the students often fail to realise what is entailed in preparing for a discussion, and a fair number regard discussion-preparation as a soft option for homework.

Having sorted out their feelings and thoughts on the topic presented, they must then work out the clearest and most precise way of saying what they feel and think. This involves a good deal of vocabulary pre-paration. They may not have the imagination to think out what kind of expressions, structures or idioms they may require, and so it is the teacher's job to suggest fields of vocabulary and idiom that they may find useful. (NOT the actual vocabulary itself; this is doing the student's job for him. The exception to this principle of course, as we have implied above, is in the use of technical terms.) The vocabulary looked up should be tabulated and studied in the way we have suggested in the previous section on essay-writing, and the student should make sure that he has the vocabulary he has learnt firmly in his mind for use in the discussion. It doesn't matter if he drags any number of words or phrases into the discussion by the hair, provided that he can in some way justify their use and explain their meaning to those of his fellow students who do not understand them. The teacher might do worse than to challenge the exuberantly enthusiastic student on such topics occasionally during the discussion itself.

They should also be encouraged to think of possible objections to their own viewpoint – again acting on the 'devil's advocate' pattern. They should consider whether a sincerely held view, forcefully expressed, may offend the susceptibilities of some of their fellow students, and, if such is the case, how the expression of the view can be made without watering down but without making it seem offensive. And they often need reminding that words like 'stupid', 'crazy', and grotesque generalisations on national character, outlook or history have no place in an ordered and sensible discussion, however heated it may become.

Preparation of the structures is more the teacher's job, of course. Ideally, of course, the structures should be so 'planted' in the themes that each sub-heading offers the chance to practise one particular structure and that the structures concerned are those which the teacher has been explaining and the class practising during the grammar-lessons that week. Incidentally, the students' mistakes, if not corrected at once, nearly always offer a valuable clue to what needs doing in the next week's structural work.

The discussion is linguistically quite useless without a follow-up. It has already been said what one part of this should consist of – correction of, and remedial exercises on, faulty structures and use of vocabulary. The expression of ideas must be reinforced in the written field by the setting of a suitable essay subject relating to, but not identical with, that of the main discussion topic. It is left to the teacher's common sense, of course, to decide whether the essay topic should touch on a subject neglected in the actual discussion, or whether, at the risk of boring the students, he should require them to investigate a well-worn subject still further.

In the case of the ideas expressed, the follow-up is more difficult. Here, we suggest, the best procedure is to approach the matter indirectly. If wildly wrong-headed ideas have been expressed, a comprehension passage should be easily found which, if carefully studied, may help eradicate them through presenting convincingly the correct, or at any rate a more reasonable, point of view. We have ourselves found more than once that the precise and spontaneous expression of a point of view by an intelligent student has caused us to reconsider our own attitude to some topics.

Strangely enough, faults of pronunciation – particularly of intonation and the strengthening of weak forms – very often seem to disappear in discussions. This is not to say that students lose their charming accents and faults of pronunciation; but these faults tend to become restricted to particular aspects – vowel quantities, rhythms and stresses. If the discussion becomes heated, it is surprising how English the intonation patterns very often become, patterns which the presence of that usual visual aid, the printed book, often upsets completely.

It is of course essential that students should be introduced to the technique of proper discussion from an early stage in their studies. The difficulty in less advanced classes is usually a variant of the *si jeunesse savait, si vieillesse pouvait* theme; i.e. the intelligent and intellectually alive elementary student is frustrated from handling worthwhile topics by lack of vocabulary and structures. At an advanced level, the trouble is more often one of lack of interest in the topic being discussed, or simple inhibiting self-consciousness.

The best way of overcoming these difficulties seems to be some form of programming the discussions so that various students in the class are given a greater or smaller opportunity to express their opinions week by week. It is reasonably simple to do this; it is rather more difficult to programme the discussions so that they lead on week by week from simple, everyday themes to those with profound implications. Nor should the rather more light-hearted, not to say flippant, theme be overlooked. There is no need for the teacher to get vexed if the discussion shows a tendency to become flippant, provided that a flippant approach can be reconciled with certain aspects of the theme under discussion. What is far more dangerous is the solemn pontificating that sometimes takes place when students are discussing something relatively unimportant. This is where the student-chairman situation sometimes breaks down, and it is the teacher's duty to intervene if he thinks that either of these two risks is being run. Because a discussion is carefully planned, it need not be solemn.

Each of the structural exercises in this course has included a number of possible discussion topics. Most of these have been of a serious nature, but most teachers – and many students – will be able to supplement them with others more light-hearted, or more relevant. To close with, here is an example of a set of headings from one planned discussion topic which the author has always found stimulates a class so much that it is usually very difficult to bring the discussion to a close – namely, Education itself.

Topic of discussion

Is modern education a waste of time?

Structures practised

Prepositions and conjunctions of time and age.
Final clauses. Modal verbs – Sequence 2.

Vocabulary areas developed

Types of school (primary, secondary, comprehensive, etc.).
Methods of teaching (class participation; heuristic method, etc.).
Vocabulary of school subjects (classics, mathematics, modern languages, etc).
Aims of society (particularly with gerunds and abstract nouns).

Headings

1 What purpose – if any – seemed to you to underlie your own education?
2 What subjects were you taught that seemed to you to be a more or less complete waste of time? Why? Was it the subject itself or the method used to teach it?
3 What subjects, both academic and otherwise, do you feel would have been useful, in which you were given either no instruction at all, or not nearly enough?
4 Do you think that school-teachers in your country are given a suitable training? If not, how do you think their training might be improved?
5 How is the educational system in your country organised and financed? Does contemporary society there seem to require or even to appreciate such a system? What changes do you think should be made to improve it?